Acknowledgements

With loving thanks to my husband, Peter, and to my children, Jason, Ethan, and Colin, for their support and understanding, which made it possible for me to do this work. I am also deeply grateful to my father-in-law, Ritchie Lowry, who got me started in all this to begin with; and to Robin Lowry, who knew all along that I could do it.

For the past twelve years I have been blessed with a wonderful family of friends here in Vermont—Patty and Scott, Jessie, Alice, Alana and Mathew—thank you all for knowing the true meaning of friendship! To my friends and coworkers as well—Linda Marks, Joan and Wil Hastings, Larry Martin, Timi Joukowsky, David Sharp, Dan Hemenway, David Haenke, Gail Jefferys—your support has been a blessing and I love you all! Appreciation also to my friends and colleagues at the Sirius Community for their light on the path.

Love and thanks to my grandmother, who is one of the wisest and most loving people I have been privileged to know; to my sister, MaryJean, who gives new meaning to the quality of strength; and to my mother, whose strong and loving spirit continues to be an active presence in my life.

A final note of thanks, and a big hug, to my editor at New Society Publishers, T.L., whose enthusiasm never failed.

Thank you to all the wonderful people who contributed their time, articles, and information to make this book possible: Paul Terry, Christopher Mogil, Roger Pritchard, Larry Martin, José Barreiro, Bernie Sanders, Victoria Bomberry, Arthur Stone, Michael Kilcullen, Peter Haggerty, Steve Zuckerman, Shelley Kellman, and my apologies to anyone I may have left out. The work is just beginning.

Dedication

To Daddy, who understands.

Economics
as If the
Earth Really Mattered

A *Catalyst* Guide
to Socially Conscious Investing

Susan Meeker-Lowry

New Society Publishers

Philadelphia, PA   Santa Cruz, CA

Inquiries regarding requests to reprint all or part of *Economics as If the Earth Really Mattered* should be addressed to:
New Society Publishers
4527 Springfield Avenue
Philadelphia, PA 19143

ISBN 0-86571-120-8 Hardcover
      0-86571-121-6 Paperback

Printed in the United States of America on partially recycled paper by R. R. Donnelley & Sons.

Cover design by Brian Prendergast.
Book design by Barbara Hirshkowitz.

To order directly from the publisher, add $1.50 to the price for the first copy, 50¢ each additional. Send check or money order to:
New Society Publishers
PO Box 582
Santa Cruz, CA 95061

New Society Publishers is a project of the New Society Educational Foundation, a nonprofit, tax-exempt, public foundation. Opinions expressed in this book do not necessarily represent positions of the New Society Educational Foundation.

Publisher's Note

Economics as If the Earth Really Mattered is the first of what we at New Society Publishers hope will be a series of books exploring the possibilities for creating an economy based on accountability. A central tenet of an accountable economy is that the people who make economic decisions should be the people—workers, consumers, neighbors, investors of time and/or money—who are most affected by those decisions. The characteristics of such an economy would probably include appropriateness of scale and local control.

Creating an accountable economy will demand much from us, our perceptions, imaginations, skills, and wills. We will need much that is new: new organizational models, new economic values and assumptions, new management techniques, and new skills. But we will probably also learn from much that is old, even nearly forgotten. Perhaps the most important lesson we can learn from our economic and natural history is respect for the complexity of human and natural systems and so a humble restraint in our actions, if not always our dreams.

Economics as If the Earth Really Mattered brings us two steps closer to an accountable economy. First, it provides a rich model or metaphor (not a prescription!). The metaphor is Gaea, a perception of the Earth as a living being, and of humans as one part of that being. Seeing the Earth as Gaea encourages us to look to the complex interactions of ecosystems as models of economic and social organization, rather than as mystifying obstacles to simplify and overcome. Thinking of the Earth as Gaea also suggests adding accountability to the Earth to accountability among humans. We are after all of this Earth; our society and economics should fit within its limits and work with, not against or in ignorance of, its systems.

Second, *Economics as If the Earth Really Mattered* provides the experience of thousands of people actively engaged in defining and creating parts of an accountable economy. In it, Susan Meeker-Lowry introduces us to concrete examples of people capturing and recycling money in the communities that need it the most, designing and testing whole new currency systems, developing businesses which are more accountable to the Earth and people affected, and much more. *Economics as If the Earth Really*

Mattered is a tremendous source of ideas and contacts. If you are intrigued by creating a more just economy, it will help you start working. If you are already involved, it will help you further your work.

Our societies and Earth are at a critical point. If we hope to create a more just and sustainable economy, we must work now—with care, reflection, and restraint, yes, but also with determination and a sense of urgency—to make such an economy possible. *Economics as If the Earth Really Mattered* challenges us to take its examples and thinking further, *to create* the living, accountable economy that will allow us—and our Earth—to continue. More than this, it provides a firm foundation for those who would take up its challenge.

We at New Society Publishers are proud to publish *Economics as If the Earth Really Mattered*.

T. L. Hill
for New Society Publishers

Foreword
Thomas Berry

It is an exciting time to be alive. After centuries of industrial exploitation, a new and more integral phase of progress has begun. The earth is achieving a new identity, a renewed vigor.

The word "progress" could be considered the central value of modern civilization. Since it was first developed in the seventeenth and eighteenth centuries, progress in terms of increased technological skills, energy use, and manipulative control over the natural world has been the goal of much human activity.

If much benefit has come about through this sort of progress, an immense amount of damage has also been done to the Earth's basic life systems. But this "progress" is so important that to be effective, any renewal program must somehow function under its banner.

The difficulty is not so much the idea of progress itself as in the limited way it is used. Progress usually refers to the power of humans to exploit the planet for solely human purposes. The vast resources of the Earth and even its most amazing splendors have been ravaged so that humans might increase their consumer economy and fight their wars. Our basic professions have become subservient to this strange effort to grind the entire natural world into a waste heap. Not only economics, law, science, and education but also religion and morality have long supported this process.

But a decisive change has begun. "Progress" begins to have a new and more integral meaning. Starting with the publication of Rachel Carson's *The Silent Spring* in 1962, ecologists, bioregionalists, naturalists, the green movement, the alternative economic movement, and even parts of the medical profession are all striving to establish a human progress that is integrated into the life systems of the Earth. This new kind of progress suggests that the water, soil, and atmosphere must all progress in their life-giving qualities; that the trees, plants, and flowers of the land should continue to expand in their diversity and abundance; that the fish in the sea, the animals on the land, and the birds in the air—as well as the humans—should achieve a more free, secure, and expansive life.

Many humans are building on this new, more integrated "progress." According to Lester Milbrath in *Environmentalists: Vanguard of a New Society*, some 12,000 environmentally oriented movements, publications, or organizations already have begun, with about 250 added each year. Our exploitive, nonsustainable economy looks increasingly backward and destructive. In law, medicine, education, science, religion, and ethics, new movements advocate our withdrawal from an industrial system that calls desolation "development."

Language plays a central role in all of this, especially in economics. When speaking of "profit," we need to understand for whom and at what cost profit exists. There is a social cost and a cost to the Earth, but only the financial cost appears in corporate bookkeeping. The financial "bottom line" must start to incorporate the second bottom line of social cost and the third bottom line of cost in terms of disrupted ecosystems for the accounting to be honest. Ecologists try simply to keep the human enterprise honest, for only so long as we keep faith with the Earth can we expect the Earth to continue the ever-renewing processes upon which all living creatures, including humans, depend.

Now that we have begun to identify the context and direction for a valid form of progress, we need specific programs for effecting these changes. The necessary confrontational and reform efforts abound. What we need most now are local, limited, creative processes growing out of and transforming the existing social order. We need precedents to guide our activities and extensive outreach and publicity to spread these models about.

Such is the work of Susan Meeker-Lowry. She understands the issues. Beyond this, she has followed the movements in recent years to establish a human form of progress integral with the progress of the larger span of life systems. She sees clearly that even while we critique the destructive forces of the past and resist their continuance to the present, we must be concerned primarily with creating the future.

To my mind, one of the most attractive and effective programs is Michael Linton's Local Exchange Trading System (see section 6.6). This effort to achieve some independence from the existing financial processes and from our national currencies is central to achieving new and more functional human communities.

By now it should be clear that a new managerial type is needed. A fourth phase of the modern managerial enterprise has begun. In the first phase, at the end of the nineteenth century and the beginning of the twentieth century, management was closely allied with engineering. Humans were trained to be compatible with machines. This was the ideal of Taylor management. The second phase was more concerned with administration. It was identified and guided by Peter Drucker after World War II, when the schools of business administration were established. The third phase is concerned with injecting humanism into the entrepreneurial context. In *In Search of Excellence* Peters and Waterman argue that a sense of corporate culture is central to managerial success.

The fourth phase that is now beginning might be considered the ecological phase. In this phase the integral functioning of the natural world is taken as the supreme model of managerial success. Of special importance here is seeing the natural world as a totally participatory process. Each member of the community rules all the other members of the community and is in turn ruled by all the other members of the community.

Earthly affairs went along well enough until the neolithic period when human intrusion into the functioning of the planet began to assume significant dimensions with the invention of agriculture, the domestication of animals, the rise of technical skills, and the establishment of village and city life. We still have difficulty realizing just why the human has become less viable as a species and the Earth itself has become dysfunctional in its major life systems. We have ventured into a position of total responsibility for the planet, a responsibility from which we cannot withdraw. What happened immediately and instinctively in the prehuman phase of the Earth must now be done consciously and with critical intelligence at the human level. This is the challenge that we face since the main natural systems of Earth have been brought under the dominant influence of human intelligence.

Fulfilling this awesome responsibility requires that we enter into a more intimate relationship with the spontaneous functioning of the planet, especially in its capacity for seasonal renewal. We need a new mystique in our relation with the Earth. Humans must learn to see themselves less as beings separate from the Earth and more as a dimension of the Earth. Humans and the Earth are totally implicated in each other. The well-being of the Earth is the only way to the well-being of the human. Once we begin to appreciate ourselves and the Earth in this context, we can begin anew to foster a mutually enhancing human-Earth relationship.

To serve as a catalyst for this process is surely one of the noblest functions we can serve.

Contents

Table of Contents

Part III   Doing It Ourselves:
Creating the Economy We Want

Part IV   Resources

Introduction

This book is primarily a handbook for action.

Our economic system often feels distant and impersonal, one of the givens of our lives. We live within its constraints, feel subject to its changes, and think we have little hope of affecting it. (Even the experts claim with increasing frequency that they don't know what's going on.)

I believe, however, that we *can* affect our economy, both locally and as a whole. I am convinced because I've spent the last five years learning about, meeting, and writing in *Catalyst* about the many people who are working to transform our economic system into one that is more sustainable, just, and life-affirming. The projects and possibilities these people are working on are the subject of this book.

The key to affecting our economy is to consciously choose to apply our values to economic interactions. If we do not choose our own values, then we subscribe by default to the values of the prevalent system. Such acquiescence is always dangerous, but these days it's also suicidal. Business as usual is killing the Earth, the source of all life.

I do not want to dictate which values or paths we should choose in our common struggle to create a more just, sustaining, and sustainable economy. I have faith that if we each search our hearts and minds, if we each open to the example of the Earth around us, we will choose paths that will contribute to a more liveable economy. But of course my perspectives and values run through this book, and in Part I, Toward a Gaean Economy, I share some of them and their source in my experience of Gaea, the living Earth. I then sketch some of the principles of a Gaean economy.

In Part II, Home Improvements: Adjusting Our Current Economy, I describe a number of ways we can influence the conduct of the corporations that dominate our economy and then present the advice of several people experienced in investing in the small-scale.

In Part III, Doing It Ourselves: Creating the Economy We Want, I tell the stories of a range of exciting projects dedicated to creating aspects of a life-affirming economy. The areas people are working in include community economics, economics of place, and economics of culture.

1

And finally, in Part IV, Resources, I collect all the resources, publications, and books I could find that might help you in your work to transform our economy.

This book is meant to be a tool for action, not an in-depth discussion and analysis of the existing economic system. Our problems are severe, and we must act. I've listed only some of the organizations and projects that are changing our economy. Many more exist, like strong blades of grass pushing up through the cracks in a cement sidewalk. All we need to do is open our eyes and hearts and see the possibilities around us in our neighborhoods and communities. A healthy world, a strong economy, justice, and peace all start at home. And life, Earth's gift to us, is the only gift we must give in return. Nothing less will do.

So, on with the work!

PART I

Toward A Gaean Economy

CHAPTER ONE

The Earth is My/Our Source

I am sitting near a brook, next to an old tree felled by beavers years ago. It is an appropriate place to write this introduction, for it is nature and the life force I feel so strongly here that are the foundation of my belief that change is possible.

It is early spring in Vermont, and although the snow has melted and the mud is drying up, spring growth has barely emerged. A flood and nearby highway improvements have changed the course of this brook, leaving debris where I sit and dying trees in the brook's new path.

Yet I can feel life pulsing here. It is bursting from the earth beneath me. The birds' songs, the rushing of the brook, the gentle late afternoon breeze dancing with the freshly budded tree branches are all promises of the potential that I know will be fulfilled by lengthening days, warm sunshine, and summer rain.

Life, death, change—this is the way of things. Being here, I see this, and I am opened to hope and a sense of what is possible—as well as to lessons of persistence.

I am fortunate to be able to come here to write, just as I was fortunate to have been raised in New Hampshire's White Mountains. We owned and ran a rather run-down ski lodge in the days before man-made snow and condominiums; it was not easy and our finances were precarious. The situation was made that much more difficult by my father's resentment of the development that began about twenty-five years ago and continues unabated to this day.

I spent much of my childhood in the woods, riding my bike to swimming holes, berry patches, secret caves, and friends' houses. My father taught my sister and I about the plants and animals in our area and how to treat the woods with care and respect. His love for them and his ease in them rubbed off on me, and the woods became the place I go to seek inner peace and to think things out.

My connection with the woods has grown into a very personal relationship with the Earth, which is an incredible gift. This Earth supports and sustains us in so many ways and on so many levels. Native Americans believe the Earth is our mother, and like our human mothers the Earth provides for us. Everything that fuels our economy and maintains our society is derived from the Earth's bounty.

But in our forays to work and the shopping mall, we often forget this. I'll always remember the first clear-cut I saw with my own eyes. I felt as if the Earth had been raped. I just wanted to spread myself over it and hold it close.

Seeing the clear-cut hurt so much, and yet I was grateful I could *feel* the pain. I felt blessed that what hurt the Earth hurt me. The pain reaffirmed my strength. It seems that when we face pain, allow it in, come *through* it, we become stronger, more whole, and more aware of who we are.

My grandmother used to tell me, "Love is the most powerful force in the universe. Love can overcome all obstacles, both physical and mental."

I believed this because it made sense and because it reassured me. It helped assuage my ever-present, deep-seated fear of being alone, of having those I love—my cat, my grandmother, my parents, my sister—die. I even used to rehearse my loved ones' deaths, knowing I could stop if it started to hurt too much. I tried to feel the pain before it became real. I did this because I knew, logically, that I would probably experience the deaths of all the people I loved, except perhaps that of my younger sister, MaryJean.

Then, almost six years ago to the day as I write this, a friend called to tell me that MJ had been very badly hurt in a car accident. As we sped to the hospital, I prayed, over and over, "Hang in there, MJ." It became my mantra.

We arrived to find my mother looking awful and my father incredibly, unspeakably sad. Mother had been undergoing chemotherapy for cancer for about a year but had been doing fine; she was cheerful and never missed work. But when my parents heard about MJ's accident, my mother asked for a painkiller for the first time and aged ten years in a week. I could see that this accident might kill my mother, or speed up the cancer's killing her. The little girl who had rehearsed her mother's death so many years ago was not at all ready for her to die—now or ever.

MJ was in a deep coma with severe brain injuries, and the doctors were convinced that she would die or at best end up as a vegetable. But my grandmother's wisdom buoyed me; I knew without any doubt that love is the greatest healer, and that nothing is impossible in love. And I knew my sister's strong, stubborn spirit. If she were to live, she would *not* be a vegetable.

I concentrated all my love and being on my sister's spirit. On my first night home, I felt her with me and repeated my mantra, "Hang in there, MJ." And I heard her reply, "I will." From that moment on, I cradled her spirit with my love, as well as I knew how, day and night. When I felt her most strongly, I would let her know that no matter how awful her body looked, her spirit could heal it. I told her I knew her purpose had not changed; she was still whole, still beautiful, still wonderfully MJ.

MJ was gradually "weaned" off the respirator, and then taken out of intensive care. We made every effort to help her awaken, from talking to her to playing her favorite music, to insisting that the nurses and doctors not talk about her (only to her) in her presence. I knew she could hear sometimes, and I could not stand her being treated like an "it." I could imagine how frustrating it must have been to be in a body you cannot use because the brain is not working properly.

MJ's coma gradually lightened, but as it did my mother became sicker. It was obvious she was dying. It seemed like she was carrying a burden only death could lessen: the burden of being too sick to be present for her child. Two hours after my mother died, MJ woke up, and the long, hard work of rehabilitation began.

These were perhaps the most difficult days of my life. I had to trust my deep sense that love can transcend and heal. I learned that this sense was not just a saying or a feeling, but the staff of life. This is what pulled me through the pain, kept me visiting my sister, helped me say goodbye to my mother, enabled me to be patient with my father.

And as I came through, my strength grew. I lost my fear of hospitals, doctors, "experts." I listened to them, asked lots of questions, and made my disagreements clear; I was, after all, my sister's advocate. But I was also changed inside. I was beginning to feel strong and to know what was real and important.

The months that followed remained hard. There were many visits with my sister as she struggled in rehabilitation, and with my father as he recovered from my mother's death. MJ eventually learned again to talk, read, write, and walk.

In the middle of all this, my third son was born. I felt like it was the birth of the Christ child all over again. Life! I felt so blessed, and surrounded by those I love, that I finally began to mourn my mother's death. I realized that I loved her for her strength, for her honesty, and for the way she loved me without judgment. Her death did not diminish me; in some strange way, she had once again given me life. I knew that to give my sons what she had given me, all I need to do is be myself and do what is important to me.

Shortly after my son's birth, my husband, Peter, and his father, Ritchie, asked me to work with them on the newsletter they were starting for socially conscious investors. Called GOOD MONEY, its motto was "doing well while doing good," and the idea was to help investors screen out companies that were doing things they did not like so that they could invest in companies that were doing things they did like. My reaction was, Of course, is there any other way?

I've always had a vision of a better world. As a child, the vision was of a magical place (a place I could actually visit sometimes when I went to the woods) where pretenses were unnecessary and only your own perceptions counted. As I grew older, I wanted in the worst way for this world to become real, but I had no idea how to help it happen. The world I lived in had to do with Vietnam, Kent State, drug overdoses, and fear and hatred of the "establishment." Like many of my generation, I experimented with various ways of reconciling the world we lived in and the world of love, compassion, beauty, and peace we knew could be.

Finally, in the early 1970s, I met Peter and we moved to Vermont to get away from the "establishment" and "back to the land." Our romantic visions of homesteading were soon shattered by the realities of gardening in clay soil and by a harsh Vermont winter. But somehow, we managed. With lots of hard work, manure, and love, we created a wonderful garden, including all sorts of my favorite herbs. We grew vegetables and poultry, we ground our own grain and baked our own bread, I birthed our first two boys at home, and we made some lifelong friendships.

And then, suddenly, the talk around the dinner table was of investing, of corporations and their activities, and of other people working on "social investing."

In some ways, this was hard to stomach. To me, corporations of any size were synonymous with the "establishment," with all that was painful and wrong in our world. They exploited people, they paid off politicians, they made weapons, they tried to make us want things we didn't need, and they turned my New Hampshire mountains into so many "parcels" to be sold to the highest bidder.

But I could see Ritchie's points. Not everything corporations do is bad, and not all corporations are equally irresponsible. One thing we could do was to educate investors so that they could make *choices* based not only on financial criteria but on each corporation's record. What does the corporation make? How do they make it? How do they treat their workers? How do they affect the environment? And so on. This wouldn't result in any overnight revolutionary changes, but it would help us begin to clean up the system, share information and skills with others, and perhaps organize a group that would be a more powerful instrument for change than any one of us alone.

This seemed pretty good as far as it went, and I was willing to help. But I did not, do not, believe that corporations, no matter how "good" they might be in particular areas, can make the kind of changes that are needed. It seems to me that true economic and social justice must take into consideration the uniqueness of individuals, communities, and diverse cultures. The only way I can see to ensure such justice and diversity is to foster the active participation of all. (I describe this perspective more fully in the next chapter.) As I looked around, I couldn't help thinking that there must be some way to get resources to those small,underbudgeted, understaffed, and unsung projects that I knew were already working for true social and economic justice.

So, after much thought and trepidation, I decided to start a regular column, "Investing in Social Change," for GOOD MONEY's supplemental newsletter, *Netbacking* (now *Netback*). In the first installment (March 1983), I wrote:

> There is another type of social investor, however, who determines his/her lifestyle and financial needs to maintain [that lifestyle] and then invests either the remainder or a certain percentage of their income to "social change." These people have been made aware, usually painfully, of the fragility of life and of our earth. Through personal experiences with death, sickness, a spiritual quest, or any number of other challenges life has to offer, they realize that there is indeed more to life than meets the eye. These people take their investments personally and look at them as an extension of their own lifestyle. They want the most good to come from their investments whether that is housing for

the poor, refurbishing our cities, trying to effect a spiritual consciousness change—whatever their own personal commitments may be. They must feel "right" about their investments each day, knowing that the present is all there really is to work with and if they don't do something to better the world today, there may be no tomorrow.

I decided that my work would be a bridge between such people and the projects that could help bring about the social, environmental, economic, and spiritual changes necessary to transform the current reality into a life-affirming one. My deep love of the earth, my convictions, and my new-found trust in myself made it possible for me to take on this new work.

It is a very powerful experience to realize that there are choices— and that we can make them. It means that things do not have to continue along their current path; they can and may, but they do not have to. And, really, the choice is ours. But to choose in accord with our values, we must have good information.

As I searched for projects to write about, I discovered many people who are looking at the "business of doing business" differently. They are using business as a tool for social change, running their businesses according to such values as cooperation, worker participation, fairness, quality, and environmental sustainability. The success of these businesses suggested that integrating social and spiritual values with the way we do business actually works! We do not have to be competitive and cutthroat to make a living.

I began to see how we can use money as a tool to make things happen. Money can be an extension of ourselves, and what we do with it can be a very personal expression of who we are and what we believe in.

To invest according to our values, we must know about the social and environmental activities of the companies in our portfolios. To support the development of the innovative enterprises and new systems, we must know about the best, most promising work being done. And businesses and organizations need to know that supporters exist, as well as how to meet the needs of investors.

When I began the column, there were few avenues a concerned investor could follow to invest in progressive business and practices. There were of course some seeds like the Briarpatch Network (a California network of alternative businesses committed to honest business and right livelihood), the Calvert Social

Investment Fund (the first socially screened mutual and money-market fund), and the Institute for Community Economics (groundbreaking work in developing the community land trust and revolving loan fund models). But soon it became clear that there was a need for a full newsletter and that the opportunities to put money to work for social change are boundless. The possibilities are everywhere: in our towns, our cities, the countryside, the Third World. All we need are new eyes to see them and the imagination and remembered understanding of the natural order of things to nurture them. We need to be at once practical and visionary.

Catalyst was born in February/March of 1984, a year after my first "Investing in Social Change" column appeared. Since then, I have watched both socially responsible investing and investing in social change mature. There are more people involved, and there seems to be a greater willingness to work together, despite differences. We are learning to plan and be patient, as well as open and flexible.

Some of the most exciting changes I see involve shifts of perception. When we begin to make choices based on values—for example, refusing to invest in companies that produce nuclear weapons—we become more open. In the words of a coworker, "Once people start making investment decisions based on their social concerns, they begin to open their hearts." A single choice based on our beliefs, successfully made and supported by others, leads us to make other choices in the same way.

In this world filled with life-threatening situations, I think humility and the desire to find common ground are very important. I believe we must not allow ourselves to fall into the us/them trap. We are all together on this Earth, for better or for worse, and we must learn to look to the humanity in each of us and accept our differences. Accepting differences does not mean ignoring them; it means not condemning people for seeing the world differently. What may seem like a very small and inconsequential change to one person may be a very big step for someone else. All movements in a positive direction must be supported.

I am also convinced that we must try to recognize what we can and cannot do. Living in Vermont, I cannot do much to make things better in the inner city, at least not directly. I can be most effective here, in my own community. This does not absolve me from my responsibility to work for justice in the wider world, but it does constrain my choices: I need to examine my options and see where my energies will have the most effect.

It is easy to despair. In the past twenty-five years, my father has watched in great pain as droves of people followed him to the White Mountains, building second homes, restaurants, strip developments, and shopping malls. He has chronicled the many destructive changes this migration has brought; he is sensitive to the ways humans can disrupt an ecosystem without actually bulldozing it under. My father and his friends all agree that development is "ruining the country," but they also despair of stopping or changing the development.

My father asks, "If everyone agrees with me that this needs to stop, and it still keeps on happening, isn't that proof that it will never change?" It's a good question, and it stops me every time I hear it. There are very powerful forces behind the development he abhors, behind the economy that is killing the Earth. And yet I keep coming back to the same answer: It is up to us to change things. We cannot wait for change to happen; we are part of the system, even the development, and we must start now, making the choices and changes we can make. As we do this, the results of these changes will ripple outward, helping us join with others to create powerful momentum for change or a new way.

This all takes time and patience, and it is often hard to see that we are making a difference. It is tempting to sit around analyzing theories and waiting for the one idea that will save us or what we love. But as long as we wait for the definitive solution, nothing will change, or rather, we will have no say in the changes. We must remember we are part of our world, that the changes we see are created by people like us.

By developing strong local economies and using local resources as much as possible, I think we can have more far-reaching positive effects. While a cooperative business in New England may not save the rain forest in any direct way, it can help reduce the demand for exotic rain forest hardwoods by supporting local craftspeople using local timber. And if the local forests are managed responsibly, with attention paid to the local ecology and long-term sustainability, the community that relies on the forest is strengthened as well.

When my oldest son, now ten, was a baby, I used to sit and watch him sleep while I cried silently, feeling such despair that even today the memory is painful. What kind of world had I birthed him into? I was terrified of nuclear war, and our violence toward the Earth felt like an attack on me and my child.

Thanks to our communication technologies, it is more and more difficult for us to pretend that starvation, acute poverty, and environmental degradation do not exist. As I examined them, it became clearer that these situations are a direct result of a global economy characterized by materialist values and inadequate methods of evaluating its own effects. Indeed, our economy and our culture are based on separations—from the Earth, from other peoples, from each other, from ourselves. Even the efforts designed to ease these situations often ignore the reality of people's lives on the community level.

Driven by fear of the unknown, we scramble to raise a wall of familiar things and people; we cut ourselves off in the name of security. And the good job we worked so hard for, the one that allows us to buy whatever means security to us, becomes a treadmill. We run faster and faster trying to keep up, to fix our appliances, to make it or move up. We have been living this way so long that it has become a cultural pattern; we can hardly imagine any other way of being. And as much as we as a society might want to develop an ability to think and to create workable solutions, the structure of our current system makes this nearly impossible.

When I cried for my son, I took my pain and fear into the garden and woods. Slowly, I began to sense a deeper meaning, continuity, and purpose. I began to see that everything affects everything else. Always. When the wind blows, it is easy to see its effect on the leaves and branches of trees. Not so obvious is the trees' effect on the wind. They lessen its force, creating a space in which other plants can root and thrive. It is a subtle power, but a dramatic one, and looking around we can see that the wind, sun, and water have created monuments as powerful as any we humans can design.

No action, good or bad, occurs in a vacuum. Just as our neglect and separation cause fouled air, water, and land, so will our love, care, and attention allow positive changes. These changes will need to be local *and* global. But since true learning seems to happen through personal experience, I think it makes the most sense to start making changes, trying new approaches, and developing new systems at home, with the people and places around us. As we develop more communitarian and responsive systems, we can apply the principles on the national and global levels. A good model can be replicated many times so long as it is tailored to local needs.

Moving beyond our walls and separation is like slowly waking from a dream. It is hard and sometimes painful, but it is also exhilarating. As we discover our connections to other people and places around the world, we find we can no longer turn away from pain and suffering. But we also find the love and beauty inherent in life on Earth. Each day offers us new opportunities to participate in healing the Earth and creating a more humane culture. We share the life of all creation. If we open our hearts to the life around us, we can begin to discover how it feels to participate with life.

Imagine: You are walking in the woods or in a park or even on a familiar street. It is a beautiful, clear day. Bright sun, blue sky, a few wispy clouds. A slight breeze stirs the leaves in your path. Your thoughts drift. First to work, unfinished business, the kids, the traffic. Then, suddenly, the thoughts fall away. You feel the warmth of the sun and the incredible deep blue of the sky. How beautiful it all is! You realize you are blessed and in your own way give thanks. And then, at just that moment, an especially large and gorgeous leaf lands right at your feet. And you pick it up, knowing somehow it is a gift.

This is the partnership we have with life. All possibilities, all opportunity are contained within it. We can accept the gift of life and meaning—and the responsibility that comes with it—or we can deny its existence and ignore it. The choice is up to each of us, each moment of our lives.

CHAPTER TWO

An Economy for the Living Earth

There's a small, human-made pond I know by a brook on the edge of a small wood. Dug years ago, it has long since been integrated into nature. What an idyllic spot! One can hear the brook, the rise and fall of the wind, the buzzing of myriad insects, a truck in the distance, a fish jumping. One can feel the wind and sun, an occasional insect, the firmness of the earth. There are cat-o-nine tails across the pond, flanked by silvery birches and dark green hemlock. The trees bend to the wind, an insect lands on the water, and a fish sucks it down.

More than anything, I am struck by the harmony and abundance here, at what the cooperation of all life has wrought. There are no expectations. There is simply acknowledgement and acceptance of the pattern.

This scene is part of what the ancient Greeks called Gaea. Gaea is the essential life force, the unknowable essence revealed as love. And love is the energy, wisdom, and desire of all living forms to be themselves. All living things—rocks (yes, rocks), plants, stars, animals, tides—know themselves, are themselves. I am not saying they are necessarily self-conscious, but rather that they live—that in themselves alone and as part of a whole, they have a purpose. The challenge for us is to learn, perhaps relearn, our oneness, our place in the web, our purpose. The challenge is to sense Gaea's essence even if we cannot know Gaea herself.

Over time, as we have struggled to understand the "laws of nature," we have come to assume that life can be explained in material and technical terms. While much can be understood this way, our reliance on this approach has drastically limited our ability to be conscious of life and to create from within that consciousness. Looking out at the world with reductionist eyes, we feel separate from all other life on earth. On the surface our lives are full of bustle and systems, but deeper down we feel a nagging doubt; deeper down, we feel alone and afraid.

This fear drives our manic systems. This fear drives us to accumulate more and more, to create weapons of death, to rape and plunder the Earth. Our economy has institutionalized our fear-driven greed.

Money was once a tool, not a commodity. We created money to facilitate the exchange of goods, an exchange that could be accomplished in any number of ways. Gradually, though, money has become one of our main measures of worth. Success means accumulating more; ruin means being left destitute. In search of money, many of us have foregone special interests or talents that do not pay. Worse, we have traded webs of relationships with communities, places, and the Earth for the transient search for the dollar. Seduced by the pleasures money can buy, or forced by economic circumstance, we have traded self-reliance for dependence on our employers. We have become commodities to be bought and sold. If we lose whatever money we have, we truly are destitute; we have nothing to fall back on.

But if we can open ourselves again to Gaea, if we can relearn our place and purpose, we can begin to assuage our fear and to see new possibilities. I believe that one of our gifts is our self-awareness. We do not just live; we perceive our living. In the space between an experience and our perception of it, we become aware.

For example, in chapter 1, had you ignored the leaf blown in your path or crushed it into the sidewalk, little would have appeared changed. Things would have gone on as before. But by accepting the leaf, acknowledging it as a gift, and giving thanks, you have changed something. You have changed your perspective. You feel a little happier. Maybe your step has an added bounce; maybe you smile to the next person you pass on the street. Life is suddenly good, and to me that is the key. Our gift and our responsibility is that we can be conscious, feeling participants in life. We can shape and feel our lives, but both responsibility and wisdom dictate that we shape them so that they fit with and contribute to the web of life, to Gaea.

As we become more aware of Gaea and more aware of ourselves, perhaps we can begin to envision a cooperative, patterned economy full of harmony and abundance. Perhaps we can envision an economy that fits the Earth as well as the human-made pond fits its spot. A Gaean economy would be whole, organic and synergetic; it would flow with the natural process of change.

One place to start our envisioning is with the processes that underlie all life. As we look carefully at the web of life around us, as we begin to trace its strands and the process of connection, we find values essential to Gaea. They lead to principles that can guide us in our attempt to create a Gaean economy.

Respect–Cooperation

In Gaea, each living thing has a place and purpose. Central to respect is awareness of the connections we are part of. Respecting Gaea means paying attention to the web of life, to the processes of connection. Respecting each other means taking the time to learn and value what each can offer and what role each can play. Respecting ourselves means searching to find our own special gifts—and then sharing them.

When we do not respect Gaea, we trample ahead, destroying the web and ultimately ourselves. When we do not respect others, we encourage defensiveness and rigidity. When we do not respect ourselves, we give up in despair.

An economy built upon respect would be cooperative. I do not mean cooperative in the sense of you and me "making nice." I mean cooperating for the life of the whole. Cooperation for the whole requires a real balance between self-interest and service. It requires our letting go of the "me" that wants and wants. It requires our learning to dance with life.

Our current economy fosters a ruthless "winner-take-all" competitiveness. We do not consider the results of this greedy consumption. We disregard our depletion of the Earth's resources—her gifts to us—our exploitation of other people, and the impact of our individual and corporate actions on our societies and cultures. Our competitive economy has contributed to our living with little creativity and individuality in a faceless monoculture.

Building a cooperative economy means working together to develop resilient businesses, social structures, organizations, and relationships that provide for our needs as *part* of a living Earth. We must start our practical search for solutions now, and we must work together. Together, we are more powerful, more creative, more effective, and more supported. One of the reasons this book is full of resources is to enable you to connect with other groups, businesses, and projects that are striving to create a humane, sustainable economy.

One example is Co-op America, a Washington, D.C., based national nonprofit organization that tries to be "America's

Alternative Marketplace." According to director and cofounder Paul Freundlich, "Co-op America is dedicated to overcoming the often painful contradiction between our politics and our pocketbook. We are committed to providing a common ground for organizations and individuals concerned with a healthier, more just, and more peaceful world."

The alternative marketplace is based on responsibility, self-reliance, environmental and economic sustainability, cooperation, and workplace democracy. Businesses, organizations, and individuals who support these values make up the membership. Members' products are marketed in a quarterly catalog. The businesses, Co-op America, and the individuals who buy *all* benefit. Traditional marketing competition is replaced by cooperation, and the results are high-quality products, reasonable prices, and the commitment to providing these with respect for the Earth's limitations and resources.

Of course, some of these businesses may still fail. They may have less than adequate cash flow, suffer from inexperienced management, or be pushed out by other, more experienced producers of similar products. They may still fail, but not for lack of opportunity and support. Cooperation for the whole provides the opportunity to develop strength, but does not guarantee strength. Sometimes the interactions in and around the pond seem harsh and competitive, yet each is part of a larger dance—of life—that goes on.

Relationship–Place

As important as the parts of the web of life are the dynamic relationships between the parts. We must pay attention to our roles in the web, to how what we give and take affects the processes. In and around the pond, the various parts of Gaea are interwoven into a complex, changing pattern of relationships and cycles.

One characteristic of the pattern is that everything is interconnected. The trees bend in the wind, but they also lessen the wind's effect on the pond and its bank. In their shelter, tiny plants, bacteria, and insects break down the needles and leaves, enriching the soil for the trees. Although we can draw temporary boundaries around specific ecosystems, they overlap and the boundaries are permeable; the web of relationships reaches everywhere.

Another characteristic of the pattern is that the relationships and cycles are always changing. Each part reacts to its environment, and the whole environment, the whole web, changes over time. As the temperature of the water changes, so does the mixture of creatures living in it. As the plants die off and rot, they contribute to the silt and, over time, make the pond shallower and warmer. There is always change here, including life and death, and the change is what keeps the pond living.

If we are to build a Gaean economy, we must build one that is flexible, that changes with time and conditions. Each place, each community, each time is unique. To create a humane, sustainable economy, we must begin by studying where and when we live. Are we in New York City, Appalachia, the desert? What is the history of our place? How are things changing? How does what our neighbors, even our distant neighbors, do affect us—and vice versa? As we look for the many answers to these questions, we will begin to find some of the many appropriate solutions for our place.

As we learn more about the complex interactions that characterize our place, we will find it harder to make decisions based on only one or two criteria (like number of new jobs, impact on the schools, or resource depletion). By insisting on knowing beforehand what we are compromising, we may find ourselves sacrificing some short-term gains in favor of longer term ones (fewer immediate jobs in exchange for those jobs having less impact on the environment and being more creative and secure). Or we may find ourselves paying more attention to the appropriate timing of a decision (a park we badly want now might be more enjoyable if we take some time to plan it and perhaps scout several sites). And we will increasingly learn to think about the larger web of relationships that affect and are affected by our decisions (slopping our wastes into the river does not help us much if we buy our vegetables from the community downstream).

Diversity–Self-Reliance

One of the most important elements of the creative change in response to changing conditions is diversity. Diversity is a key to the sustainability of the web. At our pond, the essential processes—like turning dead organisms into useable chemicals—can be accomplished by several pathways. If one is blocked for some reason, the others take its place. On a larger, longer scale, this human-made pond fits its spot as well as it does only because enough different organisms with flexible requirements could adapt to this human change to the environment.

Without diversity, an ecosystem—or an economy—is much less flexible in the face of dramatic changes. If a community is dependent on a single major employer, and that company closes down or moves (often to the Third World), all facets of the community suffer. Workers lose jobs and cannot feed their families or patronize local businesses. Property taxes go uncollected and school budgets are slashed. Compounding the problem, if the company moves where wages are lower and environmental controls fewer, the second community risks becoming dependent on the same unreliable source of work, while general wage levels suffer and pollution increases.

In a community with a diverse economy, the loss of even a major employer would not be so devastating. For the most part, the community's needs could be met by the remaining businesses and organizations. At the same time, these other businesses and organizations guarantee the community the resources to help those hurt by one company's shutting down. Similarly, communities with diverse economies are more likely to be able to control the actions of companies that try to move in. After all, they have little to lose if a company goes elsewhere.

Clearly, an important ingredient of diversity is self-reliance. I am not talking about old-fashioned isolationism. If the days of the isolated community providing all basic needs of its members ever existed, they are certainly gone now. Furthermore, so many of the Earth's problems are so large that we need each other to deal with them. But for there to be diversity, and so flexibility and creativity, we need to have reasonably independent (if also interdependent) communities, each adding its own originality to the mix.

Imagine a community totally dependent on outside resources for jobs, goods, services, support systems; Indian reservations are a good example. All the stores are owned by major chains. Although Native Americans are employed in the stores, the money they earn is sucked out of the community by the same stores. Any other money that comes into the community—say from the federal government—pours right on out, destructively, like a downpour running down a parched hill. And with the flood go the youth. Seeing that traditional values no longer work and finding no other opportunities on the reservation, they leave for the cities, for the monoculture and the isolation of corporate or "traditional" capitalism.

But imagine these same communities with local businesses and stores: any money entering the system is caught and used and reused (like rain falling in a rain forest, which recycles the moisture as its own rain). Better yet, the members create their own support systems of bartered goods, shared skills, and friendship that allow the community to maintain its identity and to respond to changing conditions. (Seeds of this exist on some reservations; see chapter 6, pages 154–155, and chapter 7, pages 210–216.)

A warning note: Self-reliance can harden into selfishness and fragment diversity into so many unrelated pieces. Changes that eat away at the interconnections of the web, that reduce diversity, can eventually ruin Gaea's ability to heal. This is the danger we face.

Harmony–Appropriate Scale

Ultimately, the web of interconnected, diverse, essential parts must be balanced in some sort of harmony. Harmony is the heart of Gaea. Harmony is the appropriate, dynamic balance of the many cycles and systems, the local and the global, life and death. For us to survive and prosper, we must align all our activities, including our economy, with the natural cycles of the Earth. To do this, we must listen to each other and to the Earth, to our place and to our communities. We must, I think, spend time in wild places where we can learn gentleness, compassion, and a deeper listening.

Perhaps the most important part of harmony for economics is attention to scale. This Earth sustains both incredibly large and incredibly small life forms. The question for us must always be: What is appropriate? For this function, what is the most productive, *sustainable* balance between large and small, short-term and long-term, local and global? Should we be doing this at all?

In our present economy, growth is automatically seen as a good thing. Whether or not it really is depends on the social and environmental effects of that growth. A certain amount of algae in the pond provides food and oxygen; an uncontrolled bloom ends with a pond devoid of oxygen and most life.

A Gaean economy would include all shapes and sizes as long as none operated at the expense of another, including the Earth. There would be many small- and medium-sized organizations and a few larger ones, where size really does increase effectiveness. Scale would be a function of our area's maximum capacity, the available resources, the needs of the community, the influence of our global interconnections, and the economics of production.

As varied as its elements would be, the core of a Gaean economy would be a web of strong local economies. To be strong, the local economies must be diverse, use local resources and talents well, and be able to recycle money rather than letting it leak out. For this to happen, local economies must be controlled by local people, by the people affected by their decisions.

In developing a Gaean economy, our criterion must always be the integrity of Gaea. If the web of life is threatened, if interconnections are ignored or severed, we must change our practices.

Looking around today, we can see it is time to change. We are destroying ecosystems, diversity, at an alarming rate. With our pollution and our monoculture, we are breaking the interconnections that keep our world alive and flexible. The "economy" we hear about on the evening news consists largely of various indices that once measured and now define the system. We know from our own experience that the gross national product (GNP), the "official" unemployment rate, and the inflation rate tell us little about what is going on in our economic lives. They tell us little about the dangerous working conditions, part-time work, increasing spirals of debt, and the informal economy that are so important to most of us.

Perhaps the most important thing to remember is that our economic system is *not* a shell built elsewhere and imposed upon us and our transactions by politicians and businessmen. While some individuals and organizations have tremendous power, we are all active participants in the economy. In a very real sense we *are* the economy. The economy begins with the work we do, the products we buy, and the often unpaid, "informal" productive work—like child care, housecleaning, bartering, and sweat equity—we do. We can begin to change our economy by taking personal responsibility and actively choosing how we invest our time, skills, and money. We can work to make existing institutions more open and accountable. And we can gather the power to really change things by working together to create new economic structures. If we wait for "experts" to come up with brilliant one-time solutions, we will simply watch—and help—our planet, ourselves, die.

In this book, I try to give you a sense of the vast number of efforts to transform our economy *that already exist*. Some people are helping investors influence the actions of corporations. Some are finding ways to invest time and money in local businesses and organizations. And many more are developing entirely new models for communities striving to provide food, housing, skills, capital, and various products to their members. Many of the most innovative projects are fully or partially in the "informal" sector of our present economy. This is the sector where we can find the space to create an economy where "the bottom line" is not purely financial.

The projects in this book are only a beginning. The transformation to a humane, sustainable economy will be difficult, fraught with confrontation, and probably slow. Just as we have participated in creating a nuclear nightmare, starving children, and toxic chemicals oozing into our basements, we can participate in creating a living economy. Despite all the horror stories and pain, I see incredible opportunity for us to remember what it means to be truly human and alive on this beautiful planet.

We must open to the life force that breathes through the Earth, join with it, nurture it, and grow with it. As we awaken from our illusion of separation, we will know that we, too, are Gaea. As we awaken, we can dance and create. Join in the dance; we need you all!

PART II

Home Improvements: Adjusting Our Current Economy

CHAPTER THREE

Having an Impact on the Corporate World

Along with political interest groups, major corporations appear to be in control of our economy. The combination of financial and political power is very hard for us to fight, especially as individuals. And no matter what our intentions are, it is hard to avoid supporting a major corporation in some way. Corporations are quick to respond to changing consuming patterns and are equally effective at creating new ones. For example, over the past few years it has become very difficult to determine which products are indeed "natural" and which have been marketed to appear that way. Simply shopping in a natural food store or a "mom and pop" store does not ensure purity or wholesomeness—we have to read all the fine print. And you can be certain that as we become more and more savvy the corporations will attempt to thwart or take advantage of that, too.

For all its power, there are ways we can affect the corporate world. In this chapter, I discuss five methods: boycotts, consumer and shareholder actions, divestment, and social investments. (There are others, but these are the ones that have proven effective.) In any case, all the activities discussed here are interim steps, tools we can use to move toward a Gaean economy.

Since the only language most corporations understand is financial, we must talk to them in that language. We cannot expect

General Electric to stop making nuclear weapons and components because we ask nicely. They are making lots of money producing those weapons, and they will only listen if we "hit them in the pocketbook." The tactics in this section do this, most effectively when used together by large groups as part of a complete strategy. The Resources section includes many organizations whose purpose is to help make this possible.

As we increase and concentrate our financial and political clout, we should be able to force policy changes or hasten failures. Companies that do not begin to change their ways of relating to communities, workers, and the environment will find that they are the dinosaurs of the twentieth century. Some realize this and, either from a genuine desire to be responsible members of the global community or from an awareness that the long-term benefits of responsibility are *real*, these companies are becoming more socially and environmentally accountable. Firms that do not make the necessary changes will be replaced by smaller, more locally focused companies that can respond to the changing climate and needs of the community.

I cannot predict how long it will take for us to use our power. It depends on how long it takes us to realize and bear the responsibility for our choices. But the longer we wait, the greater will be the toll on society and the Earth. The world of major corporations may be unpleasant, disempowering, and mind-boggling to get a hold on, but get a hold on it we must. Corporations are a part of our lives, like it or not, and we cannot make them go away by isolating ourselves and ignoring them.

Whether we make scarcely enough money to provide the bare necessities for our families, or whether we have millions of dollars to invest, each of us can make choices that affect corporations' pocketbooks.

3.1 Consumer Boycotts

One way we can vote with our pocketbooks is to start or join a boycott of a particular product or corporation. Boycotts can be very effective on particular issues, provided consumers are willing to act together over a long period of time. INFACT is a nonprofit organization founded in 1976 to hold transnational corporations directly responsible for practices that endanger the health and survival of all people. It coordinated the boycott of Nestlé in protest of that company's mass-marketing campaign to promote and sell infant formula in developing countries. Nestlé convinced hospitals to offer infant forumla to mothers and to extol it as the "modern" and easy way to feed their children. For formula to be nutritious, one must mix the correct proportion with clean water. In developing countries, the water is seldom clean, the formula is so expensive that mothers are tempted to dilute it to make it stretch, and even if the women are literate, the directions are often in English! Worse, once women start using formula, their own milk dries up, leaving them with no alternative but to continue to use the formula. It is no wonder that thousands of infants died from malnutrition and related diseases as a result of Nestlé's campaign.

INFACT coordinated hundreds of local chapters during a six and one-half year effort to force Nestlé to adopt a code endorsed by the World Health Organization for marketing infant formula. The boycott and the publicity forced Nestlé to participate in creating the code and comply with it, but some other companies—including American Home Products, Bristol-Myers, and Abbott/Ross Laboratories—continue quietly to ignore the code. Moreover, much of the damage has long since been done. Due in part to the formula companies' propaganda, a large proportion of women in developing countries have stopped breast feeding. As recently as 1986, three years after the end of the Nestlé boycott, one million infants died because they were bottle fed.[1]

Boycotting companies is like weeding a garden: we can remove a few weeds, but others remain, many with roots hidden deep underground, ready to sprout whenever we turn our attention away. While boycotts seldom root out a problem, they do increase our awareness, understanding, and vigilance. And they are a fairly simple step that we as consumers can take to control the worst excesses of corprations.

INFACT is currently taking on General Electric (GE) for its role in producing and promoting nuclear weapons. They have chosen GE because it is highly visible, is involved in nearly every major nuclear weapons system, was the first defense contractor whose indictment for fraud led to its contract being suspended, has one of the most aggressive lobbying offices in Washington, D.C., is a generous political action committee (PAC) contributor, and is the sole producer of the neutron triggers required for all nuclear bombs.

If you decide to join the GE boycott, or any other boycott, it is important to write the company to tell them why you have stopped buying their products and what they can do to win back your support. And please be careful when choosing alternate products.

In the case of GE, it is very hard to find light bulbs produced by companies not involved in nuclear weapons production—as GTE (GTE, Sylvania, Grolux, Lumalux), Westinghouse, Emerson Electric (Day-Brite, Emerson), and North American Philips all are. "Nuclear-free" light bulbs can be obtained from Duro-test (Duro-lite), DioLight Technologies (47 W. Huron St., Pontiac, MI 48508), and NOUAH (3335 S. Telegraph, Dearborn, MI 48124).[2] Take care not to jump from the frying pan into the fire!

3.2 Being a Responsible Consumer

In addition to boycotting a specific product or company, we can become more aware of the impact of our daily purchases.

One of the easiest ways to be a responsible consumer is to "buy local" as much as possible. In Vermont, we have a state-sponsored initiative that encourages Vermonters to buy Vermont products. (Oregon does the same.) At the supermarket I can purchase local milk, cheese, eggs, and other dairy products. Local bakeries distribute to supermarkets and to food co-ops. In addition, Cherry Hill Cooperative Cannery's products are available, and we even have a Vermont-based producer of processed meats like bacon, sausage, and hot dogs. Of course, many are already familiar with Ben & Jerry's Homemade ice cream. There are local craftspeople, organic farmers, and farmers' markets statewide during the season.

The point is that once we open our eyes and look at the addresses on the packages, we may be surprised at how often we can support our neighbors when we buy our everyday needs. Sometimes these products are a little more expensive than their mass-produced counterparts (for example, local eggs may cost well over one dollar a dozen, while agribusiness eggs may be as much as fifty cents cheaper), but the difference in price is in some ways an investment in the community and, in the case of eggs, in your own health.

Patronizing locally owned small businesses rather than large chains is also important. With the advent of shopping malls, our downtown areas have been drained and often rendered lifeless. Supporting local independent merchants is very important in maintaining strong local economies, with all their potential independence and diversity.

Even in locally owned mom and pop stores, most of the products are manufactured by corporations. Fortunately, researchers are collecting information about corporate activities that can help us decide what to buy in our supermarkets, hardware stores, and drugstores. One of the most useful sources of information is *Rating America's Corporate Conscience* by Steven Lydenberg, Alice Tepper Marlin, and Sean O'Brien Strub. Put together by the Council on Economic Priorities, one of the best nonprofit research organizations in the country focusing on corporate activities and responsibility, the book identifies the brand names, and rates the performance of 130 corporations. It is not a complete report card of corporate responsibility, but it does rate the relative performance of each company on each of seven issues: charitable contributions, women on boards and among top officers, minorities on boards and among top officers, disclosure of social information (their openness), involvement in South Africa, conventional weapons contracting, and nuclear weapons contracting. To fill out the picture, *Rating America's Corporate Conscience* includes the 130 corporations' policies, including their PAC contributions. Because it lists the brand names corporations use, the book is an excellent resource.

Becoming a responsible consumer is not easy. Changing habits like buying patterns is remarkably difficult. And once we change one set of habits, we often begin to notice other layers. For instance, one might begin to wonder if there are ways to avoid excess packaging, or ways to reduce the effects of our consumption on people in the Third World. Still, what we buy and from whom are decisions we control; let us use even that little bit of power.

3.3 Divestment

Divestment is a tactic used by investors to influence companies' policies and sometimes governments that depend on these companies, as in the case of South Africa. Media attention to apartheid in South Africa has made divestment a household word; and the divestment movement is having an effect. So far over sixty United States corporations have withdrawn from South Africa, and all banks, except Citibank, have stopped lending money to South Africa. This still leaves over two hundred companies doing business in that country, but the situation is changing fast and companies continue to pull out.

When it is part of a larger campaign, divestment can put a lot of pressure on companies. But as usual, vigilance is necessary. Some corporate breaks from South Africa are far from clean. For example, Coca-Cola sold its South African operations to black South African entrepreneurs and will continue sales through a

South African franchise. General Motors and IBM also plan to continue sales in South Africa, despite their official "withdrawal" from that country. The American Committee on Africa (ACOA), the American Friends Service Committee (AFSC), Interfaith Center on Corporate Responsibility (ICCR), TransAfrica, and the Washington Office on Africa have issued guidelines designed to help people distinguish between divestment and a cosmetic restructuring of economic relations. Copies of the guidelines may be obtained from ACOA.[3]

There is currently an expanded effort to force Citibank to stop loaning money to South Africa, where for decades it has been the largest United States lender. Its South African subsidiary has assets in excess of $226 million and deposits of $165 million (1985 figures). Outstanding loans to South African borrowers totalled 500 million Rand from the S.A. subsidiary and another $700 million from U.S. Citibank; these loans total over 25 percent of all loans from the United States to South Africa.[4]

After a protest in 1986, a bank spokesperson claimed, "We are doing more every day to try to end apartheid and help blacks in South Africa than can be done on any day in protests on Park Avenue in New York." Although the bank does make some contributions to black social programs and has a four-person black business lending unit, in 1985 only 15 percent of Citibank's 199 South African employees were black, 20 percent "Asian/coloured," and 65 percent white.[5]

Shareholder resolutions have been filed calling for Citibank to terminate all South African operations and to issue no new loans (including trade credits, which are still permitted by United States law). A national campaign is under way to mail protest postcards to John Reed (Citibank's chairman and chief executive officer and a member of the United States Corporate Council on South Africa), and rallies, picketing, and civil disobedience are all being used to influence the bank. So far, United States churches have closed down over $125 million worth of Citibank accounts, and in January 1987, the New York City Employees Retirement System board voted unanimously to divest from banks making loans to South Africa; at the time, they owned shares of Citicorp stock worth more than $13.6 million.

Successful divestment campaigns put pressure on the target companies, and particularly on institutions depending on the companies. Cosmetic restructuring and the willingness of less scrupulous investors to buy the divested stocks limit the economic pressure on the companies and the government, but they do not

27

necessarily stop the bad press, and divestment means we personally are not supporting a bad situation or a repressive regime. Still, it is unclear how effective divestment pressure will prove. I suspect that true justice and equality must be obtained by the grassroots efforts of black South Africans and that our place is to find ways to support their struggles.

3.4 Shareholder Action

Divestment resolutions are often forced by shareholder action, but shareholder resolutions can also be used to promote a wide range of changes in corporate policy. All owners of common stock in a corporation are entitled to vote on corporate policy and elect the directors who manage the company. Each share is worth one vote. If a stockholder cannot attend the annual meeting in person (and most do not) one votes by proxy. Before the annual meeting, management sends shareholders information about the candidates for the board and about any resolutions being submitted for consideration. One votes and mails the proxy back before the meeting.

This is more than a right, it is a responsibility. As an owner, one is responsible for the ethical successes and failings of a company as well as for its financial gains or losses. More shareholders are becoming aware of this dual role and are joining together to create more powerful coalitions to work to change corporate policy, especially social and environmental policy. Anyone who owns at least $1,000 worth of stock and has owned it for at least eighteen months may submit a shareholder resolution, a formal proposal requesting that the company take certain actions (such as disclosure on various issues or withdrawal from South Africa). The Securities and Exchange Commission (SEC) made the $1,000, eighteen-month requirement to discourage people from buying a single share of stock just to "hassle" a company (people get around this requirement by pooling funds). Despite these restrictions, many investors, especially large institutional and religious investors, choose shareholder action to push for greater corporate responsibility. Shareholder resolutions are included on the proxy statements to be voted on by all stock owners.

When submitting a resolution, one must pay careful attention to SEC regulations so as not to give the corporation an excuse to ignore the resolution. Corporations can, at their discretion, decide not to include a resolution, but to do so they must send notice, along with their reasons, to both the filer and the SEC. Regulations govern the content, as well as the submission process itself. Resolutions must meet the SEC's definition of "legitimate shareholder concern": the subject must be significantly related to the business of the company, may not be of a personal nature, may not concern ordinary business practices, and must be within the company's power to grant.

Shareholder resolutions are most effective in bringing issues and concerns to the attention of management and of the other stockholders. They are most often filed to raise awareness, rather than with the expectation that the resolution will pass. Media attention can make such resolutions more effective. So far, large institutional investors (such as pension funds) and churches have been the most effective in bringing resolutions to a vote. The Interfaith Center on Corporate Responsibility (ICCR), a coalition of approximately 250 religious institutional investors with combined portfolios totaling over $15 million, coordinates shareholder actions, boycotts, divestment, letter-writing campaigns, and vigils challenging corporations' policies. According to ICCR's director, Tim Smith, "church investors are proposing more social-responsibility shareholder resolutions to more companies than ever before in the sixteen-year history of the church corporate responsibility movement." Indeed, twice as many resolutions were filed in 1987 as in 1986! Together, these religious and institutional portfolios total over $150 billion!

Most of the resolutions filed in 1987 dealt with South Africa, requesting either that the company suspend operations in that country or cease trading or selling goods to South Africa through subsidiaries. Other resolutions concerned:

Disclosure—requests that several companies reveal specified information to stockholders.

Acid rain—American Electric Power (AEP) has been asked to disclose its plans to reduce emissions that cause acid rain. AEP controls six of the dirtiest power plants in the country according to the Environmental Protection Agency (EPA).

Images of women and minorities—their portrayal by Capital Cities/ABC.

Investments in Chile—A resolution was filed asking Exxon to adopt a policy "prohibiting further investments in its Chilean subsidiaries until the government there restores full democratic rights to its citizens, including the rights of workers to organize, to demonstrate peacefully, and to obtain fair wages and benefits by collective bargaining without police or military interference."

World debt—among the resolutions were ones to Bankers Trust, Chemical New York, and J.P. Morgan requesting that they advocate long-term loan rescheduling as well as other policies that will positively affect interest rates and other fees to developing countries.

Nuclear weapons, nuclear waste, and space weapons.[6]

When integrated into a larger effort including such things as letter-writing campaigns, boycotts, divestment strategies, and media attention, working from within the company can be an effective way of encouraging corporate responsibility.

A successful example involves the Hospital Corporation of America (HCA). When a shareholder resolution asking the company to report the number of its hospitals that have adopted infant formula distribution guidelines consistent with the World Health Organization Code of Marketing of Breastmilk Substitutes was filed, HCA agreed to distribute to its hospitals a new policy encouraging breast feeding and discouraging formula use. Since HCA voluntarily complied with the resolution, the resolution was withdrawn.[7] This is not unusual; corporations really do like to avoid bad publicity whenever possible.

Another success story: when Monsanto's contract with the Department of Energy (DOE) to operate the Mound site in Miamisburg, Ohio (the company's facility for the manufacture of nuclear weapons components) comes up for renewal on September 30, 1988, it will *not* be renewed. Wylie B. Hogeman, Monsanto's president, stated that the decision "would enable Monsanto to more fully concentrate on its major businesses." ICCR members have been questioning Monsanto about its weapons production since 1979. In 1983 they asked it for the first time not to renew its contract with the DOE.[8] (This does *not* make Monsanto a saint, however. Monsanto is a defendant denying liability in Agent Orange cases being brought against producers of that deadly chemical.)[9]

Any action that endangers the company's bottom line is bound to be taken seriously, especially if there is the threat of any publicity. To the extent that shareholders become informed and aware of their responsibility as owners (rather than being passive stockholders as most currently are), corporations will be forced to become more responsive. For maximum power and visibility, it is essential to join together with other shareholder groups and organizations. Shareholders often own stock in several companies targeted for the same reason. Although specific companies are targeted, the *issue* is the focus, which approaches the subject from a larger perspective than most boycotts.

3.5 Socially Responsible Investing

Socially responsible investing adds social and ethical concerns to the process of making investment decisions. The concept of social investing has grown and spread considerably in the past five years. Both laudatory and damning articles have appeared in such mainstream publications and broadcasts as the *Wall Street Journal*, *U.S. News and World Report*, *Money*, and the *CBS Morning News* and numerous newspapers. However new most media claim this movement is, social investing has been around in practice if not in name for quite a while. As Ritchie Lowry, president of GOOD MONEY Publications, wrote in one of the first articles on the subject:

> Throughout history people have put their wealth into objects and activities that enable them to meet daily needs and protect them from unanticipated needs in the future. They have sought to minimize the risk to the capital committed to these investments in a world that entails social and moral risks as well as economic risks. War, crime, fraud, poverty, and the like have serious moral, social *and* economic costs. There is nothing new, therefore, about the idea of making both social and economic judgments to maximize the return from and safety of an investment.[10]

In the past, church groups and religious communities were the primary supporters of socially responsible investing. Some communities, like the Amana colonies, even combined their religious and social beliefs with their way of making a living. It was not until the early 1970s, in response to the Vietnam War and, later, to Watergate that the movement began to gather popular support. In 1970, a group of concerned Methodists organized the Pax World Fund, a mutual fund that began operations in 1971. Its

31

purpose is to avoid investments in all weapons, and to support instead companies producing life-supporting goods and services. Two years later, in 1972, the Dreyfus Third Century Fund began investing in companies with "best-of-industry" records.

In the years since, the number of socially screened funds has increased to six, with fairly clear, if not all-encompassing, social and environmental guidelines for investment. In addition, the number of publications providing information for concerned investors has grown, as have the number of financial consultants and brokers who work with socially oriented clients. It was not long ago that locating a financial planner or a broker willing to even *hear* your social concerns was extremely difficult.

People involved in social investment are quick to point out that social investing means different things to different people. We are each unique and have our own priorities—there is no perfect "screen" that suits everyone. Social investment professionals also know that there are no perfect companies. Investors must make choices based on their individual value systems, and they must rank their values.

What does this mean in practice? If you were an individual investor concerned about nuclear war, the environment, the South African and other exploitative regimes, workplace issues, women's issues, and animal rights, it would be extremely difficult, if not impossible, to find publicly traded companies that are "clean" in all those areas. In the jargon of business, you would be "limiting the universe of possibilities" to the extent that nothing is left. Obviously, then, if you wished to invest in the stock market, you must set priorities and make compromises. You must decide what you absolutely cannot live with and what you *do* want to support— say, a clean environment or women-managed companies or worker-ownership. Based on your choices, you could then apply "negative" and "positive" screens to companies under consideration.

What we do with our money can reflect who we are and what we believe in, and that responsibility does not end at the point of transaction. As stockholders in a corporation, we are *owners*. A piece of that company belongs to us!

In the same way that we buy clothes or groceries on the basis of *both* price and personal taste, it only makes sense that we choose our investments with attention to who we are. If one is active in a local peace group, why hold stock in General Electric? If one belongs to a labor union (or manages a union's pension fund), why hold stock in a company that closes plants in the United States for cheaper labor outside of the country? If one supports the Sierra Club or the conservation movement, why benefit financially from a company involved in offshore oil drilling, producing toxic chemicals, or destroying rain forests?

When investing in the stock market, one can use negative or positive screens. Most investors use both. Using a negative screen means specifying activities to *avoid* supporting. (This was the way socially responsible investment started.) The following incomplete list gives some idea of the breadth of the issues various investors have chosen to avoid.

- –alcohol, tobacco, gambling
- –South Africa and other repressive regimes
- –Third World exploitation (people and natural resources)
- –nuclear energy
- –nuclear weapons
- –the military
- –handguns
- –drugs and traditional health care practices
- –violence and pornography in the media
- –animal exploitation (killing animals for research and/or for food)
- –environmental pollution
- –union busting
- –discrimination against women, minorities, and homosexuals
- –deceptive or false advertising

Issues investors have chosen to support include:

- –good pay, benefits, and working conditions
- –high-quality goods and services
- –renewable energy
- –energy conservation
- –environmental protection
- –alternative medical care
- –abortion and family-planning services
- –education and communication
- –alternative and appropriate technologies
- –local community development
- –worker equity
- –housing
- –small business

Identifying and ranking the practices you want to avoid or promote is the first step toward creating a screen. The next step is to define economic needs and goals so that investments can satisfy both your financial requirements and social concerns. You must decide whether you want income now, in the future, or both, as well as how much risk you can afford. Then decide where to look for investments. Besides the large corporations listed on the New York and American Stock exchanges, you can invest in:

- —the stock of small- to medium-sized companies that are publicly traded and sold over the counter (OTC) and on local exchanges (issued for sale in only one or a few states)
- —mutual funds
- —money-market funds
- —municipal bonds
- —government instruments
- —banks and credit unions
- —small businesses
- —other alternative investments

Many investors argue that despite their lacking the long history of the "reliable" blue-chip stocks (GE, IBM, Dow, and others), smaller companies are more responsive to change, more open to investors' and consumers' social needs, and so both socially *and* financially a better investment. *The Clean Yield,* a newsletter for social investors, focuses on these smaller, "emerging growth" companies, and their "model portfolio" substantiates this argument.

Mutual funds pool the stock of many companies to form a diversified pool of investments. This diversification protects investors from large losses due to the failure of segments of the market. There are five socially screened mutual funds that between them cover the needs of most socially concerned investors. Money-market funds require and provide more liquidity than mutual funds, and consist of some corporate investments, short-term debt, and government issues supporting such things as small businesses, construction of moderate-income housing, and student loans. There are two socially responsible money-market funds. Mutual funds usually outperform money-market funds, which are often only slightly more profitable than passbook savings accounts.

Municipal bonds are one method state and local governments use to raise money for specific projects. Interest varies according to the bond's rating and taxability and is paid every six months; the principal is returned when the bond matures (from a few months to several years). The new tax laws have altered the bond market, making it more important to assess one's tax situation before investing in them. There are now three types of bonds. Fully tax-exempt bonds are issued to raise money for such governmental purposes as the building of roads and schools. Fully taxable bonds are issued to finance "private activity"—shopping malls, stadiums, convention centers, and the like. Strangely enough, Congress includes air- and water-pollution control facilities in "private activity." Fully taxable bonds pay a slightly higher interest rate (2 to 3 percent) than the tax-exempt bonds do. Finally, there are partially tax-exempt bonds to finance projects that are considered partly public and partly private. Bonds carry ratings, from AAA insured down to C, or are nonrated. The higher the bond is rated, the lower is its yield.

The importance of bonds for social investors is that they allow us to support particular local or regional projects. There are bond funds that, like mutual funds, reduce the capital risk, but none have specifically socially responsible screens. Since bonds can be issued for anything from the construction of a nuclear power plant to the building of a new elementary school, investors must carefully examine each issue in such a fund before investing.

At the federal level, various agencies issue government bonds to finance student loans (Sallie Mae's), farm loans (Federal Farm Credit System), small-business loans (Small Business Administration), and home mortgages and housing construction (Federal National Mortgage Association, Fannie Mae's; Federal Home Loan Banks; and the Federal Home Loan Mortgage Corporation, Freddie Mac's). While not investing in the most progressive social change by purchasing government instruments, at least your money is not supporting apartheid or nuclear weapons construction.

Banks and credit unions are the places we usually put our money. They can be great investments, or they can be a concerned investor's nightmare. Large interstate banks are much more likely to have large foreign investments as well as loans to Third World countries. Local savings and loans are much more likely to invest a larger percentage of their funds locally in the form of mortgage loans, business loans, and personal loans. The Community Reinvestment Act (CRA) of 1977 requires that banks attempt to meet the credit needs of the community in which they are located. Banks must issue a public statement outlining the types of loans available to the community and also must disclose the percentage of loans made in the community. A bank with a high percentage of local loans might be a good place to open a savings account. The CRA has been a useful tool for community organizers trying to reduce the drain of capital, particularly because it allows community groups to participate in the review process a bank must go through before relocating or opening a new branch office.

Concerned investors are beginning to reach banks. At the very least, more and more banks are being asked to report where their investments are. (This is public information and the bank must provide it; ask and be persistent.) One example of a responsible bank is the South Shore Bank of Chicago. In the 1970s, the South Shore was declining, and its neighborhood had, in less than ten years, turned from rich and white to poor and black. Banks diverted money from the community, and the South Shore district was "redlined" (meaning no loans were made for anything, thus allowing the community to become poorer and poorer). In 1973 Ronald Gryzwinski, three associates, and eleven investors purchased the faltering South Shore Bank. Their holding company has three affiliates: the City Lands Corporation (a real-estate development company that rehabilitates housing for low- and moderate-income people and promotes commercial development), the Neighborhood Fund (a venture capital firm that finances minority businesses), and the Neighborhood Institute (a nonprofit organization that works to create jobs and cooperative housing.) Since 1973, the South Shore Bank has made over $75 million in development loans to the local community. Repayment on these loans is an impressive 98 percent. The total capital investment by all the divisions of the holding company exceeded $150 million as of the end of 1986.[11] The accompanying sidebar on South Shore's Low-income Certificates of Deposit is one example of their innovative work.

Some concerned investors put their savings in credit unions (which require that one be a member to participate in their programs). Community development credit unions are of particular interest to concerned investors. These are established to serve low-income communities and usually focus on people not served by other banks or credit unions. An example is the Self-Help Credit Union in Durham, North Carolina, profiled below. The National Federation of Community Development Credit Unions is a national organization that serves as a clearinghouse for general information, provides assistance and support to developing credit unions, and maintains a central fund that invests exclusively in its member credit unions. (For more discussion of community reinvestment, see chapter 6.)

As you can see, there are many socially responsible ways of investing your money in more "traditional" vehicles. Which of these you choose (if any) depends on your personal financial situation and your values and preferences. If you need help in deciding where to invest, I suggest that you consult a financial planner who is willing (or eager!) to work with ethically concerned clients. Choosing a financial consultant is like picking a family doctor. Ask your friends for suggestions, visit, and ask all your questions. (It helps to have a few written down in advance.) Take as much time as you need to feel comfortable, and do not feel forced into anything because you feel ignorant or uninformed. You may interview several planners, brokers, or whatever before you find the person or organization that is right for you.

As you search, one issue you may well face is the subject of "return." Many traditional financial planners and brokers absolutely insist that one "suffers" a loss of return as a result of a decision to invest according to values as well as financial goals. Even if you do not care about a possible loss of a few percentage points on the bottom line, professional money managers often will, since making money is their job, period. They were not trained to worry about the environment—at least not until their day is over and they are back home—and they do not think apartheid is any of their business when it comes to doing business. But professionals in the social investment movement point out that investing according to social concerns does not necessarily reduce financial return, and the numbers substantiate this. Because of the movement to divest from South Africa and because they are required by law to be financially "prudent," managers of pension funds, college and church funds, city and state funds, and the like have promoted a lot of research. For example, Ted Brown and Tom Van Dyck of Dean Witter Reynolds in California did a study for the Africa Fund in 1985. They compared 124 companies that were South Africa free to 124 companies with connections to South Africa. From 1980 to 1984 the total return for the free portfolio was 20.75% compared to 16.06% for the connected portfolio. More recently, these analysts compared 105 free companies to 105 connected companies in the portfolio of the California State Teachers and Employees Retirement System (the largest such fund in the country). Return for the free group was 36.16%, versus 20.18% for the connected group.[12]

GOOD MONEY (see pages 42–43) has been monitoring its own index of industrial stocks and utilities since 1976. It compares its thirty-stock GOOD MONEY Industrial Average to the thirty-stock Dow Jones Industrial Average (DJIA). From 1976 until October 1, 1986, GOOD MONEY's average gained 371%, as compared to the DJIA's 78% gain over the same period.

These results really are not surprising. It only makes sense that companies producing useful and safe products, treating their employees well, caring about the environment (at least enough to comply with EPA regulations), and caring about the communities in which they are located would be, overall, the best-managed and most profitable companies, especially over time. But one must always remember to use *both* social and financial criteria. Just as a financially strong company may not be a good social investment, so might a good social investment be a bad financial one. The key to socially responsible investing is balancing social and financial criteria.

3.6 Selecting a Socially Responsible Investment

Once you are clear about what you want to avoid and to support with your stock or other investments, the hard work begins. It is difficult to discover companies' social and environmental practices. Some issues, like involvement in South Africa or production of nuclear weapons and their components, are relatively easy to check out. The information is readily available (see section 3.7) and can be updated by contacting the organizations compiling the files. For example, the *Value Line Investment Survey* can tell you which utility companies use nuclear power and what percentage of total power nuclear power accounts for.

Other issues, like environmental ones, can be more difficult to sort out. The EPA keeps files of cited violations and fines, but is not always the most reliable authority on environmental protection. To get a full picture of a corporation's effect on the environment, researchers use a range of information, such as EPA reports and on-line computer data bases, obscure newspapers and journals (some of these are listed in the Resources section), reports from the companies themselves (annual reports, reports to shareholders, press releases, in-company newsletters, and the like), and regular phone queries to company executives. Even the most diligent miss some effects, and there are "secret" practices, such as illegal dumping, that surface almost daily.

To compound the issue, one person's environmental good guy may be another person's villain. One person's criterion of responsibility may be that a company reclaims an exhausted mining site, while another may question the desirability of mining at all. In general, it is safe to say that major corporations have not been the Earth's best friends.

You must therefore be very careful to do appropriate research. The many newsletters and publications focusing on the social and environmental practices of major corporations can aid both individual investors managing their own portfolios and investment professionals helping clients put their values to work in the marketplace. Some newsletters maintain "model" portfolios and rate corporations in such areas as affirmative action, environmental impact, and worker relations. If the newsletter does not describe exactly what the rating means (what the criteria are), be sure to write or call the publisher with specific questions.

Another difficulty is that the issues themselves are not cut and dried. Let us look at what it can mean to "support women's issues." One obvious tactic is to support companies that have women on their boards or in positions of power; that provide such benefits as child care, flex-time arrangements, and maternity leave with a job to return to; that have equivalent pay scales; and so on. (These practices, of course, can help all people, perhaps especially minorities.) But an investor interested in women's issues may want to look at the broader situation. The service sector, the industrial sector, and the agricultural sector (especially in rural areas and in developing countries) are the sectors that employ most women. Traditionally, these sectors pay poor wages, and women are paid much less than men for similar or equal work. Ninety-eight percent of all women workers earn less than $35,000 annually, with 51 percent of these earning less than $15,000. What is worse, many of the women are single mothers. The semiconductor industry provides a good example of the disparity between men's and women's salaries. In the United States in 1984, skilled male assemblers received $6.02 per hour, while their female coworkers received only $4.39 per hour.[13] Working conditions are frequently as poor as wages. For example, agricultural workers are often exposed to pesticides. This problem is particularly bad in developing countries, where many dangerous pesticides banned in the United States are still widely used (and promoted by companies trying to make money wherever it can be made). More often than not, especially in developing countries, women are the ones exposed to the pesticides. The effects are far-reaching. since the chemicals can cause both birth defects and genetic damage. According to a leaflet from the United Farm Workers, in the United States, "[b]abies born to migrant workers suffer 25% higher infant mortality than the rest of the population."

Even companies that do treat women workers decently may be suspect. As Carol Trenga, a researcher for GOOD MONEY, points out, "one must consider the level of occupational health education and safety precautions for workers before extolling the virtues of high-tech companies and their employment policies for women. At this point, the record is not so good." The high-tech company may provide good pay and benefits, but working long hours at computers may be hazardous to a woman's health, as suggested by increased rates of infertility, miscarriage, and birth defects among women working at video display terminals. And then there is the subtle physical stress (eyestrain, sitting all day) and emotional strain (interacting with a computer instead of people) of this sort of work.

More insidious are some of our cultural standards. Trenga notes that women in clerical and secretarial positions are often required to live beyond their means in order to maintain "professional" and polished images. The required clothing is expensive and the salaries (about $250 per week) are low. Try supporting a family on that while still "dressing for success"!

From women in management to wage disparity, from occupational health to our cultural norms, the investor interested in the lot of women is also led to the international arena. Take, for instance, the textile industry. Textile plants in the United States often relocate to developing countries where labor and environmental regulations are practically nonexistent. Trenga writes:

> Free-trade zones (FTZs) in developing countries have been described as labor camps, complete with barbed wire fences, worker barracks, and a scarcity of trade unions. Countries with very few regulations on industrial pollution usually have few regulations on work environments and working conditions as well. Young, often childless and unmarried women with good dexterity and keen eyesight are favored for jobs in the textile and electronics industries. Older women work in food processing and other industries that don't rely heavily on small motor skills. Wages are between $1.50 and $8 per day in these industries.

To compound the problem, the U.S. government encourages multinationals to expand into labor markets in developing countries. For example, the government gave aid amounting to $400 million to the South Korean textile industry. And the U.S. Agency for International Development (USAID) has encouraged the growth of high-tech labor markets in Malaysia. Some of the companies that make use of labor shops in developing countries include Sears, J.C. Penney, Hewlett-Packard, National Semiconductor, Texas Instruments, and Gulf & Western. And sweatshops exist even in this country, thanks to the threat of deportation should workers raise too many complaints about wages or working conditions. Many of the workers, mostly women, in the U.S. textile industry are migrant workers without immigration papers.

Given this complexity, what is a concerned investor to do? Trenga suggests looking at companies owned and managed by women or companies with a large percentage of women on their boards (though women do not necessarily manage companies progressively). One might also look to companies whose products and services are directed toward women (though the image of women, especially in their advertising, is not always so wonderful).

As one looks one will find some companies that have good child care and parental leave policies. Company-sponsored, on-site daycare facilities are gaining in popularity across the country. The November 1986 issue of the Council on Economic Priorities' (CEP) newsletter summarizes the state of child care in corporate America (see Resources). CEP reported that 2,500 employers (out of tens of thousands) offered some form of child care assistance in 1985.

Even from this very brief discussion, it is clear how difficult it is to maintain total integrity when investing in corporations. A company that has a wonderful employee policy may involve its workers with highly toxic chemicals. A women-owned company may promote an image of women less than desirable to feminists. Or a company with great parental leave and child care programs may be polluting the environment or be involved in South Africa. Passing one screen with a clean bill of health does not make a company saintly.

An investor who buys stock of major corporations must make choices, often painful ones. Another possible strategy is to pick the least offensive company you can find and file shareholder resolutions to change those policies you dislike. Some of the best pro-women investments are not in the stocks of corporations, but in the local development projects, small businesses, foundation programs, and the like that are the subject of the rest of this book.

What Is GOOD MONEY's Stock Average?

GOOD MONEY's stock averages have received increasing attention and publicity, primarily because of their good overall performance in comparison to traditional stock averages. During the crash of October 1987, GOOD MONEY's average dropped substantially less than the Dow! This report describes the origin, nature, and purposes of GOOD MONEY's current thirty-stock industrial average.

GOOD MONEY Publications has been in business for five years. From its founding, the company decided to design stock averages to see how socially screened investments would do in comparison to traditional ones. One of the very first handbooks, printed and sold in 1982 and 1983, described three stock averages for socially screened industrial, utility, and transportation companies. These were based upon research and analyses that Ritchie Lowry, founder of GOOD MONEY, had been doing for about two years prior to that time.

He started with the Dow Jones Industrial Average (DJIA), the easiest model to replicate, and tried to find socially responsive alternatives for a GOOD MONEY Industrial Average (GMIA). For some industries, such as computers and pharmaceuticals, this was possible. However, in other cases, such as aerospace and chemicals, there were really no socially responsive alternatives; therefore, typical favorites of social investors from other industries were substituted.

During the seven years of the GMIA's existence, changes have been made for only three reasons—ones never related to the economic performance of a company or its stock:

(1) the company goes private, declares bankruptcy, or is merged with another company;
(2) the company becomes involved in socially questionable practices or policies; or
(3) a substitution is made to better reflect the changing nature of the economy and to make the GMIA a fairer comparison to the DJIA.

In the case of all changes, a suitable substitute in the same industry was made, if at all possible, on social bases. The accompanying tables summarize these changes and the current companies on both the DJIA and the GMIA.

It is important to recognize that GOOD MONEY's average, like the DJIA, is merely an index. As such, it is subject to all the strengths and weaknesses of any index and is *not* a recommendation to buy, sell, or take any other investment action. The average is merely designed to test whether or not, over the long run, making social judgments forces investors to give up financial gains in the stock market.

Another important caution: the GMIA is not a purity index. Animal rights activists will be concerned about Hershey's use of rats to study tooth decay; divestment activists, about Johnson & Johnson's operations in South Africa; and those who wish to avoid all war connections, about Digital Equipment's selling of computers to other firms that convert them for military use. However, these companies also have strong social positives to recommend them. Though GOOD MONEY's average has something for everyone to hate, it also has something for everyone to support. In short, it is a social average, as well as being an economic and financial average.

See tables on pages 44–47 for more information about the GOOD MONEY Industrial Average.

South Shore Bank of Chicago
Investment Fund for Housing/Rehab CD-Loan Program
7054 S. Jeffery Boulevard
Chicago, IL 60649
Attn: Development Deposit Department
(312) 288-7017

With over a decade of successfully financing rehabilitation of almost 11 percent of the multifamily housing in the South Shore neighborhood of Chicago, the South Shore Bank launched the Rehab CD-Loan Program on June 1, 1985, as a response to the loss of federal rehabilitation subsidies and as a way of making a combination of interest-free and low-interest loans available for rehabilitating one thousand units of the remaining two-thirds of South Shore's housing that still needs upgrading.

The lower borrowing costs will make more rehabilitation money available per unit, and will ensure that rents remain affordable for the low- and moderate-income minority families making up 74 percent of the South Shore population living in rental housing.

Changes Made in the GOOD MONEY Industrial Average Since Its Inception

Old Company	Why Dropped?	New Company	Why Added?
Aetna Life	Ran into claims problems.	First Virginia Banks	In financial industry.
American Greetings	Did not answer question about Native American program.	Pitney-Bowes	Better representative of economy.
Coleman	Obscure company.	Miller, H.	Better representative of economy.
Cummins Engine	Defense work.	Stride Rite	New industry for GMIA at that time.
Esquire	Bought by Gulf & Western.	Meredith	Also publishing industry.
Federal Express	Should really be on a transportation average.	Flight Safety	Same general industry.
General Motors	Serious recall problems.	Honda	Same industry.
Honda	OTV problems, and foreign owned.	Subaru	More direct auto play.
Kroger	Labor and other problems.	Dayton-Hudson	Stores and old average heavily weighted toward food.
Levi Strauss	Went private.	Hartmarx	Still clothing industry.
Matsushita Electric	Foreign owned.	MMM	Big capitalized U.S. firm.
New York Times	Good journalism only.	*Washington Post*	Good women's record.
Norton Simon	Bought by Esmark.	McDonald's	Old average had too many companies.
Smucker, J.M.	Heavy food weight in old average.	Rouse	New industry.
Waste Management	Serious toxic waste handling problems.	Browning-Ferris	Did not handle toxic waste.

How the GOOD MONEY Industrial Average Has Done

Since 1987, GOOD MONEY's Industrial Average has led the Dow Jones as follows:

Date	GMIA Average	Overall Change	DJIA Average	Overall Change
12/31/86	137.60	—	1895.95	—
2/17/87	165.02	+19.9	2237.49	+18.0%
3/17/87	171.26	+24.5	2284.80	+20.5
3/26/87	172.53	+25.4	2372.59	+25.1
4/06/87	175.10	+27.3	2405.54	+26.9

However, GOOD MONEY has consistently argued that social investing is for the long term, rather than for short-term speculative profits. The comparisons for the two averages over longer periods are as follows:

Performance for last	GMIA	DJIA
10 years (12/76 to 4/87)	+531.2%	+139.4%
6 years	257.3	149.5
4 years	156.9	125.6

The conclusions? It is obvious that as many of the companies on GOOD MONEY's average mature, the rate of growth of the GMIA, relative to the DJIA, has slowed. Nevertheless, the GMIA still leads, both short- and long-term. What does all of this mean? Very simply—there is no inherent reason why investors should have to sacrifice normal rates of return by making social judgments, and, with a little bit of luck (which is true for all types of investing) they can do better by avoiding the really bad companies.

Current GOOD MONEY and Dow Jones Industrial Average Companies Compared

Industry	GOOD MONEY Companies	Dow Jones Companies
Aerospace/Defense	none	Boeing
Apparel/Shoes	Hartmarx, Stride Rite	none
Automobiles/Trucks	Subaru of America	General Motors, Navistar Int'l
Chemicals, Basic & Diversified	Minnesota Mining	Dupont, Minnesota Mining, Union Carbide
Computers	Digital Equipment, Wang Labs.	IBM
Electrical Equipment and Home Appliances	The Maytag Company	General Electric, Westinghouse
Financial Services and Banking	First Virginia Banks	American Express
Forest Products	Fort Howard Paper	International Paper
Household Products	none	Procter & Gamble
Industrial Services	Browning-Ferris Industries	none
Machinery and Machine Tools	Ametech, Norton Company Snap-on Tools	none
Metals and Mining	none	Alcoa
Multiform	none	Allied Signal

(continued next page)

Current GMIA and DJIA Companies Compared

Industry	GOOD MONEY Companies	DOW JONES Companies
Office Equipment and Supplies	Cross, A.T., Miller, Herman, Pitney-Bowes	none
Packaging	none	American Can
Petroleum Products	Atlantic Richfield	Chevron, Exxon, Texaco
Pharmaceuticals	Johnson & Johnson	Merck & Company
Precision Instruments	Polaroid	Eastman Kodak
Publishing	Meredith Corp., *Washington Post*	none
Real Estate	Rouse Company	none
Restaurants/Foods	Hershey Foods, McDonald's	Coca-Cola, McDonald's
Retail Stores	Dayton-Hudson, Melville Corp.	Sears Roebuck, Woolworth
Steel	Worthington Industries	Bethlehem Steel
Telecommunications	MCI Communications	AT&T
Tires and Rubber	none	Goodyear
Tobacco	none	Philip Morris

In addition to benefitting tenants and landlords, the Rehab CD-Loan Program also benefits investors by providing a safe, targeted investment with a guaranteed return and an annual accounting of program results.

The investor purchases a Rehab CD at the rate of 5 or 6 percent, estimated to be 3 to 5 percent below market rate. This difference between the interest rate paid to the depositor and the current market rate is allocated to the Investment Fund for Housing and becomes the source of funds for interest-free, deferred-payment loans (DPLs) to qualified borrowers. The DPL is combined with a conventional market-rate loan, such as mortgage loans or FHA home-improvement loans, to keep borrowing rates, and rents, low.

The minimum investment for a Rehab CD is $10,000 for a term of at least six months (preferably for two to five years). The bank's hope is that the effect of improved housing for inner-city residents will "combat further community deterioration," and that it will serve as a pilot program for the development credit branches the bank plans to open and for other banks throughout the country that may want to extend credit for housing rehabilitation.

The Self-Help Credit Union: A Unique Investment Opportunity
—Steve Zuckerman

Imagine how frustrating it is to watch a group of low-income individuals reopen a closed textile mill, only to flounder because no one will lend them the money to buy materials necessary to fulfill an available contract. A Burlington, North Carolina, hosiery mill, Alamance Workers' Owned Knitting (AWOK), found itself in just this situation. Many other employee-owned firms regularly face the same problem. Fortunately, the Self-Help Credit Union (SHCU), of Durham, North Carolina, has taken significant steps to alleviate such problems. Supporting SHCU efforts through membership in the credit union offers concerned individuals and organizations a very unique investment opportunity.

SHCU is a federally insured credit union sponsored by the Center for Community Self-Help (CCSH), a nonprofit organization also based in Durham. CCSH, founded in 1980, provides business, legal, and technical assistance to worker-owned businesses and other democratically managed organizations in North Carolina. Its goal is to help communities and employees save and create jobs.

specifically for low-income and minority individuals. The founders of CCSH chose employee ownership as their focus for economic development in the belief that worker-owned enterprises create more jobs. Employee ownership creates an environment where people can develop, grow, and take more control over their own lives.

But CCSH staff and the businesses they help repeatedly face a significant roadblock: conventional financial institutions are virtually unwilling to extend financing to employee-owned businesses. "Partly because they don't understand the cooperative structure, and partly because the firms are largely low-income and minority folk," explained Bill Bynum, a business developer with CCSH, "banks just won't lend them any money." The Center staff quickly saw a critical need for a lending institution designed specifically to assist cooperatively owned and managed businesses. After three years of exploration and planning, this vision became a reality in the form of the Self-Help Credit Union.

The credit union's business loans generally take one of two forms: direct business loans or worker-equity loans. The situation with AWOK, the co-op mentioned above, is an example of the former. AWOK had the opportunity to sign a profitable contract if it could guarantee delivery. But the young company had no capital with which to purchase the necessary materials. No conventional lenders were willing to risk a loan to a one-year-old effort with a somewhat novel corporate structure. SHCU, which by law must require collateral for significant business loans, arranged a loan secured at first by the inventory purchase and, later, as the goods were sold, by the associated accounts receivable. "We just work a little harder [than other institutions] to find a workable structure for difficult but sorely needed loans," explained Ms. Katherine Stern, the assistant manager of SHCU. The credit union and the Center then continue to work very closely with the businesses to make sure the loan is effective and SHCU gets repaid.

Worker-equity loans are personal loans used by individuals to buy membership shares in a worker-owned company. They are designed to serve both the businesses and the individuals involved. Obviously, such a loan provides cash with which workers can buy into a company and help to capitalize it. But even when this capital infusion is not critical to the operation, Center and credit union staffers find a personal financial investment, executed through a personal loan, very useful. "Making an individual sign a personal note is a good test of their commitment to the venture," stated Mr. Bynum. "We've seen a big difference between workers who

49

actually borrow money to buy in and those who just agree to a payroll deduction. There has to be a way for them to make a real investment."

Individuals and organizations can support these efforts through deposits in the Self-Help Credit Union. If you are familiar with credit unions, you already know some of the advantages of an SHCU investment. First, it is federally insured up to $100,000, which makes for a safe investment. Second, SHCU offers an array of competitive accounts, including a variable-rate Limited Transaction Money Market Account (with up to three checks per month), a Regular Share (savings) Account, and a variable-rate IRA. For any individuals or organizations interested in accepting a below-market rate of return to further assist SHCU development efforts, the credit union also offers fixed-term, fixed-rate Development Deposit Accounts. Thus, the credit union can meet most people's saving needs. Banking services are available in person or by mail, which adds to the convenience, particularly for out-of-state supporters.

SHCU differs from most credit unions in a very significant respect: its mission is to foster economic development efforts through business loans to democratically owned and managed businesses. "The credit union was established specifically to increase the availability of capital for grassroots job creation and business development that improves the economic stability of workers, their families, and their communities," reminds Bonnie Wright, manager of SHCU. While this credit union, like any other, serves its depositing members in every way it can, its ultimate purpose is to aid the development of its co-op business members. Thus, an SHCU depositor receives ample service and a competitive financial return, with the additional benefit of what the staff calls the "social dividend," the knowledge that deposited money is targeted for local economic development.

The Self-Help Credit Union has attracted seven million dollars in deposits, and the staff has still greater aspirations. The problem so far is that since a credit union's investments are limited by law to no more than 10 percent of its deposit base, and the nature of SHCU activities has led its board to impose a 5 percent limit, the staff has only about $350,000 to invest. Their biggest constraint today is the new regulation limiting loans to businesses to no more than 20 percent of reserves—only about $40,000 in SHCU's case. Since SHCU has considerably more deposits than many other credit unions, this affects others (and businesses in other communities served by these credit unions) even more dramatically than SHCU.

The new regulation is justified by the assumed high risk of business lending. SHCU's staff is fighting this new regulation, but has not yet been successful in changing it.

To expand its deposit base and to better serve the state, SHCU has developed an arrangement that gives members access to their accounts through the fifty-six branches of the North Carolina State Employees' Credit Union, thus enhancing SHCU's statewide appeal. The arrangement also enabled SHCU to offer checking on its money-market account and ATM access. "Although statewide access doesn't particularly help our out-of-state supporters," Ms. Stern admits, "this arrangement indicates our effort and future ability to provide economic assistance to a greater number of deserving people while at the same time providing a very attractive alternative to the investment community."

Interested individuals and organizations can join the SHCU or write for more information by contacting the office at: 413 Chapel Hill Street, PO Box 3619, Durham, NC 27701 (919) 683-3016.

Steve Zuckerman was formerly the director of development for the Self-Help Credit Union. He holds a BA in economics from Yale and an MBA from the Stanford Graduate School of Business.

3.7 A Directory for Socially Responsible Investing

Socially Screened Funds

Calvert Social Investment Fund
1700 Pennsylvania Avenue, NW
Washington, DC 20006
(800) 368-2748

Calvert offers a managed-growth portfolio (mutual fund) and a money-market portfolio. The fund avoids investments in nuclear power, defense contractors, and companies doing business in or with South Africa. Its investments support companies delivering safe products and services that have participatory management, negotiate fairly with workers, create a safe working environment, have equal opportunities for women and minorities, and have good community relations. The minimum initial investment is $1,000.

Dreyfus Third Century Fund
600 Madison Avenue
New York, NY 10022
(800) 645-6561

Dreyfus is a mutual fund that invests in companies with "best-of-industry" records in such areas as safety and environmental impact. Beginning in 1986, Dreyfus decided to avoid companies operating in South Africa, but there is no screen for weapons production or nuclear power. The minimum investment is $2,500.

New Alternatives Fund
295 Northern Boulevard
Great Neck, NY 11021
(516) 466-0808

New Alternatives is a mutual fund that invests in solar and other environmentally sound forms of energy production as alternatives to fossil fuels and nuclear power. Investments include a diversity of companies, ranging from smaller firms devoted to photovoltaic solar cells or domestic hot-water heaters to larger firms producing insulation or energy management systems. No more than 25 percent of the fund's assets will be invested in companies not listed on the New York or American stock exchanges. The fund does not invest in defense contractors or companies producing nuclear power. Other alternatives, such as cogeneration, biomass, and hydro, are also supported by the fund. Minimum investment is $2,650.

Parnassus Fund
1427 Shrader Street
San Francisco, CA 94117
(415) 664-6812

The Parnassus Fund utilizes a "contrarian" investment strategy, essentially buying out-of-favor companies that have what they call "Renaissance" qualities: high-quality products and services; market orientation that stays "close to the customer"; sensitivity to the community in which the company is located; a good relationship with its employees; and the ability to be innovative and respond well to change. Minimum investment is $5,000. (As an interesting note: some of their material is printed on recycled paper.)

Pax World Fund
224 State Street
Portsmouth, NH 03801
(603) 431-8022

The oldest of the screened mutual funds, Pax World does not invest in any company engaged in the manufacture of weapons or weapons-related products. It also avoids investments in companies engaged in the liquor, tobacco, and gambling industries. It excludes companies operating in South Africa, with the exception of those providing food and medicines. Minimum investment is $250.

Working Assets Money Fund
230 California Street
San Francisco, CA 94111
(800) 533-3863

Working Assets avoids investments in defense contractors, nuclear power, repressive regimes (for example, South Africa), and polluters of the environment. The fund supports equal opportunity, job creation in the United States, moderate-income housing, higher education, good labor relations and small business. Half of Working Assets' funds are in government securities (not T-bills) and commercial banks. The securities include Freddie Mac's, Fannie Mae's, and Sallie Mae's. The banks they invest in have strong records in the community. The minimum investment is $1,000. Working Assets also offers a "socially responsible" VISA card!

Research and Financial Management

Affirmative Investments, Inc.
59 Temple Place, Suite 408
Boston, MA 0211
(617) 350-0250

Affirmative Investments is a registered investment advisory firm specializing in advising individuals and institutions on privately placed, direct investments in socially positive enterprises. Investments may be in the form of loans, equity investments, privately placed bonds, and real-estate limited partnership interests. Minimum investment is usually $5,000.

Bank for Socially Responsible Lending
PO Box 404920
Brooklyn, NY 11240
(718) 768-9344

Conscious Investments
93 Saturn Street
San Francisco, CA 94114
(415) 621-6414

This organization offers workshops and seminars for those interested in social investing.

Council on Economic Priorities (CEP)
30 Irving Place
New York, NY 10003
(212) 420-1133

CEP is a research organization that produces a monthly newsletter and other publications of interest to social investors, focusing on various subjects related to corporate responsibility. Annual subscription is $25.

Data Center
464 19th Street
Oakland, CA 94612
(415) 835-4692

The Data Center is a subscription, research, and clipping service for information on corporations, industries, labor, plant shutdowns, Central America, and so on.

Funding Exchange
666 Broadway, 5th Floor
New York, NY 10012
(212) 260-8500

The Funding Exchange is a national organization of fourteen community-based public foundations, established to fund grassroots and activist organizations addressing such social issues as race and sex discrimination, nuclear proliferation, and economic injustice. It also sponsors conferences on socially responsible investing and publishes the *Directory of Socially Responsible Investments* ($7).

INFACT
256 Hanover Street
Boston, MA 02113
(617) 742-4582

Interfaith Center on Corporate Responsibility (ICCR)
475 Riverside Drive, Room 566
New York, NY 10115
(212) 870-2995

ICCR provides information on the practices of major corporations. Shareholder actions and corporate resolutions are major activities. It publishes *Multinational Monitor* and the *Directory of Alternative Investments* (see Resources).

Investor Responsibility Research Center (IRRC)
1755 Massachusetts Avenue, NW
Washington, DC 20036
(202) 939-6500

IRRC researches and reports on contemporary social and public policy issues as they affect corporations and produces a range of publications on business issues of concern to social investors. It is an excellent resource for information on South Africa.

Self-Help Credit Union (SHCU)
413 Chapel Hill Street
PO Box 3619
Durham, NC 27701
(919) 683-3016

Social Investment Forum
711 Atlantic Avenue
Boston, MA 02111
(617) 423-6655

The Social Investment Forum is a national professional association of advisors, bankers, analysts, investment funds, research and community organizations, and publishers active in developing the concept and practice of socially responsible investing. It will provide a list of socially responsible investment advisors in your area upon request.

Social Responsibility Investment Group
The Chandler Building, Suite 622
127 Peachtree Street, NE
Atlanta, GA 30303
(404) 577-3635

SRIG manages assets for socially responsible investors.

South Shore Bank of Chicago
7054 S. Jeffery Boulevard
Chicago, IL 60649
(312) 288-7017

Books

Bowers, Cathy, and Alison Cooper. *U.S. and Canadian Investment in South Africa*. IRRC (see Organizations).

Domini, Amy, and Peter Kinder. *Ethical Investing*. Addison-Wesley.

Foreign Investment in South Africa. IRRC (see Organizations).

Kanter, Rosabeth Moss. *The Change Masters*. Simon & Schuster.

Lydenberg, Steven, Alice Tepper Marlin, and Sean O'Brian Strub, for the Council on Economic Priorities. *Rating America's Corporate Conscience*. Addison-Wesley.

Moskowitz, Milton, Michael Katz, and Robert Levering, eds. *Everybody's Business: The Irreverent Guide to Corporate America*. Harper & Row.

The 100 Best Companies to Work for in America. Addison-Wesley.

Peters, Thomas J., and Robert H. Waterman, Jr. *In Search of Excellence*. Warner Books.

Shaw, Linda S., Jeffrey W. Knopf, and Kenneth A. Bertsch. *Stocking the Arsenal: A Guide to the Nation's Top Military Contractors*. IRRC (see Organizations).

Socially Responsible Buyer's Guide. Covenant for a World Free of Nuclear Weapons (see Organizations).

Publications

The Clean Yield
Fried & Fleer Investment Services, Ltd.
Box 1880
Greensboro Bend, VT 05842
(802) 533-7178

A monthly stock market newsletter (advisory) that focuses on publicly traded emerging growth companies. Includes updates of their "model portfolio" and "Clean Profiles." $75/year for individuals and nonprofits, $100/year for businesses.

The Corporate Examiner
Interfaith Center on Corporate Responsibility
475 Riverside Drive, Room 566
New York, NY 10115
(212) 870-2316

Monthly newsletter examines policies and practices of major U.S. corporations with regard to South Africa, labor, minorities, foreign investment, the military, and others. Regular updates on shareholder actions and the corporations' responses. $25/year.

Envest
Energy Investment Research, Inc.
PO Box 73
Glenville, CT 06831
(914) 937-6939

Biweekly newsletter focusing on developments and investment opportunities in companies providing products and services in cogeneration, alternative energy, energy management and conservation, environmental protection, and waste management. Features commentary, interviews, and company profiles. $225/ year.

GOOD MONEY
PO Box 363
Worcester, VT 05682
(802) 223-3911 or (800) 535-3551

Published since 1982, this bimonthly newsletter contains information on the ethical and social practices of publicly traded corporations. Ethical issues from animal rights to weapons production are covered regularly, as is the financial performance of socially responsible companies. GOOD MONEY also provides services to individual and institutional investors (portfolio screening) and publishes several issue papers and other reports of interest to social investors. $75/year.

INSIGHT
Franklin Research & Development Corporation
711 Atlantic Avenue, 5th Floor
Boston, MA 02111
(617) 432-6655

An advisory newsletter, published quarterly. Subscription also includes monthly market update on twenty companies, fifty in-depth briefs on selected stocks, and quarterly industry reports. $87.50/year for individuals, $175/year for institutions.

Multinational Monitor
PO Box 19405
Washington, DC 20036

Monthly publication provides information about transnational corporations and their effects here and abroad. Excellent resource for companies in Central America and other developing regions. Issues are examined from many perspectives. Recommended. $22/ year for individuals, $25/year for nonprofits, $35/year for businesses.

Value Line Investment Survey
Value Line, Inc.
711 Third Avenue
New York, NY 10017

Notes

1. The information about INFACT and infant formula in developing countries is from ICCR and INFACT press releases, conversations with Nancy Cole of Boston INFACT, and *Multinational Monitor*, April 1987.

2. *Socially Responsible Buyer's Guide*, Ann Arbor, MI: Covenant for a World Free of Nuclear Weapons, 1986.

3. *United States Anti-Apartheid Newsletter*, vol. 2, no. 1.

4. "Citibanking on Apartheid," ICCR, 1987.

5. Ibid.

6. *The Corporate Examiner*, Spring 1987.

7. Ibid.

8. Ibid.

9. *Multinational Monitor*, April 1987.

10. "Social Investing: Doing Well While Doing Good," *The Futurist*, April 1982.

11. Rob Baird, "Socially Responsible Banking: Chicago's South Shore Bank," RAIN, vol. 13, no. 1 (special issue on social investing).

12. Theodore Brown and Thomas Van Dyck (eds.), "Socially Responsible Investing: The Financial and Socio-Economic Issues," San Francisco: California/Nevada Interfaith Center on Corporate Responsibility, 1985.

13. Carol Trenga, "Women's Issues," GOOD MONEY Publications. One of a series of issue papers for social investors.

CHAPTER FOUR

Investing in the Small-Scale

Thinking of money as a means of personal expression and tool for social change leads many people to small-scale, affirmative investing, including loans, entering into partnerships, and making equity investments in businesses. Because of the perceived financial risk involved and because such agreements often involve friends or family members, this sort of investing can feel uncomfortable.

This section addresses both of these concerns. It is written by professional business and personal financial consultants who have had years of experience helping individuals and businesses clarify their personal, social, and financial goals. They agree that the first step is to "know yourself." Once you have identified your habits and priorities, it is much easier to define your financial needs and goals and to acquire the personal and technical skills needed to decide exactly what to invest in which organization.

This section is not the last word on the subject, but it is full of practical information and suggestions about sorting out your relationship with money, defining financial goals, analyzing business plans, negotiating with friends, and writing loan agreements. The issues and strategies in this chapter about lending and investing money apply to people with a lot of surplus money and to people with much less.

Investing in small-scale enterprises that we value allows us to help shape our communities since *we* decide what we support. Local investing and local buying together can play an important role in creating strong local economies that reflect our concerns.

The contributors to this section are:

Roger Pritchard, a small-business consultant in the San Francisco Bay area. He has been involved in the Briarpatch Network, providing consulting services, and counseling people interested in socially responsible investments. Financial Alternatives, 1514 McGee Street, Berkeley, CA 94703;

Christopher Mogil and Shelly Kellman, of Chrysalis Money Consultants, who work closely with individuals to set and achieve financial and life goals which integrate their personal needs and social values. Such goals have included socially responsible investing, improving family relations regarding money, effective and tax-wise social change giving, and more. Chrysalis Money Consultants, 21 Linwood Street, Arlington, MA 02174; and

Paul Terry, who works with individuals, nonprofits operating for-profit activities, and smaller businesses on business planning, marketing strategies, financial analysis, personnel, and time management. He also teaches small-business workshops, researches and writes business plans, and assists with seminar and sales presentations. Paul Terry & Associates, 1269 Rhode Island Street, San Francisco, CA 94107.

Why Invest in the Small-Scale?

Most of us assume that the safest investments are in large corporations (in stocks, money-market funds, or mutual funds), but investing in large-scale systems is not as safe for investors as it is represented to be. For instance, most investors lose money in the stock market, never mind its wilder submarkets like futures and options. Most brokers, however, make money—by convincing you to buy and sell.

It is not a system set up for honesty and clarity. The chains of information between you and those who make decisions in the corporation are long, the scale of operations is huge, your means of finding out what is happening are not good, and the intermediary salespeople do not share your interests. Mystification is normal when it comes to prospectuses, reports, and financial data, and most people do not know how to penetrate the mysteries.

Investing in small-scale enterprises offers a variety of possibilities (mini-businesses to smaller corporations) that belies its simple label. This investment sector of the economy is broad, vigorous, and, as a sector, stable. Small business is responsible for almost all job creation and is where many innovations begin.

The sector is particularly exciting because more and more people are deciding to take responsibility for their financial and social well-being by starting and running enterprises. Doing small business in a socially responsible way is joining with investing in a socially responsible way. Each helps the other.

But most businesses are not in start-up situations. Stable mini-businesses—professionals, craftspeople, small retail stores, mail order, and other single-person businesses—join small corporations in forming a solid range of opportunity for investment.

The first step in investing in the small-scale—in investing at all—is sorting out your feelings about whatever surplus money you have. Dealing with surplus money involves *work*. The steps for doing the work involve clarifying personal needs and social values (what you are against, what you are for) and learning investment skills. Only then will you have the capacity to evaluate and make investment decisions you will be happy with. In clarifying and learning, there is an *investment* involved—using one's surplus money to educate oneself and clarify one's values. And that is surely one of the most socially responsible investments you can make.

4.1 Defining Your Values and Goals

The best money decisions are fully integrated with your overall life goals. Many people view money as a "thing" separate from themselves and their lives, except as it can provide other "things" they want. Instead, try thinking of lending, investing, and giving as you view your work, your talents, your interests, your skills—as tools and resources for expressing your values and achieving your goals.

The first questions to answer when approaching an investment decision are:

1. What are my life goals?
2. What impact do I want to have in the world?
3. What do I want to accomplish in my personal life?

List general and specific answers to these questions; put aside some time to do this in a systematic way. If it seems overwhelming and hard to begin, you can start simply by producing your thoughts. Alone or with a friend, sit in a comfortable place and let yourself imagine your desired future; then write down the thoughts as they come.

Talking with someone—a friend or a counselor—often helps; choose someone who can listen nonjudgmentally and facilitate *your* getting clear instead of arguing or offering advice before you want it.

Once you have an idea of your goals, ask yourself: *How can I use money to support these goals?* For example, if your number-one personal goal is to live in a clean, beautiful area, and your most important goals for the world are environmental conservation and improvement, how can you best use your money? Depending on other goals you have listed, the creative answers you come up with could be anything from buying a suburban home and donating to the Sierra Club, to starting an environmentally sound farming cooperative, to founding or supporting a fund that gives grants to activist environmental groups.

An Example: Values About Profit

The following fictitious discussion is an example of the different ways socially conscious investors might think about profit, fit it in with their other values and goals, and apply the mix to their investment choices.

Arla: "My grandparents worked very hard for the money I inherited. They intended it to be passed down in the family. If I invest it in a way that does not make a profit—at *least* enough to stay even with inflation—I would be letting the fruit of their efforts slip away and betraying the love they showed by providing this money."

John: "My grandparents and parents also worked hard at the factory my family owns, which is the source of my wealth. But the two hundred workers they employed also worked very hard. I think it's unfair that our system gives the profits from all that work only to those who have the money or luck to own the factory—especially when some of the owners, like me, don't even work there! So I choose not to invest for interest or profit. In fact, I'm considering giving away most of the money I have coming to me from my part-ownership of the family business."

Tom: "If I don't go for as much profit as possible on my money, while everyone else in the economic system does, I will eventually fall behind and my life-style will slip. I will be able to afford fewer and fewer of the things that make me comfortable, while my friends all move into nice homes, travel more, etc."

Carol: "I've been torn about this at times. I agree with John that it is unfair that some people have the opportunity to make profits and others don't. But it's very important to me that I be able to provide my children with a college education. Saving and investing some money for profit seems like the only practical way to do that. My way of balancing my political views and my children's security is to invest in financially sound businesses that have excellent labor practices—democratic management, employee-ownership opportunities, and good on-the-job safety records."

Beth: "I feel the profit-making system is full of injustices, but I don't want the power of my money lost, either. My compromise is making loans that earn interest, but donating the interest to social-change organizations. That way the reward society gives for lending or investing money isn't 'lost'—it actually goes to work to help change a system that's unfair."

Sarah: "The profit-making system *is* full of injustices—not the least of which is the lack of security for those of us who grew up without enough money. I've earned the little money I have to invest—and what scares me is how quickly it would go if my mom stops being able to work—which will be soon. I feel like I have to *at least* keep up with inflation. To balance my desires for a more equitable system and my need for security, I invest some of my savings in a socially responsible money-market fund and the rest—at one point above inflation—in a well-established community revolving loan fund."

John: "I make zero-interest loans to a housing cooperative that helps low-income people to buy homes. If these folks had to pay interest, they couldn't do it, so my money is a very powerful tool to give a fairer footing to people who've been disenfranchised. I *feel* the money is doing *more* than if it were earning 20 percent interest."

4.2 Developing Investment Criteria

The question of profit is a good example of the values issue socially responsible investors face, because it involves social, political, personal, and life-style questions. Clarifying your values and goals in all of these areas and ranking them are the first steps in developing your *investment criteria.*

Everyone has investment criteria, although the criteria may be unconscious. Developing conscious investment criteria will help you make better decisions, even if your final decisions are gut-level ones. If you can identify them, gut-level factors can even be part of your criteria—"I want 50 percent of my money in projects that personally excite me."

As you consider different investment opportunities, keep in mind your goals and values, and the image of money as a useful tool, one of your many active resources.

How does each investment option look now? What do you envision the money accomplishing in each case? In which options do you see the money acting most effectively?

Weighing Rate of Return, Risk, and Liquidity

Another step in developing investment criteria is to decide how fluid, secure, and profitable you want your money to be.

1. How much money do I need to keep, risk-free?
2. How much do I want to invest? Lend? Give away?
3. What is the right balance of these uses of money for now?
4. How do I want that to change over the next five, ten, and twenty-five years?
5. How much can I afford to write off if necessary?

Then there are the balancing questions that put different values together:

1. How much financial *return* will I give up in order to support an enterprise that excites me—that reflects particular goals or values I hold dear?
2. How much *risk* will I take with how much of my money to support an enterprise or project that expresses my social values and goals?
3. Given my personal *and* social goals, *how long* can a borrower use my money?

Naturally, some of these questions will become clearer as you consider specific investment opportunities. But examining them ahead of time establishes a base that can be helpful in deciding whether or not to make a particular investment or loan.

Three Examples of Investment Criteria

Ron Baker, who lives modestly but comfortably on a combination of inherited wealth and income, persuaded his grandfather to put the $400,000 he was leaving to Ron into a foundation Ron would manage. When his grandfather died, the foundation was born, and Ron had to decide where to invest its assets. He established the following *investment criteria:*

1. *High return*—The fund gives away only the income on its assets, and Ron wants to maximize the money available to give away.
2. *Medium to low risk*—"I can't let the foundation's assets disappear in a flash of the stock market."
3. *Liquidity available in four years*—Ron, who has already given away principal to fund social change, may want to give more principal at that time.
4. *Local investment managers* with whom Ron can build a relationship.

These criteria are not listed in any absolute order of importance; their relative importance to Ron shifted in light of specific investments he considered. Ultimately, he chose a 50-50 balance of investments returning a fixed rate of income and those returning a variable income at a slightly higher risk. Half the foundation's money went to a well-established alternative publishing house as a three-year mortgage loan, secured with the building the company was buying. The interest is tied to the prime rate, an important deciding factor given Ron's criterion of a high return.

Ron put the other half of the foundation's assets into a stock-and-bond account managed by a local socially responsible investment manager. This manager offers a choice of social screens by which corporations are rated, and Ron is using all of them: corporate citizenship, employee relations, energy, environment, product, South African involvement, and large-scale weapons production. Within that framework, the manager will pursue the highest possible income for the foundation at low-to-moderate risk.

Abigail earns a modest salary as a community organizer and manages to save about $1,500 a year. She is the first of her family to have any savings at all and worries about having a buffer for herself and a little extra to help her family through hard times. But Abigail is also very committed to the work she does encouraging fundamental social change.

Abigail worked out a fairly explicit set of criteria. She wants her money to keep pace with inflation, be secure, be available at short notice, and if possible, support local community economic development initiatives. An unstated criterion was that her investment need little monitoring.

Abigail met her criteria by investing roughly half her money in a socially responsible money-market fund and the rest as a series of one-year loans to a well-established community revolving loan fund. The money-market fund gave her liquidity, low risk, fair return, and acceptable social screens. The revolving loan fund allowed her to support initiatives she really believed in with moderate risk, fair return, and acceptable liquidity.

Bill Weinman has many friends he considers creative geniuses. Between 1982 and 1985, he loaned and invested half his wealth in a variety of alternative business ventures run by friends and acquaintances. One friend, for instance, was working on a radical new way of diagnosing cancer; another was developing a technology to clean toxins from the environment.

Bill's lending process was informal. "Tell me about your project," he would say. If the answer impressed him, he would ask, "How much do you need?" The person would name an amount; Bill would say, "That seems reasonable," and he would put in that much money. So far he has not gotten any money back.

"All of these entrepreneurs impressed me as smart, trustworthy people," he says now. "I was not aware that making these kinds of loans was high-risk stuff."

Though Bill was not conscious of using criteria for making loans and investments, he clearly did use criteria. They were that the venture excite him personally, that it aim to advance something he believed was socially good, that the borrower impress Bill as being smart and trustworthy, that the amount of money requested strike Bill as reasonable, and that he have the money on hand. The degree of risk was *not* one of his criteria.

Looking back, Bill wishes he had researched the enterprises more thoroughly, even though he does not regret losing the money and probably would have taken some of the same risks anyway. "Some of the ventures may succeed yet," he points out cheerily. His investment criteria changed when he married and started a family.

4.3 Making Loans

Once you have set up investment criteria, you are ready to find organizations to invest in. One powerful tactic is to lend to or invest capital in mini and small enterprises that are part of a socially responsible economy. Whether for-profit or nonprofit, such enterprises try to support themselves, their workers, and their investors, while contributing to a healthy economy.

On the face of it, making loans should be a safe and easy way of investing your money in small-scale opportunities. After all, you retain ownership of the money, grant the use of it for a time to others, and take rent for it during that time in the form of interest. But people who have lent money can tell you of bad experiences—things have gotten difficult, they have been given the runaround, been burned, or lost a friend.

Why does this happen? For one thing, our society has developed powerful impediments to our making such loans with ease and assurance. *First,* banks and other financial institutions have appropriated the functions and cornered the skills of lending. We find ourselves, as individuals, feeling mystified, powerless, and naive. *Second,* we have been convinced that the system is the *only* safe place to lend, that all else is risky. *Third,* we find money (though not property) abstract and hard to own up to. *Fourth,* while banks make their loans coldly and with regard to safety, risk, and rate of return, not social responsibility, we are immersed in a tradition that tells us *as individuals:* "If something has social value, support it through gifts, donations, philanthropy—in short, through *subsidy* ." To make loans yourself, you have to unload these debilitating assumptions.

Are you reacting to the coldness of banks by going to the opposite extremes, either avoiding loans or plunging in and acting as if you were making a gift? The main cause of feeling burned is making "loans" to people and businesses when they are really taking them as a subsidy.

Do you feel that money is too abstract to be real? Then realize that money is a medium and a storehouse of wealth.

Do you feel that the system is the only safe place? Most people who have been burned in the system—and there are very many—simply blame themselves.

Are you afraid to go outside the system? Banks make loans so coldly because they rarely have good personal contacts with borrowers. You have already got an advantage: you know—or can find out—how skillful, careful, persistent, enterprising, and committed your borrowers are.

In the small scale, it is *people* that you will be mainly investing in. Successful lenders put lots of time into finding and getting to know such people. And while some will not make loans to family and close friends, others do this very well because they have observed and assessed them so closely and carefully that they can really trust their own judgment.

With this in mind, let us look at the market for loans to small-scale enterprises. There is in fact no ready market, like the stock market, and no salespeople who will make it easy for you to buy. You are going to find your borrowers by direct contact. The hardest way to make direct contact is *on your own.* Instead you will best reduce fear and hesitancy and turn the whole process into exploration and fun by getting continuing support and encouragement. Your personal network is the best place to start, and the resources in this book can help, too. Between these, you can find role models—people who have made loans already and will give you the know-how—and you can create support groups that will meet to share personal and technical concerns and thus learn the ropes.

To test the waters, put out the word that you have loan money available. Make a list of people already in business and known to you or your friends who are doing things you support and approach them. Your first loans will usually be to people under your nose that you never thought of until you decided that you really were ready to make loans.

The majority of small businesses you will know are probably pretty small and quite stable. They will include professionals as well as the obvious retail stores and restaurants; service businesses as well as small manufacturers and distributors; and mail-order people as well as artists and craftspeople. They may need help with expansion, special capital purchases, inventory maintenance, accounts receivable, refinancing previous debt, or moving their operations. If, for example, one needs a computer, it is possible for you to buy the computer, lease it and get a good tax credit, and take depreciation. Most lenders, however, prefer straight loans.

Screening Potential Candidates for Loans

The key to making a successful loan is *screening*. Before you even think about negotiating terms, get to know your potential borrowers and the business or organization they are operating.

1. Learn their plans in some detail.
2. Assess management's ability to carry out the plans.
3. Consider the stage of the enterprise: starting, stable, expanding, in a special situation, or in crisis. Screening of both start-up and in-crisis enterprises must be done carefully. Lending to strength is often the safer route—but your investment criteria might include accepting risks in the attempt to help worthy organizations in crisis.

4. Think about what the most effective loan might be: money, some tools, time, expertise, technical assistance, a referral, and so on.

When researching an enterprise, the business plan is a good place to start. If a particular organization does not have a business plan, you might want to ask for one—or structure your discussions to gather the information you expect to find in the business plan.

A business plan is the investor's blueprint of a business. It is, most importantly, a written document that includes an analysis, detailed summary, and implementation plan of the proposed project. It should help a firm anticipate and deal with problems and help you judge the enterprise's future.

The initial, *intuitive* impressions of appearance, documentation, and form are very useful. The "look" of the plan should be appropriate to the project. A video production company that uses extensive graphics and charts in their business plan indicates they know what is appropriate for such a business. On the other hand, one might wonder about the fiscal responsibility of a start-up business that spends a lot of money on embossed folders.

Be sure to discuss the plan with the managers. How closely is the plan tied to what is actually happening? What questions does the plan raise for you? How helpful and insightful are the managers' answers?

The first section of the business plan itself is the summary and review. It emphasizes the strengths, background, and opportunities in the enterprise. The summary should include the history of the business (if any), its goals, its market approach, and its "competitive advantage." Management skills and experience, financial and earning projections, and investment money required should also be included. As you read the plan and talk to the managers, try to determine whether the enterprise matches your investment criteria and whether the plan seems workable.

What are the goals of the business? Do the financial and nonfinancial goals of the enterprise match yours? At times, the personal financial goals of the management might get in the way of operating a successful business. Is the owner or manager committed to an integrated, socially responsible enterprise with both clear social goals and sound financial objectives?

70

Who is minding the business? Business experience and technical expertise are critical for success. If the venture is new, you should find out whether the managers have related prior experience and some previous business success. Small businesses usually fail because of poor management. So assessing management skills is essential.

It is also important to discover if the managers know what they do *not* know. Even after a business project is researched in depth, there are still going to be many unknown factors. A successful management is likely to admit and confront such unknowns honestly.

Finally, is the structure democratic, worker-oriented, and/or grass-roots based? Is it consistent with the statement of purpose and objectives? Are professional advisors (accountants, attorneys, bankers, technical consultants, and others) available if needed?

How accurate are the financial assumptions? Since the advent of computer-generated financial projections, business plans have doubled in length. Therefore, you must pay attention to the quality of financial documentation, not just the quantity. It is the thinking process behind the financial projections that is critical. You need to know how sales assumptions were made, what the accuracy of expense allocations is, and how good any historical financial data are.

You should also be sure that the business has an effective accounting system that consistently and accurately monitors financial operations. Finally, make certain that the people managing the business have enough *financial* expertise to handle its level of complexity.

Is there a focus on marketing? For each venture, the marketing alternatives need to be clearly identified and matched to a marketing strategy that will successfully address the business opportunity. The firm must clearly define its marketing approach (determining a market need and satisfying it) and estimate the effect marketing will have in satisfying the potential customers. Hard data, careful analyses, and a precisely targeted market are the keys to a serious, successful marketing plan.

Once you understand the enterprise and the plan, you might want to evaluate the whole in light of the following:

Critical Business Risks—Every business has inherent risks; be sure you identify, discuss, and weigh them. A new herbal tea manufacturer is trying to determine if the market is already saturated. A computerized psychological testing service is being managed by psychologists who have no business experience. A computer support business is too dependent on one experienced technician. Only one partner in a women-owned massage center has any marketing experience. None of these risks are necessarily fatal, but before you invest you should be convinced that the managers have a well-thought-out plan to deal with them.

Community and Human Benefits—Does the enterprise encourage useful employment of both people and resources? Does it provide products or services that serve the immediate community? Does it enhance local self-reliance, breaking the dependency on outside resources for development?

Action Plan—The action plan is a schedule for starting and maintaining a new business opportunity. It should be complete and realistic. A refugee-women's housecleaning cooperative scheduled language-training classes, work skills workshops, and marketing techniques development into a business plan and then did them.

Investment Opportunity—Once you are convinced that there is an acceptable business goal, capable and experienced management, clear market opportunity, and realistic financial estimates, you should find out precisely how much money is required for the project and how it will be used. The published financial statements should help you determine if the investment is excessive (extensive capital improvements or high salaries) or appropriate (efficient technology or affordable equipment). Before investing, ask: will the project succeed? will it pay a fair return? have the risks been identified?

You must take the time to read the business plan and talk with the managers. And you need to balance your own criteria against what the organization can provide. Sometimes you will need professional advice about things like taxes. And you must be sure the investment alternative you choose—stock, loan, limited partnership—is also in accord with your criteria.

Even a well-written, -researched, and -presented business plan will not guarantee success. The project is always at risk. However, management's experience and skills will increase a project's chance for success. Knowing this, you can shape intuition, first impressions, and a detailed analysis of the entire business plan into a dependable guide to social investing.

Negotiating the Terms and Making the Loan

Once you have decided to offer a loan to an organization that meets your criteria, it is time to focus on the details of the possible loan. There are some very practical things you can do that make a loan more likely to work out well for both parties.

Negotiate: Do not be afraid to actively negotiate with someone who asks you for a loan. While many of us feel a sense of obligation to lend to friends, and especially to family, with no questions asked, it is respectful to both you and to the other person to make a responsible, informed decision. Hence, you need to review your investment and loan criteria and ask for any information you need about the other person's situation. (See pages 80–86 for tips on dealing with friends and family.)

Do not hesitate to ask for what you want: Explain your needs and your thinking, and ask if it seems fair to the other person. Choose a tone that seems appropriate, but still make sure you get all the content you need to make a comprehensive, workable agreement.

Make a written contract: If you decide you *do* want to make the loan or investment, negotiate an agreement that takes both of your interests into account. Put your agreement in writing. The more explicit and specific you can be, the better. Even if the loan or investment really matters to only one party, carefully writing up an agreement helps each party clarify her or his expectations and avoid misunderstandings, while providing a record either party can refer to should there be disagreements later. The agreement should include such information as:

–*who* will pay *how much* to *whom*
–*when* and in what form the payments will be received
–whether there is *flexibility* in the payback period
–if there is flexibility, how much
–whether *interest* will be paid
–if interest will be paid, *how much*

–how the agreement can be changed
–how the parties will resolve unanticipated conflicts

Written agreements should probably be as simple as is appropriate for a given situation. If the situation is complex, if there is a significant power imbalance between the two parties, or if one party is worried, it might be worth obtaining legal or other experienced advice.

Below are three loan agreements that vary in formality and complexity. They give some idea of the range of possible agreements. Note that they are not comprehensive; they are simply frameworks you can play with. You and the other party to the agreement have to design *your own* agreement that reflects the tone and content of *your* situation.

Promissory Note

$1,000   Berkeley, California
One Thousand Dollars   April 1, 1984

Elissa Brown (Payor) promises to pay Roger Pritchard (Payee), or order at place designated by Payee, the principal sum of one thousand only dollars, lawful money of the United States, with interest thereon from April 1, 1984, at the rate of fifteen percent (15%) per annum, compounded quarterly. Should principal sum plus accrued interest not be paid by due date, there shall be a late fee of $50.00. Payor may pay off this note in full without penalty on giving one month's written notice to Payee.

Payee and Payor shall have a meeting on or about February 1, 1985, to examine Payor's ability to pay off the note when due. There will be no charge for this meeting. Should Payor be unable to pay off this note when due, or should some other trouble develop, both parties shall first try to work things out. Should this not be possible, they agree to go to arbitration with Sterling Johnson or Paul Terry, or some other person chosen by Sterling or Paul who agrees to serve. Payor shall pay for the arbitration if there are any fees.

Payor agrees to exert all moral and work efforts to paying this note off on time. Should Payor die with the note unpaid, her estate shall be responsible for its repayment.

By _____   By _____
Elissa Brown   Roger Pritchard
407 Hudson St.   Financial Alternatives
Oakland, CA 94618   1514 McGee Avenue
(415) 654-3795   Berkeley, CA 94703
                                    (415) 527-5604

This is the form of a promissory note.* First, the amount is stated. It is best to state figures both in words and numbers, as on checks. Second, the city and state are included. These establish jurisdiction. If you have an arbitrator, as in this case, the courts will back up the award, and the lender should make the jurisdiction as convenient as possible for her/himself. Third, the date of the agreement, which may or may not be the initial date of the loan, is added.

The first section of the note gives details of the promise to repay the loan. The names of lender and borrower (payee and payor) are given in full and the signatures match. The starting date is set out. The method of repayment is indicated. Then the interest rate, stated in terms of annual percentage rate (APR), plus time period for compounding, are added. Be sure the interest rate you agree on is *not* above the usury limits in your state. The courts will not back the lender up in case of trouble about that rate. The time period for compounding can range between a day and a year. (Contact your state's department of banking and insurance for information.)

The most likely challenge to this agreement is Elissa's needing more time to repay. Both the meeting in February 1985 and the late fee (which essentially helps pay for the extra time necessary to work out a new agreement) are included with that in mind. Further, two good friends whom both parties respect and trust are already named in case of irreconcilable dispute; if they cannot serve, they can name someone else.

The "security" for this loan is Elissa's moral commitment and her ability to work skillfully. This is stated *explicitly*. Had the lender wanted *material* security, that would have been included in another clause, or there would have been a separate *security*

Catalyst recommends that the note be witnessed or notarized.

agreement filed or recorded with the county or state agency in order to establish the obligation on the particular property. Had the lender wanted a *cosigner*, s/he would have been named in the body of the note and would have signed, thereby becoming "jointly and severally liable" with Elissa. The lender could, alternatively, have asked for a *guarantor*. A guarantor has better protection than a cosigner, because s/he is cleared of the obligation if the terms of the note are changed without her/his agreement—something a cosigner cannot get.

Finally, the borrower(s) sign the note. The names, addresses, and telephone numbers of all parties can be included for easy contact.

In most cases, a simple agreement will suffice. You may wish to use an attorney as a consultant to check your already written agreement for errors and omissions, or you can entrust troubleshooting to your arbitrator, if you have one. Here I will use simple loan agreements to indicate the main points to be covered. Remember that space limitations preclude more than a very brief discussion and that not every consideration is examined. For more detailed information, consult a lawyer or paraprofessional.

Loan Agreement

$2,000   May 11, 1988

Marsha Samuels has loaned Bob Samuels two thousand dollars toward producing his second record album. Bob agrees to repay the loan in four installments: on September 1, 1988, December 1, 1988, March 1, 1989, and June 1, 1989. Bob will pay 6% simple interest to Marsha.

If necessary, Bob can make the first payment on December 1, 1988, and push back the whole repayment schedule 3 months; if he needs to do this he will tell Marsha by August 1, 1988.

Bob and Marsha may agree to change this agreement, and if they do so they will write up and sign a new agreement.

Marsha Samuels_____

Bob Samuels _____

Witnessed by:_____

Loan Agreement

$10,000   April 5, 1988

For value received, I, Robin Baker, for the Haverill Community Center, hereafter (HCC), agree to pay to Betsy Hurley, or order, ten thousand dollars according to the following terms:

1. HCC agrees to pay $10,000 to Betsy Hurley, in cash, Massachusetts check, and/or U.S. bank check, in a total of ten monthly payments of $1,000 to be received by Betsy Hurley on or before the first of every month starting June 1, 1988, through the final payment on March 1, 1989;

2. HCC agrees to pay 10% per annum simple interest. Robin Baker and an advisor of her choice may elect a charitable organization as the recipient of this interest. If this option is chosen, Robin Baker will issue a check for the interest, payable to the charitable organization, and will send this check to Betsy Hurley with information about the group and its address so that Betsy Hurley can learn about the recipient organization. Betsy Hurley will forward the check to the recipient organization;

3. HCC agrees to secure this loan with the equity in HCC's building at 433 Sunshine Avenue, Chicago, Illinois;

4. The terms of this agreement may be changed only by mutual written agreement of both parties involved;

5. HCC agrees to pay all reasonable costs incurred in the collection of this note.

Robin Baker_____ _____
for Haverill Community Center

Betsy Hurley_____

Witnessed by: _____

The loan may be paid off in equal monthly payments: this is called an *amortized* loan. Or it may be paid off in one or more lump-sum payments: you will state the date(s) for payment or the circumstances (for example, attaining a turnover of $3,000 per month). State whether interest is accrued (added to principal) or paid to the lender on the date of compounding.

If you are concerned about the borrower's solidity or commitment, you may want to include an *acceleration clause*. This states that, if a payment of interest, principal, or both (as specified) is late, then the *whole* loan is payable immediately if the lender so desires. If a borrower is drifting into difficulty, this allows the lender to try to get the principal back at an earlier stage.

The borrower may want a *prepayment clause* to permit a no-penalty prepayment if things go better than expected. In this case, the lender required reasonable notice so that she could find a new borrower by the time the loan came due.

After the loan goes into operation, it is best if the lender keeps track of principal and interest owed and records payments received. Banks will provide payment books on request.

Interest on loans is taxed in the year it is due. So if you have a note where compounding without actual payment of interest takes place, you still have to pay tax on the interest *payable*.

The true strength of the written note lies both in the process that led up to it (the businesslike relationship that has been established) and in the commitment on both sides.

When appropriate, say no: Sometimes the negotiations just will not work out, and you will have to end them. This is particularly hard to do in close relationships. Sometimes, money gets linked with love and respect even when they are unrelated. Being able to say no appropriately is necessary for you to be able to say yes at other times and really mean it. If you find saying no difficult, practice it, and get someone to back you up.

Payback Problems

A common problem is the borrower being unable to pay on time. If late payment will make you uncomfortable or will not meet your needs as a lender, then you should work out a contingency plan with the borrower as part of the loan agreement. As with other parts of the agreement, find a plan you will *both* feel comfortable with.

Some popular provisions in case of delayed payments include:

–partial payments
–an agreed-upon maximum grace period, with clear communication from the borrower throughout this period

about when the lender can expect payments to begin
—a fallback emergency lender (who pays the original lender
back, then assumes the loan permanently or for as long as the
borrower is behind)
—collateral that will be liquidated to pay back the lender by
the end of a certain period of time
—a clear communication/negotiation process for changing the
payback schedule

One innovative solution is practiced by Tracy Gary, who has
made a great many loans. She and the borrower each put a little
money (say, $10 a month) into a special account. If the borrower
runs into problems in paying back the loan on time, this money
will be used to hire a financial consultant to help the borrower
figure out what to do. If the borrower never runs into trouble paying
back the loan, great—the accumulated money goes back to
borrower and lender. Tracy feels this protects her from the
possibility of a lot of extra work and aggravation.

If you as a lender *definitely need* the money back, you will want
to write into the loan agreement a secure, specific measure like
collateral that can be liquidated or a fallback lender who is willing
to assume the loan.

Think carefully before specifying collateral. Often, traditional
collateral—like a building or inventory—is an item the enterprise
you are supporting cannot afford to lose. Do you really want to
take possession of twenty thousand bicycle repair manuals—
especially if you really believe in the organization?

An alternative you might want to explore is whether the borrower
has anything to barter with you in case the repayment is not
forthcoming. Since the best security borrowers can offer is often
their skills, consider the skills as collateral! Here are three
possibilities. First, the borrowers agree that if the venture fails,
they will take a regular job in their particular skill area and pay
the loan back over time at a fixed rate. Second, the borrower offers
a list of six skills that the lender may use *if needed* as partial
repayment at an agreed value in case of default. Finally, they seek
out a three-way trade with another business or individual that owes
the borrower services or money.

Conflict Resolution

It is important that the lender and borrower agree on a method for
resolving possible, if unanticipated, conflicts. When loans are
made warmly and without implied threats, a relationship of

affirmation and support is established. If the loan gets into difficulty, the relationship is damaged. The feelings, attitudes, and intentions have to be respected if the relationship is going to survive the difficulty.

Initially, the borrower should agree to report to the lender if trouble is developing. By doing so and being open to ideas and help, the borrower steps out of the usual avoidance reaction, the relationship is affirmed, and an amicable solution is much more likely. Next, both parties agree to enter mediation and/or arbitration if things become more serious. Mediation will occur when both parties disagree but are trying to work things out; arbitration, when both parties know they cannot agree.

Together with the borrower, you might try selecting people you both know and respect who could serve as mediators or arbitrators. They should have common sense, some understanding of business, and a high regard from both of you, especially the borrowers. As many as three should be named in the agreement—and, upon commitment, should be offered compensation, usually by the borrower.

When trouble develops, the primary problem is not usually the content, but the absence of a method for making *some* decision. Closely connected arbitrators can act quickly and compassionately. However, if you do not trust this idea, seek out mediation or arbitration attorneys and community services where you live, and learn about them—or help start a service in your community. They will be more expensive, but certainly cheaper and less energy draining, than continuing the conflict process in the courts.

It is important to note that having discussed and agreed, in advance, on a method for resolving difficulty will, *in and of itself,* make your loan agreement more secure. Support has replaced an implied threat, and you will find the clause rarely needs to be invoked.

4.4 Investing in People You Know

A common fear is that investing in a venture of someone you know or loaning money to someone you know will damage the relationship: "What if the borrower is not able to pay the loan or the investment equity back? I will feel resentful; my friend will probably feel guilty; and we will end up avoiding each other or in a nasty argument that will ruin our friendship!"

Using the guidelines above to work out clear arguments will

prevent most problems and allay most of these fears. Here are some more ways to protect your relationship with family and friends when making financial transactions with them. The closer the relationship, the more attention you may have to pay to each of these areas.

Throughout the process of considering and negotiating a loan or investment, all parties should acknowledge feelings they are having about it. Listen to the other person's feelings (fear, hurt, envy, or something else) and honestly communicate your own feelings. Accepting feelings can disperse tensions. Repressing feelings may seem to work in the short term but will usually disrupt relationships over time. Explicitly communicate love and respect for the other person, separate from the financial transaction.

When saying no, communicate the reasons for your decision openly and thoroughly. Express love and respect, and be willing to listen to hurt feelings. Elaine Booker's experience illustrates the importance of communicating well and the fears one may face in doing it. Elaine, living in Cambridge, Massachusetts, was asked to lend $10,000 to a typesetting and graphics collective owned and operated by two of her friends in Santa Cruz, California. The business, Artstop, had been barely breaking even for three years. Knowing they needed capital for better equipment if they were ever to be financially viable, Artstop's owners attempted to raise $50,000. Elaine considered the loan for a month, did some research, and said no.

"Although I thought the work they were doing was worthwhile and I respected the individuals involved, the business did not appear financially viable to me," she explains. "They were asking for more money than I'd normally lend in one shot, and they were in a field in which technology changes rapidly, so there are frequent big expenditures for new equipment—otherwise you go out of business because you can't compete. I'd had little experience with that type of business, so I had Affirmative Investments, Inc. (see Resources), a firm that makes loans to alternative businesses, analyze their financial plan. The consultant said it looked like too high a risk; their firm would not make such a loan."

Elaine felt good about doing this research. In one brief long-distance phone call, she told her friends no. Later, she learned they had hurt feelings; they saw Elaine's refusal as a cold financial decision based on the consultant's recommendation. They felt that Elaine had not treated them with the respect they deserved as her friends and political allies. Says Elaine,

I should have talked with them more *openly* about my reasons. Actually, I felt very torn, because I *do* respect their work; I believe in supporting collectives; and as an owning-class person, I have a strong belief in returning some of my wealth to working-class people by supporting their efforts. At the same time, I was scared that this business would go bankrupt and I would lose all of this money that could be accomplishing good things elsewhere.

If I had told my friends all that, they would have heard the part of me that wanted to say yes as well as the part that said no, and they would have understood the *values* behind my decision.

At the time, I was afraid to voice these feelings, because I was afraid I'd then be pressured into making the loan. Now I know I made a mistake by not communicating more. I've refused other loans requested by friends without hurt feelings resulting, largely by telling them my reasons and feelings openly, and listening carefully to their feelings as well.

Be sensitive to the power differences that often exist between the lender/investor and the recipient. A borrower often perceives a lender as having more power, even though this may not be accurate. The borrower has a need, and the lender has the power to satisfy it. The greater the borrower's need and the more limited her or his options to borrow, the more acutely the borrower is likely to experience a power difference.

Once money has been loaned, the lender may worry that it will not be paid back, or that repayment will be late. The lender may now feel that the borrower has more power: the power to say yes or no to repayment. Ironically, the borrower probably continues to see most of the power in the hands of the lender to whom s/he is in debt.

Although power differences will exist as long as individuals continue to have unequal resources, we can make personal lending/ investment experiences more empowering. Whether or not you agree to a loan, explain your reasoning and the values and criteria on which it is based, so the borrower can understand your decision and not simply experience it as an arbitrary exercise in control of financial resources. If you say no or can lend only part of what the borrower needs, let the borrower know of other resources s/he might contact. When you negotiate terms of a loan, make sure that you are carefully considering how both parties' needs can best be met.

In some cases, you may want to consider making a gift instead of a loan or an investment. If you very much support what the other person wants to do with the money and you believe s/he is unlikely to be able to pay it back, you may want to offer a gift. You can also work out creative options in between a loan and a gift—for example, a loan that becomes a gift if the borrower is in the red at payback time.

4.5 Family Investment Decisions

Another challenge you may face is persuading your current family (if you have one) or family of origin to feel good about your investments. In some families, this is a big issue; it may even affect your *power* to invest. "The Finnegan money has been invested in Bunkle and Bunkle, a stable, reliable firm started by a friend of your great-grandfather, for ninety-five years," Amy Finnegan's uncle complained. He is a trustee of a trust fund set up for Amy by her grandparents; she gets $8,500 to $10,000 a year from the trust, but has no control over the $85,000 principal that the trust holds in her name.

By presenting figures about risk and return, Amy convinced her uncle and the other trustee, a bank officer, to transfer her principal in the trust to a socially screened mutual fund. "However, I would *never* be able to get them to, say, put half the principal into a worker-owned handknit sweater company," she says. "If I want to invest in things like that, I have to use the money I get each year."

Ralph sends some of his paycheck home to his parents to help them keep up with their mortgage payments. He has had a difficult time convincing his family that it is not selfish for him to invest some money in enterprises he believes in to help provide jobs while also holding a little aside for his own security or to help his family in a crisis. "I still feel guilty," he says, "but knowing I have some cushion makes me feel safer and gives me more energy to help my family work out solutions to their money difficulties. I also feel good knowing my bit of money is helping an enterprise provide services my family can use."

Here is an example of a short negotiation between relatives.

Bob: I'm excited, Marsha. I think I'm finally ready to cut my first album. It's a really big deal!

Marsha: That's great! I'm excited for you, Bob! When are you going to start on it?

Bob: Well, actually, that brings up the one thing that's a problem—I need more money. Producing a record is pretty expensive, and as a musician I don't make a lot. . . . Well, I was hoping, since you're my sister, and you have some money, and you seem to be pretty supportive of my work, that maybe you could help me out . . .

Marsha: Oh, so you want to borrow money from me. . . . This record is really important to you! How much were you hoping to borrow?

Bob: I could probably do okay with $7,000 from you. I'm gonna kick in $2,000 myself, all of my savings. And I'm going to ask my best friend, Richie, for $3,000. We could do production and press the first two thousand albums for $12,000 if we're careful. Now, if you could lend me *$10,000,* that would be *ideal,* 'cause we could press a second batch of albums. That's where you start to make a profit.

Marsha: How long do you think it would take to pay me back? It sounds like there's a fair amount of risk involved. I'm sure you *would* sell records at concerts, but it seems to me there are hundreds of albums out by musicians with small followings, and they don't sell in the stores.

Bob: I know it could be slow. But I only need to sell fifteen hundred albums at $8 each to make back the $12,000 in expenses. Let's say I continue to do about thirty performances a year, and sell, realistically, an average of twenty-five albums at each. With that *alone,* I'd make back half the expenses in a year—and that doesn't take into account the radio and store promotion we're planning to do, plus getting more gigs.

So, there is always some risk in a project like this, but on the other hand I see the audience I've already developed as a safety cushion. I could agree to pay you back *first,* and in that case I'm virtually certain you'd have your first $7,000 back within a year. Or instead of repayment, you could take a percentage of the profit we'll make after the first fifteen hundred albums are sold. It *could* take a couple of years to reach the profit point, but we think it will go much faster. You should see our promotion plan; it's really exciting! In fact, I'd be willing to work out a percentage of *all* the profit in the business—from concerts, too, for the next couple of years—if you'd prefer.

Marsha: Besides me and your friend Richie, do you have any other possible sources of financing—either people you know or lending institutions like banks and credit unions?

Bob: No, unfortunately, I don't. I don't know people with surplus money, besides you, and my credit isn't so good—I don't think I could get a loan.

Marsha: Let me explain what I do and do not feel comfortable lending money to.

Bob: Okay.

Marsha: I feel comfortable lending to close friends in emergencies, or even giving money in emergencies if I think they might not be able to pay it back easily. You are certainly someone I would help out if I knew you were in trouble.

I make other kinds of loans occasionally, to projects I support. For these loans, there has to be very little risk, and the loan must be secured by something that could be sold relatively easily, or by a clearly reliable source of income.

I love your music, Bob. But I don't feel comfortable agreeing to lend you money for the project as you've outlined it because of the risk involved. Your planning may be excellent, but tastes in the music business can change very fast, and you don't have any *other* source of income or security to put behind this loan.

How do you feel about what I'm saying?

Bob: Kind of in shock. Definitely disappointed. I don't think I'll be able to do this record for a long time without your help. And timing is *everything* in this business; my career needs this record to happen now. Also . . . I guess I thought you had a lot of money lying around in the bank, and $7,000 was an amount you would hardly miss. It never occurred to me you would be so businesslike in your requirements for lending money to *me*. [Sigh.] I guess it *does* make me wonder whether you believe in me and in my music.

Marsha: There is no question that I believe in you, and that I *do* think you're a very talented musician. I'm sorry this could give you any doubt about that. But you definitely did have some misconceptions about how I handle my money. It's a precious resource, and I feel strongly that I want it all to be invested in things that do make some positive social contribution, but without much risk that the money will be lost. I have dreams of my own of what I could do with the money someday; I don't intend to work many more years as a software designer, even though the pay *is* great.

Bob: Hmm. I *am* sorry I made those assumptions about you; it really wasn't fair. You know, I think if I work at it, I might be able to meet your criteria. There may be some people, like Uncle Ned, I could ask to back up this loan, so if I was having trouble making payments they could pay you instead. And I could ask the cooperative credit union I belong to for a couple of thousand dollars. I'll check out these options. Suppose I came back to you with a proposal that takes your criteria into account and asks for less—say, $3,500?

Marsha: I'd be happy to consider it. If I decide I am seriously interested, we can talk about interest then. I appreciate you listening well to what I said about the way I use money. You know, whether or not I make a loan to you, I'm willing to help you in other ways. Would you like me to think with you about other sources of money, and ways to improve your credit? Or about alternative timelines in case the financing takes a while?

Bob: Yeah; let me see what other resources I can dig up around here, and I'll get back to you. Thanks.

4.6 Examples of the Range of Possibilities

Here are some samples of the wide variety of small enterprises you might want to invest in.

Ben & Jerry's Homemade, Inc.
Route 100, PO Box 133
Waterbury, VT 05676
(802) 244-5641

Ben Cohen and Jerry Greenfield are folk heroes in Vermont because of the unusual (and fun!) history of their premium ice cream company. Incorporated in December 1977, B&J began hand cranking their delicious ice cream in an old gas station in Burlington. The two young entrepreneurs had been friends since high school and always loved ice cream. After deciding to go into business together, and honing in on ice cream—not just any ice cream, but the best—they took a correspondence course from Penn State University for $5 (really!). This, plus Ben's experience as a night mopper at a Friendly's ice cream store, made up their total relevant experience. Undaunted, they each came up with $4,000, borrowed another $4,000 from a bank, and were off. Their secret to making the best ice cream around is, according to Ben, "Just use the best ingredients and use a lot of them." This formula proved popular, and their small store/manufacturing plant was often sold out before the end of the day.

Their business became a Burlington highlight, with its brightly painted exterior—the now familiar spotted cows, cartoon-like and cheerful—and Ben and Jerry grinning behind the counter. As soon as the business began to turn a profit, the two men decided to run free films on summer evenings to show their appreciation. In addition, they gave away ice cream at charitable functions, something the business continues to do. (In fact, they now have a full-time person whose job it is to line up events at which to give away scoops of the delicious treat!)

A year and a half after B&J's opening, restaurants began to request the ice cream in bulk containers to sell to customers. At this point they expanded and purchased an old ice cream delivery truck with almost 250,000 miles on it. In 1980, they decided to manufacture pints of the ice cream to sell in stores. Since then the company has expanded considerably, going public in 1984—at first making their stock available only to Vermont residents because they wanted the people who made the company a success to own it. A second offering, made in 1985, was advertised on their ice cream containers—a most unusual way to sell stock. Both offerings were used to build and then expand their large plant in Waterbury, Vermont. The second offering was not limited to Vermonters, although seventy thousand shares were set aside for the existing shareholders to purchase. At this writing, no one has lost money by investing in Ben & Jerry's. The company continues to grow, and its market is expanding nationwide. The quality of the ice cream is still excellent, and there are now over thirty-five flavors. The most recent, Cherry Garcia (after Jerry) is extremely popular (and a personal favorite, although I must admit I have not tasted a B&J's flavor I did not like.) Also, part of the profits from its sale go to the Grateful Dead's own nonprofit foundation.

Ben & Jerry's success has not gone unnoticed by their major corporate competitors. In 1984 the Pillsbury Corporation, which owns Häagen-dazs, tried to prevent Ben & Jerry's from distributing their ice cream in the Boston area by telling distributors that if they carried Ben & Jerry's they would lose their profitable Häagen-dazs line. This prompted the young company to ask "What's the Doughboy afraid of?" on bumperstickers, t-shirts, and their retail pints. Ben & Jerry's prompted the Federal Trade Commission to investigate Pillsbury's apparently illegal trade practice, and Pillsbury finally settled out of court without admitting wrongdoing.

In 1985, the Ben & Jerry's Foundation was organized to make grants to promote human rights, community organizations, community-run businesses, and community celebrations. States Ben, "I'm trying to send a message to other businesses that it's viable to run a business where profit isn't the only motivator. We're interested in doing something new and different, like showing money as contributing to and not stealing from the society." In addition to summer films, B&J's sponsors the Fool's Fest in Montpelier, Vermont, an annual summer event that brings together local residents, clowns, jugglers, craftspeople, mimes, social change organizations, musicians, and dancers for a weekend of revelry and fun. Ben & Jerry's often scoops out free cones at baseball games, concerts, and fundraising events of various kinds—"It allows us to spread joy by giving it away. That's a great thing about a business when you have a product that people love. Ice cream brings people up. It makes us happy."

The company provides excellent working conditions, reasonable salaries (with no one—including Ben and Jerry—earning more than five times the least-paid worker), a profit-sharing plan, full health benefits, and stock options. Dress is casual and the atmosphere loose and informal.

Ben & Jerry's 1987 annual meeting was held under a circus tent surrounded by hundreds of helium-filled balloons, a graphic example of the energy and sense of fun inherent in the business. Shareholders voted for a stock split designed to protect their company from any takeovers and learned that manufacturing has begun in two other states to keep up with demand. "One thing I've always been real proud of is our commitment to the community. Our fear is that if the stock began to turn over, our new shareholders would not have that commitment and the whole reason for being this company would end." The out-of-state plants (in Maine and Rhode Island) still use Vermont dairy products.

B&J's continues to innovate. Recently, to help deal with the growing problem of what to do with the gallons of dairy refuse they produced, Ben & Jerry's has gone into business with a local farmer. They loaned Earl Mayo, Jr., of Stowe the money to buy over two hundred piglets and then gave him the dairy waste, which is excellent pig food. Mayo will repay the loan once the pigs are sold. The contract includes the provision that "at least one of the pigs must be named after Ben, and one of the pigs named Jerry, and one of the pigs named Ed Stanak." (Stanak is the district coordinator for Vermont's Act 250 land use and development law, with whom Ben & Jerry's worked for over seven months to find a solution to the waste dilemma.) According to the company's general manager, Fred "Chico" Lager, "the pigs enjoy all the flavors except Mint Oreo Cookie. I don't think it's the Oreos; they just don't like the mint. We're thinking of maybe feeding them on different flavors, and people can order a different flavor of pig."

Although providing premium ice cream (or flavored pigs) may not be everyone's idea of an essential business, the way this company began, its community orientation, its sense of fun, its responsible treatment of its employees, and its financial success are all wonderful examples of the possibilities for corporations in this country. If companies like Ben & Jerry's can succeed, it should pave the way for more entrepreneurs guided by their values and a spirit of celebration, a most worthwhile contribution indeed.

Peace Fleece/Soviet-American Woolens
RFD 1, Box 57
Kezar Falls, ME 04047
(207) 625-4906

Peace Fleece is a unique business founded in 1985 by Maine sheep farmers Peter Hagerty and Marty Tracy as a way to promote peace and to show that people—businesspeople in particular—can work together even if governments will not. Peace Fleece blends Soviet wool with American wool in equal amounts. The skeins are then sold with knitting instructions and a booklet, printed in Russian and English, telling the story of the business.
Peter's story:

> At the end of World War II, my father moved from Dorchester, Massachusetts to the South Shore, married, and began a furniture business. I grew up in the Kennedy era and, after finishing Milton Academy and Harvard, was expected to move into politics. But I was profoundly affected by the Vietnam experience and sickened by the values I saw around me. Along with many of my contemporaries, I rejected the "system" and moved to a small rural town in Maine. There I married and began logging and farming. By living close to the land, growing my own food, harvesting my own fuel, I intended to minimize contact with the capitalist system. Marty and I had two children, and through my family and my work, I grew to know and respect my neighbors. However, something was missing. It became increasingly difficult to reconcile my privileged background with my daily work. I began to see that the greatest gift my parents had given me was the knowledge that I could accomplish whatever I wanted in life. And I also began to feel that perhaps by rejecting the "system" so completely, I had severely limited my options. It takes a lot of energy to "hide out," especially if you're not even aware that you are doing it. But I also held fast to my ideals.
>
> As my daughter turned eight, I realized a few things: I was going to die someday; everyone has a story to tell (but

you have to listen to hear it); and the threat of nuclear war is the primary survival issue facing us today.

Peter began to feel despair over the possibility of nuclear war. "What was the point of raising all these lambs, growing all this feed, if all at once the sky should light up and everything I valued disappear?" he asked. Together he and Marty worked through this despair and created Peace Fleece—something they personally could do to help increase understanding between people.

When they began working on the idea of importing Soviet wool, everyone said the chances were slim. Peter decided his best course would be to travel to the Soviet Union, so in August 1985 he went on a tour with other U.S. farmers. Amazingly, on his first day, he met two businesspeople who took him directly to the headquarters of Firm Runo, the government-owned corporation that handles the U.S.S.R.'s five-year plan for cotton, wool, and synthetic fibers. There Peter met Director Nikolai Emelianov, with whom he discussed Peace Fleece and their lives and families. "It is difficult, this Peace Fleece. Our country needs all the wool we can find . . . but perhaps we can do something," Emelianov said. (The Soviet Union must import wool from Australia and New Zealand to provide enough warm clothes for its people.) Before Peter left, the two were able to work out a deal; the men shook hands and parted friends.

The first shipment of wool arrived in January 1986 and was blended with American wool, carefully spun, and dyed into beautiful, rich colors to be knit into caps, mittens, sweaters, and the like as symbols of cooperation and peace. Peter writes:

> Last year, I watched as two multinational corporations worked overtime to import, free of charge, the first shipment ever of Russian wool into the United States. I listened with interest as my politically conservative wool broker in Boston berated the U.S. government for levying a punitive tariff on our "Communist wool." "We'll refuse to pay it. Damn them, it's just stupid!" Marty and I watched as knitters around the United States began working with our yarn, as the *Wall Street Journal* featured us on the front page, as the Boston business community decided that "war was bad for business" and began expanding trade with the Russians.

Although they still raise sheep, Peter and Marty's life has changed considerably since their business began. Soviet-American Woolens is a major force working for cooperation between U.S. and Soviet businesspeople. Peter has taken three tours to the Soviet Union, tours that promote understanding and friendship as only person-to-person contact can. Marty now offers hand-dyed yarns as well as commercially dyed ones. There is a Peace Fleece video (put together from coverage by NBC and CBS News); stories on the 1986 summer farm tour to Rostov and Krasnodar in a ten-part CBS report on the U.S.S.R.; and "Peace Fleece—Trust Through Trade" buttons ($1), part of the proceeds from which are donated to a Soviet-American youth organization that sponsors workcamps on collective farms in the Soviet Union.

Recently, Soviet-American Woolens sponsored the first of several trade conferences for U.S. and Soviet businesspeople. Peter recorded some of his impressions:

> Albert Melnikov, a businessman, grandfather, and chief trade negotiator in Washington for the U.S.S.R., must be in his mid-sixties. He's not the first Russian I have ever met, but I had never met one quite like him before. Born about the same time as my father, he lived through the war against fascism, through Stalin, and now Gorbachev. I was to share the podium with him to reaffirm a role that American corporate industry can play to save the world from nuclear war. "Building Trust Through Trade" was the conference's motto. To get to this position, both Albert and I had to pocket some old beliefs about the capitalist system. I listen to Albert's voice as he talks about survival—human and economic survival. I watch the faces of the audience. For most people in the room, Albert is the first Russian Communist they have ever met. I find myself praying quietly for a leap of faith. A friend of mine once said that "to play ball in business today, you have to take risks. There are no winners on the sidelines." As Albert closed his talk, I wondered if we still had a game to play. It soon became obvious, however, that I needn't have worried. The room at the Parker House was full of players!

Peter sums up his experience like this. "The past two years have saved my life. I've nurtured a global perspective, the center of which is still my home and family. I have rediscovered a part of myself. With each new day comes a new story and a new opportunity to listen."

Things have come full circle in Peter's life. "One day, not long ago, I returned to my family business, which my brother now owns. As he and I walked through the factory, we came upon a large pile of elaborately packaged birch plywood. The label on the stack registered its port of origin and it was written in Russian.

'It's the best product of its kind on the market,' my brother John smiled. 'Dad started buying it years ago.' "

Spruce Mountain Design
26 State Street
Montpelier, VT 05602

Spruce Mountain Design is a small-scale hydroelectric development and consulting firm. It was founded in 1980, two years after Congress passed legislation designed to encourage the development of renewable energy by independent power producers. Spurred by the oil embargo of 1973 and the consequent sharp rise in oil prices, the legislation mandates that power produced by nonutility developers (who take on the risks as well as the benefits, rather than passing losses to the consumers as utilities do) must be purchased by utilities. The amount the utilities pay to nonutility developers is set by state utility boards and based on the "avoided cost." When the legislation was passed, oil was expensive and the amount paid to the nonutility developers was high. With the drop in oil prices (and so "avoided cost"), independently produced power is financially less attractive. Still, many people believe the drop in oil prices is temporary and that the alternatives will once more become financially viable.

In Vermont, the Vermont Power Exchange (VPX), supported by fees paid by the independent producers, purchases their power and sells it to the state's utilities. Currently 1 percent of Vermont's power is produced by these independent developers.

John Warshow and Mathew Rubin, the partners in Spruce Mountain Design, met while protesting Vermont Yankee, the nuclear power plant in Vernon, Vermont. As members of the Clamshell Alliance, they had been arrested while protesting the Seabrook, New Hampshire, nuke and were vocal opponents of the development of nuclear power. Eventually, they decided that the best way to protest nuclear power was to prove the economic viability of alternatives. Drawing on John's experience studying hydropower possibilities in Vermont for the U.S. Department of Energy and Mathew's as an energy conservation consultant, they became business partners and applied for a license to use an abandoned flood-control dam in Montpelier. The license, plans, and property were subsequently sold to a local utility.

With the profits from that sale (and additional borrowed money), they began to develop their first hydro site: an 860-kilowatt dam on the North Branch of the Winooski River in East Montpelier.

This site, as well as most of the two hundred other sites in Vermont that used to supply all of the state's electricity, had been abandoned with the advent of cheap oil and the development of nuclear power, once touted as being "too cheap to meter." They purchased the site from Green Mountain Power, which had stopped using it in 1970. Renamed "Winooski Eight," the dam came on line in the fall of 1986 and now produces 3.1 million kilowatt-hours of electricity per year. The only noticeable change at the site is the new brick powerhouse at one end of the dam. And the price that Vermonters pay for this power is fixed, by law, for thirty years.

John and Mathew's second small-scale hydro site is in downtown Springfield, Vermont. The site last produced power in the 1950s. The new powerhouse produces two million kilowatt-hours of electricity a year. This site is a "run-of-the-river" project, meaning it relies on the natural flow of the river to drive the generators, rather than on storage and release of impounded water.

Their third and largest project is located in Winooski on the Winooski River, north of Burlington. Once construction is completed, this site should produce twenty-two million kilowatt-hours annually, enough electricity to supply approximately five thousand homes.

Hydroelectric projects can have large, often negative, effects on the environment. John and Mathew have received a lot of praise for their community and environmental awareness, as well as for their care in construction and design. Their handling of the Winooski site is a particularly revealing example of their environmental concern. The site of the Winooski One Hydroelectric Project is the home of the much-cleft anemone, a small plant whose last Vermont habitat is the rocky ledges at the proposed dam site. Warshow and Rubin plan to spend over $55,000 extra to move the location of the dam's powerhouse fifty feet to the north to protect the patch of plants. They have donated an additional $50,000 to the Vermont Agency of Environmental Conservation's endangered species/nongame fund to be used to protect the anemone and other endangered or threatened species in Vermont. State personnel will monitor the anemone's population and report annual counts to the Agency of Environmental Conservation. Although some plants will have to be removed for the project, their seeds will be collected for permanent frozen storage in a seed bank while state officials study the feasibility of propagating other plants from the seeds.[1]

"We see things both from the environmental perspective and the need to have a profitable, well-engineered project," Warshow recently stated. "We are committed to showing that you can develop alternative energy without wrecking the environment. Vermont has a very high environmental consciousness. That's the reason I live here."[2] Rubin agrees, saying he believes the state has "a right to hold developers to the highest standards."[3]

John told me that these three projects will most likely be the extent of his hydro development in Vermont, although he will continue to act as a consultant to other developers. He admits that small-scale hydro is not environmentally perfect and believes that we must develop other alternatives, such as wind and cogeneration. When asked about waste-to-energy mass incineration plants, he agreed that the ideal solution for dealing with wastes is source reduction rather than incineration, especially since plastics and other toxics are typically burned along with all other waste. He has no doubts that Vermont could be energy self-sufficient even without Vermont Yankee. He is committed to work for that eventuality in a manner that does not endanger the Earth.

4.7 For More Information on the Small-Scale

The following list of organizations, books, and publications is provided to help you locate additional resources on the topics covered in this chapter. Use the Resource section at the end of the book to get the complete listings for the groups and written materials below.

Organizations

Ben & Jerry's Homemade
Chrysalis Money Consultants
Consumers United Group
Financial Alternatives
Funding Exchange
Haymarket People's Fund
Paul Terry & Associates
Peace Fleece/Soviet-American Woolens
Spruce Mountain Design

Books

Joan Anzalone (ed.), *Good Works: A Guide to Careers in Social Change*

The Briarpatch Book: Experiences in Right Livelihood and Simple Living

Annie Cheatham and Mary Clare Powell, *This Way Daybreak Comes: Women's Values and the Future*

Duane Elgin, *Voluntary Simplicity*

Gift Giving Guide

Guide to War Tax Resistance

Victor G. Hallman and Jerry S. Rosenbloom, *Personal Financial Planning*

Paul Hawkin, *The Next Economy*

Inherited Wealth: Your Money and Your Life

Invest Yourself: A Guide to Action

Bernard Kamoroff, *Small-Time Operator*

Charlotte Kirsch, *Facing the Future: A Financial Guide for Women Left Alone*

Greg MacLeod, *New Age Business: Community Corporations that Work*

Peg Moran, *Invest in Yourself*

Carole Phillips, *The Money Workbook for Women*

Michael Phillips, *Honest Business*
　　　　The Seven Laws of Money
　　　　Simple Living Investments for Old Age

Robin Hood Was Right: A Guide to Giving Your Money for Social Change

Christopher Schaefer and Tijno Voors, *Vision in Action: The Art of Taking and Shaping Initiatives*

E. F. Schumacher, *Small Is Beautiful*

David Shi, *The Simple Life*

Philip Slater, *Wealth Addiction*

Publications

In Business

Notes

1. *Times-Argus* (Montpelier, VT), 22 March 1987.
2. *New York Times,* 12 April 1987.
3. Ibid.

PART III

DOING IT OURSELVES: CREATING THE ECONOMY WE WANT

CHAPTER FIVE

Investing in Social Change

Most investors consider making any connection between social concerns and investment capital "investing in social change." I do not think this is enough. Investing in *social change* means changing the root causes of the problems we are concerned about. To achieve this we must invest our time, energy, skills, and ideas—as well as our money.

I have spent the past five years researching grassroots, small-scale, decentralized projects working for peace, economic justice, the preservation of wildness, the protection of the environment, and the constructive use of resources and "waste." I have chosen this route because I believe that corporations are part of and the source of our problems. As I have met more and more skillful, incredibly committed people working both here and in the Third World to heal some of the damage done by corporations, I have become more and more convinced that to save this Earth and its communities, we must transform our corporate economy.

Large corporations are often totally unresponsive to the needs of their workers, to their communities, and to the environment until they are forced to "toe the line" by new laws and regulations or by an embarrassing media exposé. Industry leads the battle *against* acid rain legislation and *for* increased production of nuclear weapons. It does this by forming political action committees (PACs) and contributing huge sums of money to the campaigns of sympathetic (or soon to be) politicians, by appealing via the mass media to the public's need for national security and a high standard (not *quality*) of living, by debunking private organizations' reports, by covering up the truth until forced to 'fess up by an accident or circumstances (Union Carbide—Bhopal; A.H. Robins—Dalkon Shield; Chemie Grunenthal—Thalidomide), and by the simple power of economic and political strength.

I applaud the corporations that are making gainful strides in such areas as worker participation, safety, the environment, and community relations. Social investing, as discussed in the previous two chapters, is a useful tool and an interim step that can help us get from where we are to a more humane and Earth-based economy. It can begin to wake us up to the gross irresponsibility of much of corporate America and help us learn more about the effects of our financial activities on the rest of the world. It also opens the debate over whether we "should" integrate money and values. (Most people that I've talked to believe we should at least try!) It begins the essential process of making connections between our actions and world circumstances while preserving the so-called security of the financial bottom line. And, once in a while, social investing makes a difference in some corporations and gives us a hint of the extent of our economic power.

Social investors point out that since corporations have amassed so much economic and political power, we can make great strides by pressuring companies to change their policies and act more responsibly. I think what we need now is much more than a change of policy—what we need is a change in perception and a corresponding change in the structure of our economy. Although legislation and regulations can alter perception and structure a little, they do not penetrate deeply enough into the root causes of exploitation and injustice to give rise to the structural changes I feel are necessary.

What differentiates social investing from investing in social change is a commitment to the value of the individual within the context of the (human and Earth) community. Raising workers' salaries from $12,000 to $20,000 may be an improvement, but it is not social change. Social change might mean developing a worker-owned or cooperative business that would incorporate worker and community input into its decisions. Preserving the environment or cleaning up toxic discharges is an improvement, but social change involves developing technologies that do not leave us with toxic discharges in the first place, and further, involves our changing our orientations so that we see "waste" as a valuable resource to be reused rather than dumped. Social change is not just saving the rain forest: it is developing a culture that provides for the needs of the people *and* the rain forest. Social change means recognizing the importance of history and of other cultures and the absolute necessity of diversity. Social change takes into account (and celebrates) the small differences between and the nuances of each of us within our communities; it does not expect to franchise (or clone) itself around the world.

"Traditional" social investors sometimes object to investing in social change by noting the difference in financial return. No matter how sympathetic they may be toward the plight of the poor or the small-business-person, many investors and financial professionals claim they cannot afford to invest in social change. It is absolutely true that saving for our children's education, for retirement, or for unexpected emergencies is very important. I certainly want to offer my sons financial security. But I also want to leave them a world they can revel in. I want them to be able to roll down a mountainside of wildflowers as I did as a girl. I want them to have the opportunity to fulfill their hopes and dreams creatively. I want them to be able to make their own decisions, and control their own lives, without having to always answer to a corporate or political power. And I would like them to be able to earn a living doing what they love, not what they feel they must do to get by. How can I not afford to invest in social change?

I see no greater risk than the folly of ignoring the needs of the Earth. And I see no higher return than that of a future that sustains all life joyously on a living Earth. The innovative, catalytic projects I discuss in the rest of this book provide hope, inspiration, and the beginnings of the solid foundation of such a world. These projects can help our children have a future worth living.

5.1 An Example: Investing in Social Change in South Africa

Some Americans (certainly not all!) feel that U.S. corporations can actually do some good in South Africa. They feel that better salaries and working conditions for black South Africans would alleviate some of the unrest. As we know, the situation there is deteriorating rather than improving. Simply providing a better working environment and more money does not increase black opportunity or bring about equality. It has not touched the injustices of apartheid; instead, U.S. corporate investments have reinforced it. South Africa's white political leaders use U.S.-made goods (Ford trucks, IBM computers, and so on) to further entrench the apartheid system. The South Africa Freedom Fund is an example of a U.S.-based effort that has a better chance of making some difference.[1]

South Africa Freedom Fund
Grassroots International
PO Box 312
Cambridge, MA 02139
(617) 497-9180

Anti-apartheid activists insist that the system cannot be reformed. It must be scrapped. They are demanding not only the integration of buses and beaches, but also a restructuring of the country and a fundamental democratization of the entire society.[2]   —Dan Connell
Executive Director of Grassroots International

Grassroots International (GRI) is a nonprofit social change organization that funds community-based relief and development programs in Africa, the Middle East, and the Philippines. GRI operates the South Africa Freedom Fund as part of its South Africa program. This program works in collaboration with OXFAM Canada and is based upon partnerships with groups in the United Democratic Front and members and service groups of the Congress of South Africa Trade Unions. The purpose of the fund is to support the growing anti-apartheid movement in South Africa and to help build a free, democratic, nonracist society there.

Projects are under way in the following areas:

Community Organizations—Black South Africans have rejected the "township councils" chosen for them in 1983 and have begun to organize new civic associations, parents' crisis committees, women's organizations, youth groups, and the like. Since many community leaders have been arrested, "street committees" have been elected to protect against disruption in the event of an alternative leader's "detention." GRI is committed to supporting these organizations. Specifically, it has pledged to support the Natal Organization of Women (NOW), which publishes a community newsletter and health education packets and offers workshops and such survival projects as gardens. GRI also supports the Durban Youth Forum, which coordinates classes and seminars

99

that give unemployed young blacks the skills and motivation to organize and operate self-help projects and community services in township ghettos.

Trade Unions—GRI is committed to helping workers fired from a factory owned by a British multinational after they went on strike in support of demands for trade union rights. Although the one thousand dismissed workers continue their struggle against BTR (Rubber Products) Sarmcol, they have established small survival cooperatives to support their families. The Sarmcol Workers Co-operative grows vegetables, makes bulk food purchases, produces silk-screened t-shirts and buttons for anti-apartheid groups, and runs a free health service.

GRI supports the Technical Advisory Group, an independent organization of researchers and professionals who work in consultation with major trade unions. TAG has provided research and assistance to the National Union of Mineworkers for negotiations on improved contract provisions for its members' health and safety.

Alternative Media Services—GRI supports papers in East London (*Veritas*) and in Johannesburg (*South Africa Student Press Union*).

Educational Outreach—A powerful exhibition of banned photographs depicting the nonviolent anti-apartheid struggle inside South Africa is available for educational use throughout the United States. The collection of twenty-two recent photographs, entitled "Taking Sides in South Africa," is from Asrapix, a multiracial group of prominent South African photographers. The exhibit has toured a number of U.S. college campuses.

Medical and Material Aid—Paramedic training by the multiracial National Medical and Dental Association in first aid, emergency treatment, and crisis intervention counselling for victims of police and army repression.

As a matter of policy, GRI does not accept any government funding and will not accept any contributions from corporations doing business in or with South Africa. The Freedom Fund is a unique opportunity to fight apartheid while supporting grassroots efforts for a nonracist, free South Africa. GRI publishes a newsletter that is sent to supporters who donate $25 or more.

Notes

1. The following is reprinted from *CATALYST*, vol. 3, no. 3, **and** updated.
2. *Christian Science Monitor*, 9 April 1986.

CHAPTER SIX

Community Reinvestment

A community's economy is like a bucket of water—the fewer the leaks, the healthier the economy. Just as a bucket full of holes can hold no water, a community whose money and resources flow out to other communities cannot sustain itself. Although all communities have some leaks, in a healthy economy the leaks are few, and the money and resources coming in balance those leaving. Money circulates within the community, being earned, spent, and invested there. As the leaks increase, the community must scramble to keep the balance. This becomes an endless, frustrating cycle, making big "one-shot" deals tempting.

When a community needs more jobs, capital, or housing, community officials often hire outside consultants, who proceed to develop a plan with minimal input from the community or even the individuals who will be most affected by the plan. It is not surprising that such plans rarely plug the leaks.

Practitioners of this sort of economic development might propose large housing projects as the solution to inadequate housing. If all goes well, such a plan *may* lead to more housing, but it is unlikely to take into account the social fabric of the community and the diversity of neighborhood cultures. Moving people from their familiar social networks into a large, unfamiliar complex can wreak havoc in their lives. Their housing may be improved, but not their sense of community.

Similarly, communities sometimes see big business as a panacea for problems of jobs and capital. While a large auto plant looks good when many people are unemployed, the competition (according to the Rocky Mountain Institute, some twenty-five thousand cities compete annually for a mere five hundred plant sitings) makes the effort expensive and often frustrating. More important, the price—in terms of corporate tax breaks, environmental concessions, and loss of independence—of enticing big business often outweighs the benefits. And given big business's tendency to run away to areas with cheap labor and/or few pollution controls, there is little guarantee a plant will stay for very long.

Nor is our federal government very reliable. While many federal programs have provided much-needed funds and technical support, most have been cut—probably never to return.

By focusing on the needs of the community as a whole and by drawing on its resources, community reinvestment efforts attempt to plug leaks and create healthy, self-reliant, local economies. Community reinvestment has always been a good idea, but with the federal government's withdrawal of support, the increasing disparity between the haves and the have-nots, and general economic dislocation, community reinvestment has come of age.

Community organizations are working with state and local governments, community members, and private and institutional investors to develop strategies and projects to create strong local economies while addressing economic, social, and environmental injustice. Self-reliance and sustainability are integral to these new projects—financially, socially, and environmentally. Money and other resources are hard to come by and must be used prudently. These efforts also involve as many different sectors of the community as possible, which gives people a sense of ownership of and commitment to a project and increases the likelihood that it will fit the community's needs.

This chapter examines some ground-breaking projects and models for community reinvestment, with particular attention to land and housing, jobs, availability of capital, and energy and resources, including waste.

6.1 Land and Housing

In this country, land is a commodity to be sold to the highest bidder. Its value rises as we develop it, causing land values and taxes to rise in surrounding areas. In turn, rising taxes often force people to sell undeveloped land to developers. This vicious cycle exploits the land and the people. Consider the following statistics compiled by Alanna Hartzok for the Henry George School of Social Science in May 1986:

  –An acre of land in the San Francisco Bay area costs between $50,000 and millions of dollars.
  –One square yard of land in prime urban areas costs as much as an acre of rural land.
  –In 1970 the average cost per acre of farmland was $196; by 1981, it was $790 (figures from U.S. Department of Agriculture).

Fewer and fewer people can afford to own land or homes. Farmers and homeowners alike are facing bankruptcy and foreclosure because of rising property values. The large prices paid by developers tempt cash-poor landowners to sell. As high-rise buildings, parking lots, industrial parks, and shopping malls cover the Earth, we lose more and more productive and beautiful land. The developments sprawl and the increase of dispossessed people undermines the possibility of stable, supportive human and natural communities.

One important approach to housing problems is organizing for rent control, tenants' rights, and more emergency shelters. But organizers are increasingly looking toward longer-term solutions.

Housing Cooperatives

Some communities are turning to housing cooperatives to enable low- and moderate-income people to own homes at a reasonable cost. In a housing cooperative, the building is owned by the cooperative corporation and the resident members own shares proportional to the value of the unit they occupy. In a market cooperative, members can sell their shares for full market value. In a limited-equity cooperative, the resale value of each share is held below market value to ensure that the housing will continue to be affordable.[1] The limited-equity feature does not limit the participation or responsibility associated with cooperative ownership. Co-ops can be started by individuals, organizations, or local governments. Often residents of a neighborhood get together and, with some technical assistance from an advocacy organization and financial backing, organize to purchase a building themselves.

Cooperatives, as well as the land trusts described below, often increase the strength of a community as the participants work together for common goals, develop their skills, share what they already know, and support each other through the inevitable rough times. Chuck Matthei, Director of the Institute for Community Economics (ICE), observes that "while many cooperatives begin as 'partnerships of convenience,' members typically find a high level of companionship, mutual aid and 'social security' during the process of development, organization and management."[2]

Access to affordable, decent housing is the goal of many community organizations; lack of such housing is one of our nation's pressing social problems. The American dream of home ownership is often just that—a dream. Even renting is becoming more difficult as gentrification overtakes whole neighborhoods. Displacement, often resulting in homelessness, is a reality for more and more Americans. Advocates for the homeless have estimated that as many as three million people are homeless in this country. One-third of them are families. Emergency shelters cannot keep up, even in warm weather.

Community Land Trusts

The community land trust (CLT) model was developed by Robert Swann and Ralph Borsodi in the 1960s to address the issue of land tenure. In a paper entitled "The Possessional Problem," Borsodi wrote that "the only way to make possible a truly good life for mankind is to utterly abolish the principle of absolute ownership of land and other natural resources, and completely replace it with agreements of tenure in trust. No amount of legalization can provide an honest title to any portion of the earth."

Although the CLT model is a relatively new organizational structure, the concept has its U.S. roots in the tradition of the early New England "commons"—land held by the community "for the common good." Today, this means protecting land from development, as well as preserving farmland and wilderness. The "commons" is similar to nonprofit landholding organizations that hold the land for conservation purposes, but differs in that the land is open to all members of the surrounding community for common use. Individual memberships are not bought or sold.[3]

In Robert Swann's words:

> The CLT has a purpose which goes beyond simple preservation of land. It recognizes that human beings are ultimately a part of the total ecological reality, and that in order to reach ecologically sound goals, we must also support economically sound objectives. For this reason the CLT encourages an approach to land use planning which includes a mixture of housing and farmland in ways that are mutually compatible and supportable.[4]

The purpose of a community land trust is to strike a fair balance between individual and community interests, combining features of both private and community ownership. The trust is a nonprofit corporation with open membership and an elected board that typically includes residents of trust-owned lands, other community residents, and public-interest representatives. The trust acquires land in perpetuity through purchase or donation, thus removing the land from the speculative real estate market.

The trust then leases the land on a long-term or lifetime basis. Leaseholders (which may include families, individuals, businesses, cooperatives, and community organizations) pay a regular lease fee based on "use value" rather than "full market value." While leaseholders do not own the land they use, they may own buildings and other improvements made. CLT's often help the leaseholders obtain ownership of buildings by arranging affordable financing. An agreement is usually signed between homeowners and the trust that provides for the terms under which a home may be sold. These generally include a provision restricting the amount of appreciation that the seller may receive. For example, if one builds a house for $30,000, one may be able to sell it for twice that in ten years, depending on property values in the area. If the home were in a land trust, one would be able to sell it for $30,000 plus a reasonable amount for inflation and any capital improvements. One does not make a large profit, but one knows that one has not adversely affected someone else's chance for affordable housing, either. By limiting equity, the CLT allocates the value created by the homeowner to the homeowner and the value created by the community to the community.[5] It also addresses the need for affordable housing by asking homeowners to sign agreements that if they decide to sell, their price be based on use value rather than on what the market will bear.

There are now many successful CLTs in both rural and urban areas. The model is being used by neighborhoods, intentional communities, organizations concerned with the plight of our agricultural lands and wilderness, and even city planners. The CLT model is being adapted to fit many situations. Here are a few examples.

Institute for Community Economics
151 Montague City Road
Greenfield, MA 01301
(413) 774-5956

Founded in 1967, the Institute for Community Economics (ICE) has become one of the most active and effective organizations working to enable low-income people to participate powerfully in the economic development of their communities. ICE is committed to working for the systemic changes necessary for self-reliance. Its deep belief is that residents of a community must be involved in economic development and be the primary beneficiaries of that development. Toward this end it provides technical assistance to groups in community organizing, the acquisition of property, legal agreements, and financing. Advice on low-cost housing design, training in appropriate methods of construction, and low-cost skilled labor during the early stages of a project are also services of ICE.

ICE recognized early on that the main obstacle for low- and moderate-income people and organizations is the lack of capital. Without credit and/or a track record, they find it impossible to obtain financing from more traditional sources like banks, credit unions, or even partnerships with investors. Furthermore, high interest payments usually only undermine the success and potential social impact of grass-roots projects.

To solve these problems, ICE began to work with two models, the community land trust (CLT) and the revolving loan fund (RLF). Robert Swann and Ralph Borsodi developed the CLT model in the 1960s to address the issue of land tenure and in 1967 formed the International Independence Institute, which later became ICE.[6] (see page 132 for ICE's other work)

South Atlanta Land Trust
1523 Jonesboro Road
Atlanta, GA 30315
(404) 525-2683

The South Atlanta Land Trust (SALT) provides an excellent example of the positive impact the land trust model, combined with limited-equity housing, can have on a rapidly deteriorating community. SALT also demonstrates that working closely with residents, community members, and local government can greatly improve the chances of both getting the work accomplished and creating the kind of environment that brings people together.

Created officially in 1982, the land trust has a much longer history. South Atlanta was once a prosperous middle-class black community of more than seven hundred single-family homes, most of them privately owned. In the 1960s, both Clark College and Gammon Seminary moved, and the community began to decline. The City of Atlanta purchased the 450-acre Clark College campus for a large public housing project and planned more public housing in South Atlanta.

According to Craig Taylor, staff person for SALT,

Economics as If the Earth Really Mattered

Atlanta was in an all-out push to build a lot of public housing as a means of controlling certain neighborhoods, and South Atlanta was one of the real hotbeds of black activism in the fifties. The effort was to keep on and condemn the property of homeowners, to build more public housing units, and destroy South Atlanta. At that point the South Atlanta Civic League was formed. They raised a dollar from every household—over five hundred dollars—hired an attorney, and were successful in defeating the efforts to condemn their community.

Still, the community continued to deteriorate. Families moved and children grew up and left, too. Houses were abandoned when the elderly died. Absentee landlords and trucking firms and other businesses began buying property. Over two hundred units of housing were lost between the mid 1950s and the early 1980s, and there are now 230 vacant lots in South Atlanta. During the same period, home ownership dropped from almost 100 percent to 35 percent!

The South Atlanta Civic League continued to resist this decline, mostly by tearing down old, empty houses, which were seen as hazards. That led to the question of what to do with all the vacant lots.

In 1981, the Trust for Public Land held a seminar attended by a group of neighborhood leaders. There they learned about the community land trust model. L. D. Simon, president of the Civic League since its beginning, remembered, "We saw businesses moving in on the residents, pushing them out. . . . If we owned the land we could block them from coming in." At this point, they contacted ICE and began the process of developing SALT.

Since the primary focus of the Trust for Public Land's seminar had been open space for communities, at first SALT still focused mostly on cleaning up vacant lots. But since houses continued to be vacated, the need for affordable housing was great, and real estate prices were low, SALT realized that many of the vacated houses could be rehabilitated if they moved quickly.

The first house was purchased in the fall of 1983 for $6,000, and the City of Atlanta granted the CLT a block grant for the rehabilitation. During the rehabilitation process, the contractor reported that over two hundred people asked about the house's availability. And the Wheelers—the home's new residents—said that in the first week alone, forty-nine people wanted to know how they, too, could get such a house.

SALT now has a well-established track record and several innovative programs to provide low-cost, decent, long-term housing to people whose incomes vary from extremely low to moderate; they even have a program designed to provide homes for the homeless.

Neighborhood Preservation Project   This project focuses on acquiring and renovating vacant houses for moderate-income (between $15,000 and $20,000) residents. So far, it has completed eleven units. SALT employs its own construction crews, thus providing jobs as well as houses. Currently, three work crews and a construction supervisor are on the job. When licensed work is required, the Project tries to hire minority subcontractors. The houses renovated under this project sell for about $40,000.

Since most prospective home-buyers for SALT houses do not qualify for regular bank mortgage loans, SALT has worked out a creative financial arrangement with two local conventional lenders, Trust Company Bank and Georgia Federal Bank. SALT enters into a mortgage agreement with the bank based on an 80% loan-to-value ratio and then provides a 95% wraparound mortgage to the buyer. This requires SALT to tie up 15% of its funds for each house in long-term mortgages. SALT is thus committed to finding arrangements that will make it possible for the buyers to borrow the money directly from lending institutions. So far, the Georgia Residential Finance Authority has agreed to make 7¼% fixed-rate thirty-year mortgages to SALT homebuyers.

Low-Income Housing Project   The need for housing for very low-income families became apparent when many who applied for the $40,000 homes could not afford them. This project aims to help those with incomes between $8,000 and $15,000. SALT received a Community Development Block Grant from the city to subsidize this housing. It used the money to move and rehabilitate eight houses scheduled for demolition in conjunction with a noise abatement program around Atlanta's airport.

ICE loaned SALT the money to purchase a one-acre tract of land on which to locate the eight houses. These homes sell for $30,000 and priority is given to female heads of households. Trust Company Bank arranged a blanket mortgage to cover all eight houses, and SALT then made separate wraparound mortgages with the individual buyers. Monthly payments on these mortgages is less than $300, including taxes, insurance, and land-lease fees.

To supplement this project, SALT plans to acquire at least six units that very low-income families can rent at reasonable rates.

Cooperative Housing Project   The target groups for this project are the elderly and young mothers with small children. SALT acquired sixteen units of multifamily housing that had once been Gammon Seminary's married student housing and had subsequently been sold to a notorious slumlord. ICE loaned SALT the $110,000 necessary to purchase the building, and the City of Atlanta provided $5,000 per unit at no interest to rehabilitate it. The city forgives 10 percent of its loan each year so long as the units remain accessible to low-income tenants. The remaining $120,000 necessary for rehabilitation came from a local bank, Citizens and Southern Bank. The permanent loan came through the Federal Home Loan Mortgage Corporation. This project demonstrates the kind of creative financing that can be assembled to make low-income housing possible.

SALT plans to reorganize the project into a limited-equity cooperative once the rehabilitation is complete and the units are occupied.

New Construction Pilot Project   SALT is now beginning to build four three-bedroom homes—three for moderate-income families and one for a low-income family—on some of the vacant lots in the neighborhood. This is quite an event in South Atlanta, since no new homes have been built there for at least twenty years. SALT's goal is to construct at least eighteen new homes per year; it also hopes that this project will pave the way for better working relationships between lenders and nonprofit developers. The Georgia Residential Finance Authority has agreed to provide permanent financing for the first four houses, again at a 7¼% fixed rate for thirty years.

Operation New Start   Homelessness has virtually doubled in Atlanta in the last two years, and many of these homeless people are families. Under the leadership of the mayor's office, Operation New Start was conceived as a transitional housing program. Using housing from the airport area (being moved as part of a noise-abatement program), homes will be moved into the city and made available to homeless families. SALT was chosen to implement this program because of its experience with moving houses, its ownership of vacant land, and its proven ability to manage this kind of housing. SALT is working in conjunction with Fulton County, the City of Atlanta, and Economic Opportunity Atlanta. The houses are being moved free of charge by some of Atlanta's housemovers. SALT will develop permanent housing for those moved into the transitional homes.

Doing It Ourselves

Atlanta Mayor Andrew Young has described SALT as a "united community effort," drawing upon "all of the resources that are available: that's human resources, city resources, religious community resources and neighborhood resources." The project provides other communities facing similar problems with a wonderful model for a really broad-based, innovative, and effective community reinvestment program.

Community Land Trust in the Southern Berkshires
195 Main Street
PO Box 276
Great Barrington, MA 01230
(413) 528-1737

The Community Land Trust in the Southern Berkshires (CLTSB) was founded in 1980 with a commitment to making land available to year-round residents for housing, agriculture, and cottage industry. It buys land and leases it to residents at the lowest rates possible. Each plot of land comes with a land-use plan based on the needs of the community, local zoning ordinances, and the ecological characteristics of the land itself. Sites are leased for ninety-nine years; leases are automatically renewable and inheritable (fairly common among this sort of CLT).

According to CLTSB's literature:

> How the land is utilized and developed determines the character and vitality of any community. As is the case here in Berkshire County, economic pressures from outside the community, such as an overheated second-home market and skyrocketing interest rates, price land out of the reach of many of the community's full-time residents and in turn erodes community control over the development of its own land.

The Trust's first piece of land was purchased in 1980 and now provides cluster housing for four families on ten acres. The second piece, obtained in 1986, is a larger tract (twenty-one acres); a detailed development plan has been designed and approved by the Great Barrington Planning Board. The twenty-one acres are divided into four zones. Zone 1 is the "development zone," characterized by houses, roads, and utilities. Zone 2 (three separate sections) will be wooded spaces. Any cutting within these areas "must increase the zone's usefulness as a wooded recreation area and must be approved by the Forest Row Lessees Association" (Forest

111

Row is the name of the development). Zone 3 is a smaller area designated for recreation and such livestock as chicken or goats. Zone 4 consists of eleven acres called the "wild zone." No cutting, fires, hunting, or building will be allowed. This plan provides for minimum ecological impact, adequate recreation areas of various sorts (open and wooded), and privacy. The land in zone 4 is ecologically sensitive and the plan provides for its perpetual protection.

Housing construction is complete. There are two quadruplex units, three duplex units, and four single-family sites. The quadruplex units sell for between $75,000 and $85,000, while the duplex units sell for $110,000. Mortgage money is available at 5½% from Massachusetts's newly formed Home-Ownership Opportunity Program for first-home buyers. The single-family sites will be leased to residents who will design, finance, and arrange construction themselves.

The units or homes may be sold for what it would cost to replace the house, but profits created by fluctuations in the real estate market are prohibited. In addition, the deeds state that residents must live in their homes at least six months of the year, preventing the houses from becoming second homes for vacationers.

A Fund for Affordable Housing is being implemented as a second mortgage pool for first-home buyers living and working in the southern Berkshire region. The fund is designed to complement the Commonwealth Homeowner's Opportunity Program with a more flexible, locally controlled program able to respond efficiently to the housing and income pressures unique to the southern Berkshires. Surprisingly, much of the capital for this fund has come from second-home owners in the area. Second mortgages are available at 7% interest for first-home buyers earning less than $30,000 annually. The homes financed in this way must be owner-occupied and priced below $100,000. Financing is made only for units with a provision for limited equity. Individuals may invest in this fund for a three- to five-year term and earn 6½% interest. Investments are secured by a second mortgage made by the Fund. A variety of interest payment plans and terms are possible, and the minimum investment is $1,000.

This project is another example of how CLTs and limited-equity financing can work together to satisfy the needs of a community. It also demonstrates the flexibility of the structure as it is applied to a rural area. The Fund for Affordable Housing was implemented because second mortgages are often necessary for moderate-income people to purchase homes at all. In western Massachusetts, where land values are skyrocketing because of increasing development and recreational use (which attracts wealthier people who can afford second homes and vacation condo retreats), projects such as this help to keep small rural towns intact and in the control of local residents.

6.2 Jobs

Creating new businesses and ensuring the vitality of businesses already operating in a community are very complex and often difficult tasks. But they are essential elements to the well-being of a community. Many cities in the United States are suffering incredibly because of plant relocations, industry-wide failures, and the changing nature of the economy. Plant closings, especially in the "rust belt," are causing the reappearance of ghost towns. In many communities, especially in the South and the Midwest, unemployment haunts more and more people. As usual, blacks, other minorities, and the young are hit the worst.

In addition, many, if not most, Americans are dissatisfied with their jobs, simply "putting in time" until the day is over, the weekend arrives, or they can retire. It is rare to find someone who is doing what s/he loves *and* earning a decent living at it. As a result, it is not surprising that we feel we should at least be able to "have" luxuries and conveniences as rewards for our servitude. While these rewards can help us relax or forget, the relief is often transitory; the daily grind reasserts itself. Even the few well-paid are often dissatisfied with their working lives. We feel out of control—and we often are.

Cooperative businesses and worker-ownership are two of the most promising tools we have to regain control over our work lives *and* to revive our communities. Cooperatives have been around for a long time, and most states have laws governing the form and structure they can take. Basically, regardless of her or his financial investment, each person in a cooperative has one vote. This insures that nobody can overpower the decision-making ability of anyone else. For this to work, the cooperative must have excellent communication systems and checks and balances, and the membership, especially those with the most money invested, must share a high level of trust. The Resources section lists several organizations that help set up cooperatives and offer technical and financial assistance.

There are many levels of worker ownership, some of which have more possibilities than others. Employee stock ownership plans (ESOPs) are often nothing more than pension funds. Workers have the stock, that is, the ownership, but they often have no responsibility, not even voting rights. True worker ownership involves ownership *and* responsibility. Workers participate in the decisions of the company and are affected by the consequences, good and bad, of their decisions.

The most successful transitions to worker ownership are those in which the managers provide training in worker ownership and management for the employees. The transition takes time. Just as managers must learn to see the long-term effects of their decisions on the workers, the community, and the planet, so must workers learn to make decisions that ensure the health of the company as a whole—not just their short-term benefit. Decision making is a skill; effective worker-owned companies recognize this and take the time to learn what is involved. In addition, successful worker-owned companies have found that when their members earn their ownership, it means much more. When ownership is given rather than earned, the stock or other equity is usually considered strictly for its financial value and used as just another commodity.

The Industrial Cooperative Association (ICA) provides technical assistance and training to companies wishing to become cooperatives or worker owned. ICA also has a revolving loan fund that lends money to workers to enable them to purchase stock in their companies. Interest rates and repayment schedules are tailored to individual need and are very reasonable.

The Philadelphia Association for Cooperative Enterprise (PACE) is another landmark organization. It assisted workers in Philadelphia A&P food stores in converting them to worker-owned O&O supermarkets. The conversion changed the necessarily adversarial relationship between "management" and "workers" and so involved difficult but ultimately productive discussions with the union.

The NCB Development Corporation provides technical assistance to cooperative businesses and has an investment portfolio that includes worker-owned businesses as well as revolving loan funds and projects of nonprofit organizations. According to Terry Simonette, vice president and senior lending officer, NCB makes loans to

> businesses that make sense. The development corporation isn't a philanthropic or grant-making institution. We think

of ourselves as a venture capital firm for cooperative businesses. We're planting the seeds for all kinds of cooperative business growth. That means we're making long-term investments in co-ops that have the potential to grow into solid business enterprises. We're investing in the ways and means by which more people can gain economic empowerment by working together for the common good. [7]

As communities begin to look at what is available within their borders and begin to look at workers and jobs with an eye toward new possibilities, worker ownership and workplace democracy will become not only appealing but essential in developing healthy and productive economies.

Worker Owned Network
50 S. Court Street
Athens, OH 45701
(614) 592-3854
Contact: June Holley

We believe it does not work to simply create new businesses with cooperative workplaces only to set them adrift, isolated in our economy with the deck stacked against them.
—Marty Zinn
one of the organizers of WON

Some people in Appalachian Ohio have come up with a solution that should be applicable to other areas of the country. The Worker Owned Network (WON) is providing assistance to low-income people who want to create their own jobs by starting worker-owned businesses that will operate in a just, democratic, and personal way.

WON began about three years ago, with volunteers working with a group of welfare mothers starting a homemaking/home health aide service. In spring 1985, WON incorporated as a nonprofit organization and gained tax-exempt status. WON's first funding came from the State of Ohio, and the network added three more businesses: a Mexican-American restaurant, a natural foods wholesale bakery, and a cleaning service. WON staff are now helping a group of local women form a craft cooperative and doing a feasibility study with a group of machinists. As each business gets under way, it helps the next one take its first steps.

The Worker Owned Network aims to address the pressing needs of a region with 20 percent unemployment (over 50 percent among Native Americans) and to play a part in aiding the revitalization of the local economy. WON sees itself as a model of community-based economic development fostering initiative and self-determination among low-income people.

WON's main work is to offer technical assistance and cooperative training to worker-owner groups. Since employees in a worker-owned business must make many decisions together, they need to acquire such group process skills as leading effective meetings, planning, decision making, problem solving, and conflict resolution. WON's training includes skill building in these and other social processes to enhance cooperative work relations within the worker-owner group, as well as such technical business skills as marketing strategies, financial projections, and costing and pricing. WON also assists each group in creating its corporate structure, writing its bylaws, and developing business policies. The network's computer systems are available to each business.

The founders of WON were inspired by the Mondragon cooperatives in Spain to create a system of support services and to build on community relationships so that no small cooperative enterprise would have to exist in isolation. (For more information on Mondragon, write: The Trusteeship Institute, Baker Road, Shutesbury, MA 01072; or The Alternative Center, 2375 Shattuck Avenue, Berkeley, CA 94704). WON's staff has also learned much from several U.S. groups: the Industrial Cooperative Association in Boston, the Philadelphia Association for Cooperative Enterprise, and the Center for Community Self-Help in Durham, North Carolina. The network hopes to establish other support services, such as its own financing institution for its growing number of businesses, and to meet worker-owners' needs for day care, housing, and health insurance through cooperative efforts.

The Worker Owned Network is primarily funded by grants but is building a local funding base for the long term. Donations from grassroots fundraising, contributions from the businesses in the network, and fees for services outside the network are growing.

For those interested in learning more about WON, ask for their packet of materials ($3) or register for their periodic one- to two-day seminar on site ($35).

6.3 Capital

Capital is more than just cash. It is time and skills (some of which can be converted into cash). Capital is what it takes to get a project off the ground and to respond to changing situations. The time and skills of the participants are the core of any enterprise. But, in our economy, the cash is often the deciding component. Here I want to discuss different ways of raising capital.

In the past, cash capital has been raised by obtaining loans, selling shares in a corporation (equity), limited and equity partnership, and winning grants from the government and private or public foundations. Often, these sources are combined. These days, several of these methods are combined to come up with the total financing package. Public/private partnerships are becoming more common to finance housing and business development. Often, individuals or institutional social investors like churches are playing crucial roles in such projects as low-income housing developments and land trusts that combine the trust with limited-equity housing.

There are also alternative financial institutions that facilitate the financing of social-change projects. These include revolving loan funds, loan collateralization programs, and even alternative currency. Such institutions, along with progressive banks and community development credit unions, are some of the most exciting catalysts around. They provide excellent educations for community members without previous experience in financial matters, their funds can be applied to meet the particular needs of their community, they give people a local investment option, and, if set up properly, they give the community control over some of its assets.

For a Good, Safe Investment, Think About Your Local Minority-Owned Bank
—Michael Kilcullen

If asked to describe an ideal alternative investment, what would it be? Perhaps one that pays market rates, is risk free and convenient, yet also promotes housing and business development in low-income neighborhoods. Consider for a moment placing a deposit in a minority-owned bank or savings and loan. They are:

> *High Yielding*—Rates paid on deposits are generally compatible with those paid by other banks. Minority-owned banks (a term by which I include savings and loans) are for-profit businesses and therefore must pay market rates if they intend to continue operating.

> *Safe*—All deposits in minority-owned banks are fully insured up to $100,000 by the federal government.

117

Convenient—There are nearly two hundred minority-owned banks around the country, with most offering the same services you would find elsewhere.

Socially Responsible—Minority-owned banks can be generators for economic development and positive social change in their communities.

Minority-owned banks have been around for close to a century. The early banks were founded to promote savings and provide financial services for blacks in their own communities—areas entirely neglected by traditional banks. Their numbers surged during the 1960s and 1970s in response to the civil rights movement. Minority-owned banks came to be viewed as a vehicle to combat discrimination and to redress economic disenfranchisement. Today, minority-owned banks have combined assets that exceed $7 billion. Sixty percent of these banks are black-owned, 33 percent are owned by Hispanics, and the rest are owned by women, Asian-Americans, and others.

Most minority-owned banks are very small. They serve below-average-income communities and are run by people with roots there. As a result they are less inclined toward community disinvestment, that insidious practice in which banks limit or avoid lending to low-income, "high-risk" communities, yet freely take deposits and fees from them to support the banks' activities elsewhere. As a result, these low-income communities, the ones with the greatest need for capital, are denied access even to their own. Moreover, with their capital continually being siphoned off, these areas remain impoverished.

Minority-owned banks can be effective in countering this process. From the data available, it is clear that on average minority-owned banks historically have been very responsive to the needs of their communities. Specifically, they provide:

(1) mortgages in allegedly "red-lined" areas underserved or neglected by traditional banks;
(2) sorely needed loans to small local businesses;
(3) training and employment opportunities to community residents; and
(4) credit and financial services to small savers who might otherwise be totally ignored.

Furthermore, minority-owned banks can provide such important intangibles as serving as role models and stabilizing forces in their neighborhood.

Thus, it appears that an alternative investor gets money, security, convenience, and community development, but there are catches. First, a deposit in a bank is lumped together with all other deposits to form the bank's lending base. Therefore, it is hard to see the direct effect of the investment. Nevertheless, it does contribute overall to the bank's operations and ultimately to the community. Moreover, the cost to the alternative investor is minimal, most likely just the time involved in switching banks.

Second, and more problematic, is that not all minority banks are socially responsible. On average, minority-owned banks are, yet the range can be great. Some are progressive catalysts for change, while others are as active in disinvesting as their mainstream counterparts.

The question is, therefore, how to separate the wheat from the chaff. The place to start is with the bank itself, and to consider the following:

(1) The annual report and any public relations pieces—Look at what the bank says about itself. Perhaps it gives out a description of its community involvement—something of which it is proud—or a breakdown of its lending activities.

(2) Its statement on business policy and goals (often given in the annual report)—Buffeted by high interest rates, deregulation, growing competition, and changing technology, banks, especially small ones, have been finding it difficult to make a profit and sometimes even to survive. One viable business strategy is for small banks to focus on a particular market segment, or niche, in which they have some advantage. By exploiting this niche, by serving it better than anyone else, the bank can successfully defend its "turf" against even its largest competitors.

For minority-owned banks this means developing expertise and finding opportunities within their own communities, which, because of prejudice or ignorance, are missed by their competitors. There are many minority-owned banks that follow this strategy, develop the synergy between the community's interests and the bank's, and have above-average profits. So, you should give special attention to the bank's business strategy for good insights into its community role.

(3) The Community Reinvestment Act (CRA) files—This is a statement containing comments on the bank's community involvement that is open for public viewing.

(4) Home Mortgage Disclosure Act Data—This is a published list of the bank's mortgages. It can be a very good source of information, though it is tedious to look through.

(5) Bank Management—Take a trip to the bank and talk with the staff, or write a letter to the president. A good question to ask is what civic activities the staff are involved in (for example, the local Y, church groups).

You will probably be frustrated in getting exactly the information you need from the bank for two reasons. First, these banks are small, understaffed, and have limited public relations materials and capabilities. Second, the banks are generally run by entrepreneurs—men and women proud of succeeding in a highly competitive environment. Thus, the bank's management might not think in terms of social contributions and therefore could be confused by your requests. Be persistent.

Next, consider such nonbank sources of information as local newspapers, which can be useful and objective. A national publication that might be helpful is *Black Enterprise Magazine*. It has an annual review of black banks in June and sometimes has focus pieces on select banks. Another excellent source of information is people in the bank's neighborhood (for example, local community development groups or churches), who would certainly have an opinion one way or the other on the bank.

After gathering all the information you are inclined to gather, look it over to see what pattern emerges. Those banks that are active in their communities will probably have supporting data like commendations by the local newspaper or a nearby pastor, while those without good records will have little or nothing to show. Be skeptical if the bank makes great claims, yet the people you have spoken with say otherwise and the CRA file is empty.

Another thought: if you find a bank you feel comfortable with, then in addition to your deposits think about other indirect investments in the bank, such as using the bank's nondeposit services (checking accounts, IRAs, insurance, and so on). You can also support the bank by giving it all your business, especially if the product is good. In addition, tell your friends; those contributions add up.

If you wish more information on minority-owned banks, you may obtain the report on which these findings are based, *Church Investments in Minority-Owned Banks and S&Ls* ($3 including postage from ICCR Clearinghouse, Room 566, 475 Riverside Drive, New York, NY 10115). The report includes a complete list of minority-owned banks. The list is also available from the banks' trade associations: National Bankers Association, Suite 240, 122 C Street, NW, Washington, DC 20001—for commercial banks; and American League of Financial Institutions, Suite 1001, 1435 G Street, NW, Washington, DC 20005—for savings and loans.

Michael Kilcullen, who holds an MBA from Harvard, has worked as an investment research analyst for the Morgan Guaranty Trust Company. He has a personal interest in minority community development and is a consultant to several community development organizations in the New York City area. He may be contacted through ICCR (address above).

Dwelling House Savings and Loan
501 Herron Avenue
Pittsburgh, PA 15219
(412) 683-5116

Dwelling House Savings and Loan has the unusual motto "The institution that serves your need, not your greed." It loans money to poor, mostly black, people who would not qualify for loans at other banks.

Once, the Dwelling House Savings and Loan Association was a very different operation, part-time and disorganized. In 1957, Robert Lavelle, then a real estate developer in the area, went into Dwelling House to obtain a mortgage for a client. Despite the client's excellent qualifications the bank was unable to make the loan because all of its money was committed to paying back investors who had left. Angry, Lavelle gave them advice on how the bank could be run better. At that moment, literally, Lavelle was made a director and the bank's secretary. Lavelle recognized that the bank needed federal insurance to grow, but to do this it needed to prove that it was self-supporting. It needed a separate, ground-floor location, and it needed to be open full-time. So Lavelle partitioned his real estate office, moved the bank into the new space, and opened it full-time.

Dwelling House then had three black directors, six white directors, and assets of only $67,000. By 1968, the directorship had changed to its present seven black to two white ratio, assets had climbed to $130,000, and the campaign to become federally insured had begun. The drive revolved around a subscription campaign to recruit people who pledged to save once the bank was insured. By 1970, they had succeeded in collecting enough pledges to obtain insurance. Dwelling House Savings and Loan was off the ground.

Dwelling House's lending policy is based on person-to-person contact and trust. Lavelle says, "The banking rule is you lend at the highest rate you can to get to people at the lowest risk. Under that rule, how can a black person, a poor person, or a deprived person get a loan? When they first come in, we go through the same procedure as any bank. Only after that we have another dimension of trying to help a person. At that point, we say, 'You don't meet the criteria. What can you say to make me lend you this money?' You really get them to face themselves and to know why we're going to do it."

Lavelle believes that marginal loans must be made because the needs of the black community must be met. He asserts that home ownership helps bring about quality schools, more and better services, and better police protection. This, in turn, generates a need for small businesses, which provide young people with positive examples and jobs.

Since 1957, the bank has authorized over six hundred mortgages, as well as some home improvement loans and loans to churches. Anyone can deposit in Dwelling House by paying postage both ways. "Everyone's mail box is our branch office," says Lavelle. The bank pays 5½% interest ("plus human") and is insured to $100,000.[8]

Self-Help Credit Union
413 E. Chapel Hill Street
Durham, NC 27701
(919) 683-3016

The Center for Community Self-Help was begun in 1980 to provide technical assistance to worker-owned and other cooperative businesses. It has developed a network of such businesses that has come to be known nationally as a unique model of rural economic development. In 1984 the center created the Self-Help Credit Union (SHCU) to provide loans to these businesses and to developers of low-income housing. New groups seeking to develop worker-owned firms and existing loan recipients also receive assistance.

As of January 1987, SHCU held $5 million in deposits, and had made loans totalling more than $1 million. For investors, SHCU offers regular savings accounts, money-market accounts, IRAs, and certificates of deposit at market rates. The credit union is one of the few socially responsible lenders that can offer positive social investments and federal insurance on deposits up to $100,000. In addition, tax-deductible gifts of $5,000 or more are sought to provide reserves for the higher-risk loans.

Examples of SHCU's projects include loans to the North Carolina Council of Churches for migrant farmworkers' housing, to a low-income cooperative hosiery mill to purchase their building, and to a worker-owned restaurant employing low-income women.

Self-Help Association for a Regional Economy (SHARE)
E. F. Schumacher Society
Box 76A, RD 3
Great Barrington, MA 02139

Self-Help Association for a Regional Economy (SHARE) is a loan collateralization program supporting small businesses in the Berkshires that are socially and ecologically sustainable. Located in Great Barrington, Massachusetts, the program works in cooperation with the Great Barrington Savings Bank to provide low-interest loans to individuals and small businesses that meet the following criteria:

> Businesses must be from the region. To the extent possible, they must use local materials and employ local people to produce goods to sell to a local market.

> The goods/services offered must be needed by the regional community. Priority is given to businesses producing food, clothing, shelter, and alternative energy and providing health and transportation services.

> Businesses must use appropriate-scale technology and must *not* be environmentally damaging.

> Businesses must have responsible relationships with workers and with the community. Priority is given to cooperatives and businesses with a high degree of worker participation.

> Financial criteria include a sound business plan that demonstrates the capacity to repay the loan, good bookkeeping methods, and the inability to qualify for a traditional bank loan.

Loans up to $3,000 are made from SHARE's credit fund. People join the credit fund by opening a ninety-day notice account (6 percent interest) at the Great Barrington Savings Bank and designating it a SHARE account. The depositor agrees that SHARE may use up to 75 percent of the balance as collateral for loans made from the credit fund.

The bank makes the actual loans, based on the decisions of SHARE's directors, and collects the payments. Because the loans are fully collateralized, the bank can make them at rates well below the usual. The rate is 10 percent—the 6 percent the accounts earn plus a 4 percent yearly service fee.

SHARE is a nonprofit organization incorporated in 1982. It draws its inspiration from Ralph Borsodi's efforts to develop a local currency. In the 1970s, Borsodi successfully developed a small alternative currency project, The Experiment, in Exeter, New Hampshire. His currency was called "constants," and he worked in cooperation with an Exeter bank that agreed to act as the "money changer," exchanging dollars, which Borsodi provided, for the "constants" that Borsodi issued. The value of this alternative currency was regularly compared to the value of the dollar. Since it was backed by such commodities as silver, agricultural products, and energy, its value remained constant, protected from inflation. The Experiment was popular with local residents and merchants alike and even brought reporters from *Time* and *Forbes* to Exeter to interview Borsodi. Unfortunately, Borsodi had to stop his work because of ill health (he was in his eighties at the time).

Robert Swann, one of the founders of SHARE, worked with Borsodi during the years of The Experiment and decided that the point was not the physical "alternative currency" but the creation of regional self-reliance. In his view, "If, as is presently true all over the world, local deposits in dollars were not sucked out of the local area into the huge metropolitan areas and into the big corporations which can afford to pay the highest interest rates, then even dollars could be made to serve a more useful purpose."

In line with its basic beliefs, SHARE supports cottage industries, small farmers, and very small businesses. Since SHARE is really a community-based project, its activities include more than simply making loans. SHARE members work together to support the businesses they have decided to back with their accounts. Their support includes word-of-mouth marketing to friends and acquaintances, asking store owners to stock SHARE businesses' products, and moral support. Members receive a monthly newsletter that keeps them informed about SHARE's activities and how businesses are doing.

Recipients of SHARE loans include:

Jim Golden, to build a barn for his two draft horses. Many farmers prefer draft horses to tractors since they do not tear up the land and they can go places big machines cannot.

Sue and Wayne Sellew, to enable them to upgrade their cheesemaking equipment to meet state guidelines. Although their goat cheese, Monterey Chevre, is excellent, their lack of credit history made a traditional loan difficult.

Kites of Four Winds, so that owners Nick and Sallie Van Sant could take advantage of a 50 percent markdown on fabric offered when a major fabric maker closed. The business nearly doubled profit rates because of the low-cost fabric and paid back the loan in six months.

Bonnie Nordoff, who knits specialty clothing at home. Her first SHARE loan established credit with a wholesaler, while the second upgraded her knitting machine. When she needed a third loan, she was able to receive a traditional bank loan thanks to her credit history with SHARE.

Community Supported Agriculture (CSA), a community of consumers who have banded together to employ one full-time gardener and several part-time helpers to produce biodynamically grown vegetables. The shareholders of CSA have committed to paying a portion of the annual budget for the running of a market garden. Each week throughout the summer, shareholders receive a portion of the week's harvest. CSA encourages its members to help in the garden and include in the price of a share ten somewhat negotiable hours of work over the course of the summer.

SHARE has brought over seventy new depositors to the Great Barrington Savings Bank. Support within the community has grown consistently over the years, creating a much greater awareness of "what's here and what's not here" as well as discussions about "what kinds of businesses do we want to support." SHARE is an excellent way to bring community members into the process of choosing their future. And the $100 minimum (subsequent deposits can be for any amount) ensures that virtually anyone in the community can participate.

SHARE is committed to helping other communities develop similar projects. It will furnish a packet of information and legal documents for $10 to those interested in working on this in their regions.

Churches and Community Development Credit Unions: A Burgeoning Partnership

A fast-growing movement within the ecumenical community is church involvement with community development credit unions (CDCUs). On a grassroots level, individual parishes and neighborhood church coalitions are coming together to organize, sponsor, and create CDCUs. On an institutional level, national denominations, Roman Catholic orders, and regional and local judicatories, synods, and dioceses are placing significant numbers of federally insured market-rate deposits in CDCUs.

Stripped of their financial resources, low-income neighborhoods are considered too high a risk for lending by "prudent" investors. As a result, neighborhoods are denied access to capital needed to rebuild, and the cycle of poverty endures. There is no money, no credit, and no development.

There are, however, institutions that not only lend in these high-risk zones, but are proud to do so. **Union Settlement Federal Credit Union** is one. This twenty-eight-year-old East Harlem institution has assets of over $2.5 million and lends virtually exclusively to local residents, workers, and businesses. Two-thirds of its outstanding loans are small (under $1,000) and are made to community residents (70 percent of them Hispanics, 22 percent blacks, 70 percent women). These loans are for financing education, consumer durables like refrigerators, or home improvements. The Union's remaining credit is extended to small businesses, nonprofit organizations, and residents purchasing or rehabilitating East Harlem housing.

When the Manufacturers Hanover Trust Company announced the closing of its generations-old branch on Manhattan's Lower East Side (which served a hundred-square-block area with a population of over fifty thousand), the neighborhood residents rallied. Faced with a strong community reaction, but finding no other bank willing to move into the site, Manufacturers agreed to donate the property to a community development credit union—the **Lower East Side People's Federal Credit Union**—formed by local residents with the assistance of the Lower East Side Catholic Area Conference and the National Federation of Community Development Credit Unions.

Consider, too, the **Brooklyn Ecumenical Cooperative,** a coalition of thirty-five churches in and around downtown Brooklyn that has taken the message from the pulpit to the pocketbook. In the past two years, Brooklyn Ecumenical has raised over $1 million to lend solely to its one-third black, one-third Hispanic, and one-third white low-income membership.

In the Bronx, members of a coalition of over fifty churches and community groups (the **Northwest Bronx Community and Clergy Coalition**) have recently started their own credit union.

Such grassroots credit unions are aimed at strengthening local community development. It is a phenomenon increasingly finding a role in neighborhoods around the country as residents pool their savings in nonprofit financial cooperatives to provide affordable loans and credit facilities to members in need. Other benefits include:

> CDCUs promote savings by providing federally insured depositories without huge minimum balances or high fees.
>
> CDCUs offer vital low-interest loans. The maximum rates are generally 12 to 15 percent. These interest rates are far less than the 20 percent charged by many banks, or the far higher rates demanded by finance companies or other credit sources (for example, loan sharks) that prey upon low-income people.
>
> CDCUs often have check cashing, payroll deductions, insurance, and other needed, yet often unavailable, services for the small saver.
>
> CDCUs provide intangible benefits: education in savings, credit and financial planning, training in bookkeeping and management for resident members, and, as in most work done by volunteers, development of a cooperative ethic and community spirit.

The bottom line here is that all of these services are provided to people who generally would not have them available—or have them only with inordinate transaction charges. In making credit union loans, a member's character is often as important as income criteria. Thus, credit unions extend credit to first-time borrowers (such as recently divorced women) and others regularly turned down by banks.

But credit union boosters see them as far more than just a financial intermediary providing credit services to those whom others deem "unbankable." Institutions like Northwest Bronx, Lower East Side People's, Brooklyn Ecumenical, and Union Settlement become catalysts for community change, with influence and effects extending far beyond the cash transactions themselves. While neighborhood income from paychecks, social security, and public assistance tend to wash away because of high prices and disinvestment, credit unions act to anchor resources within the neighborhood.

For instance, commercial lending sources charge two to four times a credit union's rates. These substantially higher interest charges are immediately siphoned out of the community, leaving the neighborhood with less money to spend and recycle. Credit unions reverse the process. First, they charge less, thus increasing the cash members can then use in their own community. Second, whatever surplus in interest the credit union does charge is distributed to the members as dividends.

Nor can credit unions mimic the banks' practice of disinvestment—taking savings from a low-income neighborhood and using them to support activities elsewhere. Legal barriers—not to mention moral ones—prevent a credit union from discriminating against its own community. It must lend only to its members, who live within, or are tied to, the community; and as one-member, one-vote cooperatives, local control is assured over credit union resources.

This can be extremely significant. Impetus for the Northwest Bronx Credit Union came from a study showing that for every dollar deposited with a bank in the Bronx only $0.02 was re-lent to residents. *Two cents!*

Increasingly, community development credit unions are becoming involved in providing mortgages for neighborhood residents to buy or rehabilitate their own dwellings and thereby mitigate the effects of displacement caused by speculation and gentrification.

The Brooklyn Ecumenical Cooperative, for example, is using its credit union to resist such pressures in downtown Brooklyn. The group grants and processes mortgages for eventual sale to a secondary market. Through such sales it can recycle capital back into its credit union for new mortgages. Brooklyn Ecumenical has also started a special depository program to provide some of the financing for the rehabilitation of eight thousand abandoned city-owned units that it seeks to reclaim for cooperative housing for low- and moderate-income families.

While churches at the grassroots level have a long-standing involvement with supporters of community development credit unions, institutional support by churches has also been strong and is growing. Members of the Interfaith Center on Corporate Responsibilty (ICCR) have been making investments in CDCUs for nearly two decades. The U.S. Catholic Bishops, the American

Baptists, the United Methodists, the United Presbyterians, and the Marianists are but a few with long-standing involvement with CDCUs.

The reason is that *deposits in CDCUs are the safest, most direct means to benefit in a fundamental way low-income communities.* Most ICCR members place nonmember deposits in a community development credit union. According to their charters, credit unions have limitations on who can become a member, but allow nonmember deposits. Depending on the size of the deposit, rates, and maturities, these deposits can be competitive with banks; moreover, they are fully insured by the federal government up to $100,000.

For further information on Community Development Credit Unions, contact the **National Federation of Community Development Credit Unions** (Cliff Rosenthal, NFCDCU, 29 John Street, Room 903, New York, NY 10038; (212) 513-7191 or 1-800-437-8711). An umbrella group of community development credit unions from around the country, NFCDCU provides training, technical assistance, capital development, management support, and marketing and regulatory advocacy services to credit unions nationally. The federation also operates a CDCU capitalization program and places and monitors church investments in CDCUs around the country according to the needs of the church investor. This program provides capital on an ongoing basis to community development credit unions.

Churches interested in CDCUs or in the area in general should contact ICCR's **Clearinghouse of Alternative Investments** (475 Riverside Drive, Room 566, New York, NY 10115, (212) 870-2316). ICCR is a coalition of 235 church groups interested in or making deposits in CDCUs or other community-based investment opportunities. ICCR publishes the country's most comprehensive directory of alternative investments, containing a four-page description of each CDCU and other groups that receive church support. The clearinghouse also regularly publishes a news packet with developments and church activity in the field and holds networking, brokering, and skill-building meetings.

6.4 Revolving Loan Funds

One of the most exciting developments in recent years is the incredible growth of community-based, social-change-oriented revolving loan funds (RLFs), which have been responsible for leveraging millions of dollars for projects that might not have been possible otherwise. They support and finance low-income housing, cooperative and worker-owned businesses, the projects of community development corporations (CDCs), community land trusts, limited-equity co-ops and limited-equity housing, appropriate agricultural development, the creation of worker-owned co-ops in Mexico and other developing countries, and even a revolving bail fund for Central American refugees. They provide individuals and such other investors as religious institutions and businesses the opportunity to support community investment consistent with their desire for social and economic justice, without the hassle of evaluating projects individually.

In the past three years, the number of RLFs has increased from about twelve to almost three dozen, and more are being planned. Their combined assets total more than $30 million.

RLFs are nonprofit corporations that pool monies from lenders and make loans to projects that further the funds' goals. RLFs usually make loans at below-market rates to projects without access to such traditional sources of capital as banks, credit unions, or other lenders. Many funds allow investors to set their preferred rate of return, usually from 0 to 6 percent, depending on current interest rates, their preferred term (most funds prefer a minimum of two to three years), and the repayment schedule. In addition, several funds allow lenders to target their money toward a specific area or even a particular project.

All the revolving loan funds described in this section provide technical assistance to borrowers. This can range from guidance in developing a business plan, to locating the best contractors for a job, to providing ongoing accounting and planning services. This technical assistance is the loan's and the investor's greatest protection. Despite the seemingly high risk of their loans, most of the funds have experienced no defaults and most have never failed to meet their obligations to lenders.

RLFs often help projects obtain financing from traditional sources. Sometimes they can help a group or organization package their project so that it fits standards and criteria acceptable to banks and other financial institutions. More often, however, the RLF provides seed money and other support to help a project assemble a total financing package that eventually might include loans from other RLFs, equity financing (investors buying shares of a project), bank loans, and perhaps cooperation between the public and private sectors.

Besides helping to finance projects, RLFs give participants the opportunity to develop a sense of solidarity and mutual support. They can create a strong local community or neighborhood economy and increase stability.

Most people with low incomes do not have savings, but they do find money to pay often exorbitant rents and to buy food and clothes. The amounts of money are substantial. For example, if a family pays $350 a month for rent, that is $4,200 per year; over thirty years, this amounts to $126,000! And that does not take into account any rent increases or that most of us rent for a lifetime, not just thirty years. This is enough to buy a house—or part of a housing cooperative. By providing up-front capital and technical assistance to ensure payback, RLFs help capture the money that flows through a community and turn it into projects like housing cooperatives and land trusts.

As you read through the individual stories and resource listings for the various revolving loan funds, imagine the social change that would occur if, instead of thirty RLFs, there were ten times that. Imagine what such a fund could do in your community. Imagine the changes if small, cooperative, neighborhood businesses started cropping up in previously rundown areas. Imagine the opportunity provided to low-income people if they were no longer being drained of all their hard-earned money to pay rent to an absentee landlord. Imagine how powerful people would feel after winning a struggle to purchase and rehabilitate an old building into cooperative apartments, with access for the handicapped so that people of all ages could live there and develop a real community—a "common unity" of support and purpose.

These are the kinds of changes that RLFs can catalyze. They are truly grassroots solutions to very real problems, and their strength is their flexibility in adapting to the unique needs of each community. The model has been created. It is up to us to put it to good use.

Despite new tax regulations lowering the amount that can be deducted for money contributed to tax-exempt organizations, all *loans* up to $250,000 to a nonprofit organization (which includes, of course, the RLFs in this section) are exempt from the rules regarding imputed interest. Under this exemption, if you make a below-market-rate loan to an RLF, you will not be assessed at the imputed T-bill rate on your taxes. For example, if you lend money at 2 percent and the T-bill is 7 percent, you are now required to report only the 2 percent interest earnings. On any loan amount exceeding $250,000 to any single fund (a problem most individual investors will not encounter), you must report those interest earnings at the T-bill rate, regardless of the actual rate you specified. However,

even these investors can report the difference between their rate and the imputed T-bill rate as a charitable gift, remaining tax-liable only for the interest they actually earn. This exemption was fought for by the Institute for Community Economics and the National Association of Community Development Loan Funds. As ICE's director, Chuck Matthei, stated in the *Boston Business Journal:* "We are the private sector initiative the government called for to solve the social problems. It's unfair to penalize us."

The Institute for Community Economics (ICE)
151 Montague City Road
Greenfield, MA 01301
(413) 774-7956

The revolving loan fund (RLF) model is perhaps ICE's best-known work. Their own fund was initiated in 1979 after years of working in community economic development and alternative financing. They saw a need for a bridge between investors and projects in need of capital and recognized that lack of capital often stalled or halted projects. Initially, their fund was established with no endowment, operating for its first three and one-half years entirely with loaned capital. Today, twenty-one donations have provided an endowment, or permanent capital pool, of $232,262. (Donations, which are tax-deductible, enable a fund to be flexible in meeting the needs of very low-income borrowers.) Currently, the fund is capitalized at over $7 million!

ICE loans nationally. Their role in providing technical assistance to community groups means that they are skilled evaluators of borrowers, able to accurately assess their needs and capacities. Their excellent technical assistance team works closely with borrowers, monitoring them and troubleshooting if needed. Their working relationship often extends through the whole loan period. The fund also serves as an intermediary between community groups and local lenders who wish to invest in their communities but do not want to manage loans and projects themselves. Projects supported by ICE include nonprofit corporations developing affordable rental housing, limited-equity co-ops, community land trusts (rural and urban), and worker-owned businesses.

In 1985, ICE sponsored the first National Conference of Community Development Loan Funds. The conference grew out of ICE's providing technical assistance to community groups wishing to initiate local and regional revolving loan funds like ICE's. Over thirty funds (those in operation and many in the planning stages) sent representatives, and out of this conference came the National Association of Community Development Loan Funds (NACDLF) (see page 134).

The New Hampshire Community Loan Fund (NHCLF)
Box 666
Concord, NH 03301
(603) 224-6669

The NHCLF provides a wonderful example of the kinds of community organizing and coalition building that revolving loan funds facilitate. Founded in 1984, the fund was assisted by and modeled after the Institute for Community Economics' revolving loan fund. It makes loans and offers technical assistance to New Hampshire organizations, tenant groups, cooperatives, and other self-help economic development projects unable to obtain financing otherwise.

NHCLF has been instrumental in making affordable housing available to low-income New Hampshire residents. In 1986, the fund helped residents purchase three mobile home parks. In both Greenville and Weare, NHCLF loaned the tenant groups the necessary up-front money for the "good faith" deposits on their parks. The tenant groups raised the rest of the money themselves.

In Milford, the residents of the Town and Country Mobile Home Park ended a two-year battle of rent increases and eviction notices by buying their park and preventing the site from becoming a new condominium development. Raising the money came down to the wire. With only eleven days left, $1.4 million was still outstanding. NHCLF took the lead in finding these funds, piecing together money from twenty-eight lenders to provide nearly half of the amount needed.

The fifty-eight families who live in Town and Country have low incomes, and many rely on fixed incomes. They have formed a homeowners' cooperative with an elected board of seven to operate the park. Committees on finance, operation and maintenance, special fund, membership, and park rules do most of the work. The board receives training and continuing technical assistance from both the NHCLF and the Mobile Home Owners and Tenants Association. The residents use the special fund to help some of them afford the fee increase necessary to cover the costs of interest payments on some short-term loans. The special fund is supported by raffles, yard sales, and food sales held by the residents.

In 1986 NHCLF leveraged over $5.7 million for affordable housing for 284 families who can now control their housing costs and conditions. For example, NHCLF helped one struggling family with nine children escape eviction, buy their house, and end up with payments less than half of any rental. NHCLF also supplied the "missing piece" of the downpayment so that the New England Non-Profit Housing Corporation in Manchester could acquire twenty-seven units, mostly family size, and remove them from the speculative cycle of rental housing.

In addition to assisting community groups in meeting basic human needs and providing access to capital, the fund also provides a "hassle-free means for people with capital, or who manage capital, to put it to work locally in line with their values and ethics."[9] So far, lenders have provided enough capital to enable the fund to make all the loans the board wanted to approve. The fund has many exciting projects under consideration for the future, providing continuing opportunities for concerned investors to put their money to good use.

National Association of Community Development
Loan Funds (NACDLF)
151 Montague City Road
Greenfield, MA 01301
(413) 774-7956
Contact: Greg Ramm

NACDLF grew out of the First National Conference of Community Development Loan Funds, sponsored by the Institute for Community Economics in October 1985. Although the funds support different types of community development projects, they are all working to address the issue of poverty, the patterns of ownership and control (of housing, land, and business), and the inequitable distribution of capital in our communities. Member funds are also committed to "responsible stewardship of investment resources and sound business management."

NACDLF has a threefold purpose: to assist those who need capital most, to provide opportunities for responsible community investment to those with capital, and, by example, to encourage and challenge those who manage capital to overcome prejudice and increase the capital available for community based projects.

The organization serves as a resource center for information concerning member funds and community investment in general; increases public awareness of community needs and possible solutions; provides information, training, technical assistance, and peer evaluation to loan funds; and coordinates efforts to open up new sources of capital.

NACDLF also offers an "Associate Membership" to individuals and organizations that support its purpose and philosophy but are not involved in revolving loan funds.

Women's Institute for Housing and Economic Development, Inc.
179 South Street
Boston, MA 02111
(617) 423-2296
Contact: Joan Forrester Sprague

The Women's Institute (WI) was founded in 1981 by three women (a lawyer, an architect, and a banker) to provide expertise in housing and business development to grassroots women's organizations, which, although well-intentioned, often lack the skills necessary for the successful implementation of sustainable enterprises.

The institute's services include:

Transitional Housing Development—Transitional housing for women and their children provides the necessary link between emergency housing and permanent housing. The best models include a supportive housing environment, access to child care, and opportunities for job training. WI's *Manual on Transitional Housing*, published in 1987, is an excellent resource on the subject. In addition to the chapters defining the need and describing different models (right down to the floor plans!) and the special groups they best serve, the book details the steps necessary to develop transitional housing—gaining community support, finding a property in a suitable neighborhood, discovering funding sources, managing the operation and determining what will be required of the residents, and so on. Actual projects from around the country are described and a list of resource organizations is included.

Venture Planning Assistance—This is another service provided to community organizations in housing and business development. Services include: needs and capacity assessment; goal setting; budgeting; financial packaging; negotiating with government, community, and business; property acquisition (including site evaluation and investment advice); preliminary architectural design work; assistance in selecting architects, contractors, and engineers; and more. A 1984 publication, *A Development Primer*,

135

discusses the issues of women and housing and business development. The subject is approached in a practical manner, and it is made clear that with adequate information and assistance, when necessary, women *are* doing it! We are developing organizations and businesses with the goals of empowering women both personally and financially and we are having some impact. This book examines the similarities and differences between housing development and business development, gives advice on how to proceed, and provides real-life examples and a good resource list.

Participatory Training Workshops—These workshops are designed for women's groups, community-based organizations, and social service agencies interested in housing or business ventures. They are intensive workshops custom-tailored to the needs of specific groups. For more information on WI's projects and publications, write to them at the address above. Tax-deductible contributions are also most welcome.

6.5 A Directory of Revolving Loan Funds

A recommended resource for community loan funds is *The Community Loan Fund Manual*, prepared by the Institute for Community Economics. This newly published manual (350 pages, in a loose-leaf notebook) draws on experiences in the development of several community loan funds and in the management of ICE's own revolving loan fund. The book discusses in detail key aspects of developing and managing a community loan fund and includes case studies of funds in New Hampshire, Boston, and Philadelphia. If you are starting a revolving loan fund in your community, this is an invaluable resource ($45 plus $2 postage from ICE, 151 Montague City Road, Greenfield, MA 01301).

The information on revolving loan funds that follows is accurate as of the fall of 1987.

CALIFORNIA

The Low-Income Housing Fund
55 New Montgomery, Suite 223
San Francisco, CA 94105
(415) 777-9804

Doing It Ourselves

Founded: 1984

Purpose: The Low-Income Housing Fund (LIHF) was established to increase the amount of capital available for low-income housing at affordable rates and terms. The fund has several programs designed to assist developers of low-income housing: LIHF is a lender of its own funds; it is a financial intermediary that arranges financing from other sources; it administers a small mortgage guarantee program and an investor program that generates subsidies; and it provides technical assistance to developers of low-income housing.

Size and Record: By January 1987, LIHF had made twelve loans of its own totaling $822,000, creating 419 units of housing. In total, LIHF has been involved financially with the development of 861 units of low-income housing having a total development cost of over $25 million. It has had no defaults.

Investment Opportunities: LIHF's preferred method for leveraging capital is the Interest Rate Writedown, based on reducing the interest rate on mortgage financing for low-income housing to a more affordable rate for a specified period. The mortgage financing, or the underlying loan, is obtained from available sources (for example, private institutional lenders or mortgage revenue bonds) for as long a term as possible, preferably twenty to thirty years. The interest rate on this financing is then subsidized for a shorter period of time, up to twelve years, through an investment made by a socially concerned investor willing to accept a substantial but below-market rate of return (up to 7 or 8 percent). The investor's funds are placed in a certificate of deposit (CD), which earns a market rate of interest. The returns from the CD are split between the investor (at the required below-market rate) and the nonprofit housing development corporation, which receives most of the remainder of the difference between the return and the market rate in order to subsidize the interest rate of the underlying loan.

Examples of Projects: ASIAN, Inc., is an established nonprofit organization specializing in business development, with some low-income housing activities, too. It had negotiated a sales agreement on a thirty-one-unit apartment building housing low-income, predominantly Southeast Asian families. Because of lengthy negotiations needed to secure permanent financing, $9,500 was needed to extend the escrow period. LIHF's loan for that amount gave ASIAN the needed time and ensured that they would not forfeit their $10,000 nonrefundable deposit. Community Housing Developers, a nonprofit corporation in San Jose, was also assisted by LIHF in its effort to establish a transitional housing facility for low-income battered women and their children.

Northern California Community Loan Fund
14 Precita Avenue
San Francisco, CA 94110
(415) 285-3909

Founded: 1986

Purpose: The Northern California Community Loan Fund (NCCLF) was established to address the long-term needs of low-income communities by supporting projects and models that allow their residents to build equity and contribute to an indigenous economic base. It was also created to serve as a bridge between socially conscious investors and projects in need of capital, as well as to be a forum for public education on community investment and economic justice. NCCLF seeks to create greater understanding of the importance (and the means) of community investment, which will lead to changing the established patterns of investment.

Size and Record: NCCLF is a new fund. About $300,000 has been pledged toward start-up investment capital from foundations, individuals, and private brokers. Contact NCCLF for the latest developments. The fund is a project of the Vanguard Public Foundation, a member of the Funding Exchange Network.

Investment Opportunities: Individuals and institutions may loan money to the fund, specifying the terms of their loans. A minimum of $1,000 for at least one year is preferred. Interest paid will not exceed current bank money-market rates.

COLORADO

Catherine McAuley Housing Foundation
1601 Milwaukee Street
Denver, CO 80206
(303) 393-3806

Founded: 1983

Purpose: Catherine McAuley Housing Foundation (CMHF) was established by the Sisters of Mercy, Province of Omaha, and is affiliated with Mercy Housing, Inc., the Sisters of Mercy's nonprofit housing corporation. It was founded to serve as a financial resource base for affordable housing and community development projects and to act as a catalyst for attracting resources to selected projects. Its projects empower people, improve the quality of life, strengthen the family, and promote systemic change.

Size and Record: Over $1 million has been invested in the foundation since its inception, and $608,000 has been lent to eleven borrowers since its first loan in 1985. The foundation serves eighteen states: Arizona, California, Colorado, Idaho, Iowa, Kansas, Minnesota, Missouri, Montana, Nebraska, Nevada, New Mexico, North Dakota, Oregon, South Dakota, Utah, Washington, and Wyoming. It has had no defaults.

Investment Opportunities: Individuals and institutions may lend $2,500 or more to the foundation for a minimum of three years. Many loans have been received without interest requirements, but interest-bearing loans are also accepted. Donations, too, are gratefully received.

Examples of Projects: Loans have been provided to such enterprises as "sweat equity" construction of single-family homes, rehabilitation of dilapidated homes, and nonprofit housing.

CONNECTICUT

Cooperative Fund of New England
108 Kenyon Street
Hartford, CT 06105
(203) 523-4305

Founded: 1975

Purpose: To provide loans to cooperatives in New England, with an emphasis on those with low-income membership. To provide a socially responsible investment option.

Size and Record: The fund had investments of approximately $160,000 as of January 1987 and had made more than $450,000 in loans since 1975. Its losses since its inception have averaged less than one-half percent. The fund also has over $30,000 in "first loss money" (investors who have agreed to assume losses first if there are any).

Investment Opportunities: Individuals may lend the fund $1,000 or more for at least one year at any rate between 0 and 6 percent.

Examples of Projects: A loan to Cherry Hill Cooperative Cannery, Berlin, Vermont, to replace its heating system and consolidate debt. Cherry Hill is a producer/consumer co-op providing high-quality commercial canning of local produce and community canning facilities. Boston Food Cooperative—a moderate-sized retail food co-op, one of the first in New England— was lent money to renovate its building as part of a major revitalization effort. Gandhi Peace Center and Institute—a charitable organization in a depressed area operating a free food-distribution program, an approved rest home, and self-help activities for the very poor—received a loan to finance a cooperative craft-marketing project and to consolidate debts.

DISTRICT OF COLUMBIA

Jubilee Housing Loan Fund
1750 Columbia Road, NW
Washington, DC 20009
(202) 332-4020

Founded: 1974

Purpose: The Jubilee Housing Loan Fund (JHLF) finances the purchase and renovation of large apartment buildings in Washington, D.C., for use as low-income housing. It was established to help break the cycle of poverty through loans from caring people. It is part of an integrated community working with such needs of low-income families as jobs and job skills, health care, parenting, preschool education, and programs for the elderly poor and homeless. Loan funds are invested in buildings that JHLF purchases. No loan funds go toward operating expenses.

Size and Record: The Loan Fund is capitalized at $1,375,795; the average interest rate paid is 2.05%. There are 424 depositors. The smallest loan is $25, the largest is $50,000, and the average is $2,435.

Investment Opportunities: There is no minimum-amount requirement for lending to JHLF. The investor sets the desired rate of return from 0 to 6 percent. Interest, if requested, is paid on a predetermined schedule and investments are repaid whenever the investor wishes. Loans are backed by JHLF's equity in its buildings, and a reserve is kept in liquid investments in order to honor withdrawals.

Examples of Projects: Since the fund's inception, over eight buildings have been acquired and renovated. Over one thousand adults and children live in 258 apartment units in the buildings. In 1985, the first Samaritan Inn, a halfway house for street people, was furnished. An additional building has been acquired for the second inn; funding is needed to renovate and furnish it. A third inn, for women, is planned.

GEORGIA

Koinonia Partners
Route 2
Americus, GA 31709
(912) 924-0391

Founded: Koinonia Partners (KP), a religiously oriented farming community, was founded in 1942. Its Fund for Humanity (housing fund) was set up in 1968.

Purpose: The construction of affordable housing for low-income families in rural Sumter County, Georgia. The fund pays for construction of the single-family houses, which it also helps build. Construction costs usually run about $25,000. The houses are then sold to qualifying families at cost with a twenty-year interest-free mortgage. Payments are kept around $100 per month.

Size and Record: Since 1969 around 160 houses have been financed; payments coming in from these mortgages provide the money to build more houses. Tax-deductible donations provide about one-third of the funds needed each year, and loans provide about one-fourth of the needed funds. All monies are in a revolving fund for the years ahead.

Investment Opportunities: Individuals may lend the fund any amount at no interest, repayable on thirty days' notice for amounts under $5,000 and on sixty days' notice for larger amounts. In practice, however, loans are repaid within several days.

Southeast Reinvestment Venture
159 Ralph McGill Boulevard, NE
Room 412
Atlanta, GA 30365
(404) 659-0002, ext. 276

Founded: 1986
Purpose: The Southeast Reinvestment Venture (SERV) is a nonprofit loan fund subsidiary of the Fund for Southern Communities, a progressive membership foundation. Its primary goal is to provide affordable and accessible capital to community-based nonprofit organizations—including co-ops, community land

141

trusts, and community-owned or -organized businesses—involved in housing development. SERV operates in Georgia, North Carolina, and South Carolina.

Size and Record: As of January 1987, SERV had not yet made a loan, though one was pending.

Investment Opportunities: Individuals and organizations may make loans to the fund. Contact SERV to discuss your specific needs.

Examples of Projects: SERV's first loan will be to the South Atlanta Land Trust in the amount of $72,500 at 6 percent.

ILLINOIS

Anawim Fund of the Midwest
1145 W. Wilson Avenue, Suite 2424
Chicago, IL 60646
(312) 989-6233

Founded: 1985

Purpose: The Anawim Fund is a collaborative interfaith effort of church-related and other nonprofit member organizations that have pooled financial resources and make credit available to businesses and programs that address the needs of the poor and disadvantaged. Anawim is a biblical term for "God's poor" or "little ones." Anawim is particularly interested in supporting the development of cooperatives and alternative work structures. It serves Wisconsin, Illinois, Iowa, and Minnesota.

Size and Record: Anawim has forty-three members, who have loaned the fund $302,000. Its first loan was made in 1986.

Investment Opportunities: The member organizations may lend to the fund. Individuals may become "Friends" and donate funds and provide technical assistance to borrowers. Individuals aware of the fund may encourage nonprofit organizations or religious institutions of which they are part to become members and thereby contribute to the fund's work.

Examples of Projects: Anawim's first loan, of $25,000, was made to the Midwest Center for Labor Research of Chicago, whose mission is to create and retain jobs and stability in declining industrial communities. The loan will help finance a project on worker ownership that will educate and train business and community organizations in the potential of employee ownership and will directly assist three to five businesses in their efforts to convert to this model.

KENTUCKY

Human/Economic Appalachian Development Corporation
PO Box 504
Berea, KY 40403
(606) 986-1651

Founded: 1987

Purpose: Human/Economic Appalachian Development Corporation (HEAD) was formed to assist cooperatives and worker-owned businesses, nonprofit and community development corporations, land trusts, and individuals. There is little capital available for community projects since absentee landlords control much of the region's resources. HEAD's projects are grounded in a cooperative philosophy and spirit. In 1980, HEAD began operating a federally chartered and insured community development credit union, the Central Appalachian People's Federal Credit Union (CAPFCU). Today, the credit union has over 900 members and over $1 million in assets. It has made $1.3 million in loans, most at 12 percent or less. CAPFCU has been able to make about 10 percent of its loans for development and job creation projects; federal regulations make this percentage difficult to exceed. The Revolving Loan Fund is designed to expand this critical area.

Size and Record: HEAD is capitalized at $220,000 and has $185,000 in loan commitments.

Investment Opportunities: Deposits are being sought from individuals and institutions. Loans to the fund range from $500 to $20,000. Individual arrangements are made; loans are designed to fit specific needs.

Examples of Projects: HEAD has made smaller loans to a craftsperson for a building; to a video store; to two craft cooperatives; to a candy-making business. The largest loan to date is to a nonprofit sewing factory in Virginia which will employ thirty workers.

MASSACHUSETTS

Boston Community Loan Fund, Inc.
25 West Street, 2nd Floor
Boston, MA 02111
(617) 451-2050

Founded: 1984

Purpose: To provide loans at below-market rates to qualified community-based projects that build or rehabilitate affordable housing in Boston for lower-income people, and to create new sources of capital for this purpose by accepting loans at below-market rates from individuals and organizations that wish to make socially responsible and safe investments. The Boston Community Loan Fund (BCLF) also has a commitment to eliminate racial and ethnic barriers across the city and to provide fair housing and open access for all citizens.

Size and Record: The BCLF has received $434,000 in loans from thirty-six lenders; loans range from $1,000 to $150,000. The BCLF has made thirteen loans that have helped build or preserve over 435 units of housing for poor people in Boston. Five of these loans have been repaid, and all other payments are on schedule.

Investment Opportunities: While lenders may specify the terms of their loans, the BCLF generally does not accept loans for less than $1,000, for periods of less than one year, or for higher than current bank money-market rates. Unrestricted loans are preferred.

Examples of Projects: The BCLF has provided a range of financing and technical assistance to nonprofit organizations developing housing. Its loans have included a bridge loan to complete construction and ensure syndication of a low-income, limited-equity cooperative, a permanent mortgage on a battered women's shelter and transitional house, and share loans to public housing tenants to purchase cooperative units in a limited-equity cooperative. The BCLF provides technical assistance to borrowers, both for development and on an ongoing basis. It also works with other organizations and individuals involved in nonprofit housing development and social change.

Institute for Community Economics, Inc.
151 Montague City Road
Greenfield, MA 01301
(413) 774-7956

Founded: The Institute for Community Economics, Inc. (ICE), was founded in 1967. ICE set up its revolving loan fund in 1979.

Purpose: The fund was established to link community groups and potential lenders. Loans are made for a variety of projects, especially for low-income housing, cooperative housing, community land trusts, and cooperatively owned businesses. ICE provides technical assistance to the organizations it works with. It developed the community land trust model, as well as the model many RLFs in this section are using.

In addition, ICE technical assistance teams help community groups all over the U.S. to establish their own revolving loan funds. Examples include the New Hampshire Community Loan Fund and the Burlington (Vermont) Revolving Loan Program.

Size and Record: ICE is currently capitalized at over $4.5 million. Since 1979, ICE has made 141 loans, 79 of which have been repaid; there has been one default amounting to less than $2,000.

Investment Opportunities: Individuals may lend to the fund at whatever rate and term of years they choose. The average interest rate requested is around 5 percent, although many lenders offer less. Lenders may also specify a project they would like their money to support.

Examples of Projects: The People's Laundromat in Camden, New Jersey, was purchased by concerned citizens of North Camden to keep an important service in an economically depressed neighborhood. Though the laundromat came to operate efficiently with the help of neighborhood volunteers, its twelve-year-old washing machines needed to be replaced. As a nonprofit business in a low-income community, it could not get financing from conventional sources. A loan of $3,500 from ICE funded the purchase of the essential equipment.

The Boston Aging Concerns Committee purchased a burned-out lodging house that it planned to renovate as a twenty-three-unit shared-living home for the elderly. Commitments for financing were received from the city and a bank, but the process of completing contractual arrangements proved slow, and there was fear that the project would stall altogether. A five-month bridge loan from ICE allowed construction work to proceed, encouraged other lenders, and assured the success of the project.

With support from the Lower East Side Catholic Area Conference, groups of Lower East Side residents have organized as limited-equity co-ops to homestead abandoned buildings. Once co-op members have completed necessary demolition and cleanup activities, it is possible to get title to the buildings from the city and arrange financing to complete the rehabilitation process. Before initial activities can proceed, however, money is needed for dumpsters, tools, and other immediate costs. ICE loans have provided front money for nine buildings. In October 1986, ICE made a loan to two specific homesteaders' cooperatives to complete renovations on these co-ops—the first to reach this stage.

Western Massachusetts Community Loan Fund
145 State Street, Suite 500
Springfield, MA 01103
(413) 739-7233

Founded: 1986

Purpose: The Western Massachusetts Community Loan Fund (WMCLF) was established to provide low-interest loans to qualified community-based projects that increase and/or preserve the supply of low-income housing and to finance businesses owned and operated by low-income people that provide employment for such persons within their local community. The fund serves the four western counties of Massachusetts: Hampden, Hampshire, Franklin, and Berkshire. Groups eligible for loans include nonprofit corporations, cooperatives, community development corporations, and other organizations and individuals engaged in projects consistent with the purposes of the fund.

Size and Record: WMCLF is just beginning its capitalization effort. It was created by a merger between the Fund for Affordable Housing in Western Massachusetts and the Task Force on Community Reinvestment. A number of local groups received assistance from these two organizations.

Investment Opportunities: Individuals and institutions may lend to WMCLF. Lenders may specify the terms of their loans (number of years, interest rate, and schedule of repayment). Lenders may also designate a particular type of project, a specific geographic area, or even a particular recipient. Donations are also welcome.

Worcester Community Loan Fund
PO Box 271, Mid-Town Mall
Worcester, MA 01614
(617) 799-6106

Founded: 1985

Purpose: The Worcester Community Loan Fund (WCLF) was established to provide technical assistance and loan capital to community organizations developing affordable housing and the economy of Worcester County. Loans can be made to community land trusts, limited-equity cooperatives, community development corporations, community-based organizations, and housing-related businesses that are in partnership with or part of CDCs.

Size and Record: WCLF is a new fund and made its first loan of $180,000 with money loaned to the fund by two local churches and the Institute for Community Economics.

Investment Opportunities: Individuals may lend to the fund; there are no minimum requirements for amount or number of years. Interest paid ranges from 0 to 5 percent.

Examples of Projects: WCLF's first loan was to the Jeremiah Hospice Sheltering Program for adult males who have been deinstitutionalized. The funds were used to prevent the razing of the program's building and for rehabilitation.

MINNESOTA

Women's Economic Development Corporation
Iris Park Place, Suite 315
1885 University Avenue West
St. Paul, MN 55104
(612) 646-3808

Founded: The Seed Capital Fund (SCF) was founded in 1984. The Growth Fund was founded in 1986.

Purpose: The nonprofit Women's Economic Development Corporation (WEDCO) was created in 1983 to help low-income women develop and successfully run their own businesses. The organization provides individual consulting services, training work groups and business-related classes. Women are assisted by staff who understand the unique problems associated with being a low-income woman. WEDCO sets its goals to help employ as well as empower. The SCF makes loans ranging from $200 to $10,000 directly to women business owners, or WEDCO may act as a guarantor for a woman with a banking institution. The businesses must be at least two years old and moving into a new stage of growth.

Size and Record: The SCF has a capital base of $650,000. The average loan is $5,000. Three to five applications per month are processed by a seven-member, volunteer committee. Interest rates are two points above prime for small loans and terms range from thirty days to three years. Eighty-five loans have been made, twenty-five repaid in full, six written off, and the rest are current. The Growth Fund has a capital base of $300,000. Its loans range from $30,000 to $125,000.

Investment Opportunities: Those who loan money to the Funds may set their own rates and terms, subject to market considerations.

Examples of Projects: The SCF has loaned money to a fundraising and communication business which raises more than $1 million a year for activist groups; a book sales and distribution company; a hand-woven fabric business; a building restoration business. The Growth Fund's first two loans were made to a florist and a food manufacturer.

NEW HAMPSHIRE
New Hampshire Community Loan Fund
Box 666
Concord, NH 03301
(603) 224-6669

Founded: 1984

Purpose: The New Hampshire Community Loan Fund (NHCLF) makes loans to New Hampshire organizations, tenant groups, cooperatives, and other self-help economic development projects unable to obtain financing otherwise. Borrowers also receive technical assistance.

Size and Record: As of January 1987, loans by the NHCLF totaled over $1.2 million, primarily for affordable housing projects by low- and moderate-income people. NHCLF has made nineteen loans to date.

Investment Opportunities: Individuals may set the time, rate, and payment schedules for loans to NHCLF; these will be accepted if they can be used to meet current community needs for capital. Loans must be for at least $1,000 for a minimum of one year. Generally, interest is for no more than the money-market rate, with interest-only payments during the loan.

Examples of Projects: The owners of the Town and Country Mobile Home Park in Milford, New Hampshire, sold the park to a condominium developer late in 1984. Huge rent increases and eviction notices were given. Two years and a court battle later (a technicality between the seller and the developer), the situation still presented a dire threat to the low-income families living there, with not one family able to find a place to move their home. The average income of the families is well under $10,000 a year and most are elderly or families with young children. NHCLF helped them form a cooperative and make the owner an offer in excess of the developer's. The developer prevailed in court, so the cooperative offered to buy the park at a price that reflected a 100 percent return to the developer. The offer was refused. Meanwhile, they conducted negotiations to buy another piece of land, but the land was abruptly donated to the town, which refused to sell it. The developer finally signed an agreement giving the residents eleven days to obtain financing of $1.4 million! Loans provided by NHCLF and ICE made the purchase possible.

NEW YORK

Capital District Community Loan Fund
33 Clinton Avenue
Albany, NY 12207
(518) 436-8586

Founded: 1985

Purpose: The Capital District Community Loan Fund (CDCLF) was created to stimulate and encourage housing development and economic opportunities for low-income and other disadvantaged households, to provide education, financing, and technical assistance, and to create alternative models of finance for housing and economic development. Loans can be made to cooperative and nonprofit corporations engaged in developing or managing housing that will be affordable for lower-income people on a long-term basis; to nonprofit and worker-owned businesses, and to consumer cooperatives. Technical assistance is also provided.

Size and Record: CDCLF has received $140,000 in loans.

Investment Opportunities: Loans are accepted from individuals and from institutions. Loan amounts, terms, and payback procedures are determined on a case-by-case basis. A lender is able to set the terms of a loan according to his/her own needs, within the boundaries of what CDCLF can expect to use productively in the community. In general, a loan will not be accepted for less than one year or at a rate higher than 5 to 6 percent. Lenders may also specify a use or restriction on their loan.

Examples of Projects: Three loans have been made so far, all to existing nonprofit groups for specific development projects. One was for a portion of construction financing for a home ownership program, the other two were bridge loans, one for the rehabilitation of abandoned property for use as permanent housing for homeless families and individuals. Several other loans are being negotiated.

Catskill Mountain Housing Revolving Loan Fund
PO Box 473
Catskill, NY 12414
(518) 943-6700

Founded: 1981

Purpose: Catskill Mountain Housing (CMH) was founded to improve housing conditions for low- and moderate-income residents of Green County, New York. The fund provides resources for people to help themselves in solving their housing difficulties by making short-term, low-interest loans for rehabilitation, small home repairs, and ownership. Borrowers also receive comprehensive technical assistance to help them make the most cost-effective use of their money. They are given money management counselling, if needed, to assist in meeting their loan obligations.

Size and Record: CMH is capitalized at $24,250. It has loaned a total of $32,524 in seventy-two loans, fifty-one of which have been repaid. The average loan is between $500 and $1500.

Investment Opportunities: Individuals can lend $50 or more for at least one year. Interest received can be between 0 and 5 percent. Money is loaned at 6 percent. All supporters can recommend general guidelines for the use of their money. The fund combines the many loans and tax-deductible contributions made to it to leverage major, long-term support from government, bank, foundation, church, and business sources.

Examples of Projects: A $995 loan was made to a single parent with two teenagers to leverage a $47,000 mortgage. The money was provided to pay closing costs. A $500 loan was made for furnace repair to a single parent of two whose house was so cold that the water in her cat's dish froze.

Leviticus 25:23 Alternative Fund, Inc.
Mariandale Center, Box 1200
Ossining, NY 10562
(914) 941-9422

Founded: 1983

Purpose: The Leviticus Fund is a consortium of church-related organizations whose purpose is to make low-interest loans to projects and organizations that benefit the poor and are in need of financing. People affected by projects must be involved in decision making, large numbers of people must benefit, and projects must serve the victims of racism, sexism, or ageism.

Size and Record: Members are tax-exempt, nonprofit organizations that also support the fund technically by providing assistance in the investigation, evaluation, and follow-up of projects. The fund now has thirty-eight members and is capitalized at $630,000.

Investment Opportunities: Tax-deductible contributions may be made to the fund. Nonprofit organizations may become members and support the fund financially. Write to the fund for more information.

Examples of Projects: A loan of $15,000 will enable the East Patchogue Alliance in Bellport, New York, to purchase a house from the town of Brookhaven in order to rehabilitate and rent it to a low-income family. A loan of $50,000 will enable New Community Corporation in Newark, New Jersey to construct one unit of its affordable-housing project—one of three such projects, each to include fifty-four units. New Community Corporation has done extensive community revitalization work in inner-city Newark since 1973. A loan of $25,000 will be used for start-up costs for a minority-operated business in Philadelphia.

OHIO

Cornerstone Loan Fund
PO Box 8974
Cincinnati, OH 45208
(513) 871-3899

Founded: 1986

Purpose: Cornerstone Loan Fund (CLF) was established to provide low-interest loans to nonprofit low-income housing groups in Cincinnati.

Size and Record: As of January 1987, CLF had received about $33,000 from twenty-nine initial lenders. They have made two loans.

Investment Opportunities: Individuals and organizations may loan $100 or more to the fund at interest rates of their choice from 0 to 7 percent and for terms of their choice from five to ten years. Donations are also possible.

Examples of Projects: Owning the Realty, Inc., received CLF's first loan, of $14,900, for the acquisition of a building that will provide four units of low-cost housing for the poor. A second loan, for $4,700, went to Camp Washington Community Board, Inc., to facilitate the purchase of a two-family house in Camp Washington.

OREGON

Association for Regional Agriculture Building the Local Economy (ARABLE)
PO Box 5230
Eugene, OR 97405
(503) 485-7630

Founded: 1984

Purpose: ARABLE was established to create a rural-urban partnership in agricultural development, to provide access to capital for intensive small-scale farming operations (especially organic farming), and to provide technical assistance, enabling those with the greatest experience in one area to share it with others. ARABLE also is concerned with new market development, consumer education, technical assistance of various kinds for producers, and supporting policies favorable to agricultural development in local and state governments. To my knowledge, ARABLE is the only program of its kind.

Size and Record: ARABLE is capitalized at $150,000. It has made fifteen loans totalling nearly $100,000 since its first one in 1985 with no defaults. ARABLE serves Lane, Linn, and Benton counties in Oregon.

Investment Opportunities: Individuals and organizations may lend money ($25 minimum) to ARABLE; up to 6 percent interest is paid quarterly. General membership is open to anyone; however, no more than 25 percent of ARABLE's total assets may be from outside its geographic area.

PENNSYLVANIA

Delaware Valley Community Reinvestment Fund
924 Cherry Street, 2nd Floor
Philadelphia, PA 19107
(215) 925-1130

Founded: 1984

Purpose: The Delaware Valley Community Reinvestment Fund (DVCRF) was established to make development capital accessible and affordable to low- and moderate-income communities in the Greater Philadelphia area. The fund also provides technical assistance to community organizations involved in housing and economic development. Specifically, the fund finances and assists organizations that use strategies of social action, advocacy, and community development to address such issues as affordable housing, worker and consumer ownership, energy conservation, affirmative action, expanding the job base, and quality health care and education services. Groups must address these issues in a systematic way.

Size and Record: Information not available.

Investment Opportunities: The fund accepts loans from individuals and institutions, usually at interest rates of 0 to 4 percent and for terms of three to five years. Interest is paid annually or semiannually; principal payment is at maturity. Operating funds for DVCRF are provided through tax-deductible grants and contributions. Investors may place special provisions on their loans designating the geographical area, type of project, or even a specific recipient.

Examples of Projects: A $10,000 loan at 5 percent to Centro Guayacan of West Chester, Pennsylvania, a community-based Hispanic community development corporation. This organization offers job, language, and literacy training for unemployed and low-income men and women. The loan bridged existing Chester County contracts and allowed for the financial stabilization of vital programs; it was repaid in full. A loan of $30,000 for working capital at 7 percent to Jubilee Crafts to allow them to purchase inventory from Third World cooperatives was repaid in November 1986. A $25,000 loan at 7 percent to Concerned Citizens of North Camden for the rehabilitation of the third, fourth, and fifth houses in their land trust.

Fund for an OPEN Society
311 S. Juniper Street, Suite 400
Philadelphia, PA 19107
(215) 735-6915

Founded: 1975

Purpose: To provide affordable mortgages to people in changing, racially mixed neighborhoods—single-family or multi-family—that promote and maintain integration.

Size and Record: OPEN has participated in $2.9 million in mortgage loans, $2.5 million with OPEN funds and the additional $400,000 leveraged from other sources. OPEN's mortgage loan fund offers both fixed-rate and floating-rate mortgages. OPEN also has a high-risk revolving loan fund, capitalized from gifts, for emergency help to families facing displacement.

Investment Opportunities: Individuals can invest in the mortgage loan fund either through OPEN's notes, which carry a fixed rate of interest (between 6 and 8 percent) for terms of five to twenty years, or through its floating-rate notes, which are sold for ten- or twenty-year terms at interest rates adjusted annually to current Treasury rates. The twenty-year floating-rate notes earn a premium of one-half of one percent.

Examples of Projects: Contact organization.

153

SOUTH DAKOTA

The Lakota Fund
PO Box 340
Kyle, SD 57752
(605) 455-2500

Founded: 1986

Purpose: The Lakota Fund will provide loans and technical assistance to new and existing businesses on the Pine Ridge Indian Reservation. The fund will assist some of the poorest people in the United States—the Oglala Lakota (Sioux) who live in Shannon County, in the heart of the Pine Ridge Reservation. In 1985 the county had an unemployment rate of 85 percent. It has not improved. There are more than 20,000 tribal members on a reservation the size of Connecticut and fewer than sixty businesses owned by Native Americans! The fund will help the development of small business by providing capital, technical assistance, and a "business environment supportive of businesses, consumers, and Lakota culture." It will essentially work with two kinds of enterprises. The first is the microbusiness, similar to those in the Third World. These loans will be very small, from $50 to $100, for traditional entrepreneurial activities like selling pecans and beadworking and other crafts. For example, a wild-turnip gatherer might be loaned money for gas so that she could gather turnips, braid them (the traditional way of storing them, like garlic braids), sell the braids for enough to repay the loan, and still have money left to put more gas in the truck and do it again. This time, though, there is no loan to pay back, so the gatherer begins to support herself and the family. The second kind of enterprise to receive loans will be such businesses as mechanics and barbershops, which require more skill, more business knowledge, and more money. Both kinds of business development need to go hand in hand to be helpful to Native Americans and supportive of their culture.

Size and Record: Capitalization in progress at time of publication.

Investment Opportunities: Individuals and institutions may lend (preferably $1,000 or more) for three years at rates between 0 and 5 percent. This fund, working with people from the Institute for Community Economics, is now becoming capitalized and needs your support. The fund is a project of First Nations Finances, formed in 1979 to help Native Americans gain control over their resources and development in ways consistent with their traditions, values, and culture.

Examples of Projects: Contact organization.

VERMONT

Burlington Revolving Loan Program
Community and Economic Development Office
City Hall, Room 32
Burlington, VT 05401
(802) 862-6244

Founded: 1983

Purpose: The Community and Economic Development Office and the Burlington Revolving Loan Program (BRLP) were created by the administration of Mayor Bernard Sanders to help direct and plan for healthy economic growth in Burlington. The primary objectives of BRLP are to enhance employment opportunities for Burlington residents, revitalize neighborhoods, and stabilize the local tax base by stimulating new private investment in the city's small- and medium-sized business sector.

Size and Record: $400,000 has been invested in BRLP, and fourteen loans have been made; one has been repaid, and all others are on schedule.

Investment Opportunities: Although BRLP's financing has so far been from federal grants, loans from individuals and institutions are being sought. Money is loaned to businesses at 60 percent of prime, and the maximum return to investors will be at 60 percent of prime as well. (Of course, loans below this rate are desirable.) A minimum of $10,000 for at least two years is preferred.

Examples of Projects: Loans have been made to a health food store, a glass blower, a laundry, a worker-owned maternity dress manufacturer (Wild Oats), a videotape duplicator, an ad agency, and a toy store.

Vermont Community Loan Fund
PO Box 827
Montpelier, VT 05602
(802) 223-1448

The Vermont Community Loan Fund (VCLF) was in the development stages at the time of this writing. Work began in 1987 and the fund expects to be operational by spring 1988. The fund will make loans to community-based development projects that increase or preserve the supply of affordable housing or support locally based economic development opportunities for lower-income Vermonters. The fund will also provide technical assistance. Loans of greater than $1,000 and at rates between 0 percent and the current money-market rate are sought. VCLF worked with the Institute for Community Economics and has assembled a committed core of people that have made the fund's existence possible. Write them for more timely information.

WASHINGTON

Cascadia Revolving Fund
4649 Sunnyside North, Suite 348
Seattle, WA 98103
(206) 547-5183
In Tacoma, (206) 588-8254

Founded: 1985

Purpose: Cascadia links socially responsive investors (who make loans to the fund) and small businesses, nonprofit organizations, and cooperatives (who borrow from the fund to improve their operations).

Size and Record: $200,000 in the fund from fifty depositors. All loans are screened by a loan review committee for financial viability. Technical assistance is arranged or required when necessary for success. Borrowers must be located in the Puget Sound region and must meet the following criteria: produce essential, high-quality goods and services; promote ecological sustainability and regional self-reliance; support worker democracy, ownership, and safety; employ or serve low-income and minority persons; and spring from a vision of social and ethical values.

Investment Opportunities: Terms are individually negotiated. Minimum deposit is $500, for at least a six-month term. Twenty-five percent of the fund is held in reserve. A loan-loss reserve is building as well.

Examples of Projects: Loans have been made to Puget Sound SANE, an antinuclear lobbying group, to help with a short-term cash flow problem, and to Seal Press, a small publishing firm collectively owned by four women, for publishing a book that helps children who are experiencing violence in their homes. A loan was recently approved for Abundant Life Seed Foundation, an organization that protects pure, nonhybridized seed strains and makes them available for direct and mail-order purchase.

MEXICO

Worker-owned producer cooperatives are being funded through the work of two dedicated individuals, Estelle and Mario Carota. The Carotas are professional consultants in community development and public participation in development plans. About twenty-five years ago they went to Mexico with their children to work on projects with the poor. More recently, they have begun working to develop cooperatives with young campesino parents. To this end, they established a revolving loan fund that makes interest-free loans to existing co-ops or groups wanting to organize a new one. They are using the Mondragon cooperatives in Spain as a model. The fund committee has decided that any loan is made on the condition that the borrowing co-op must agree to lend back 10 percent of its annual profits to the fund to support the development of other cooperatives. So far, about ten co-ops have been formed, many of which are in production; a catalog has been assembled to market such products as woven garments, blankets, and hand-knitted sweaters. Other cooperatives produce chickens, lumber, and ground corn. You can help by lending any amount, interest-free, to the fund. For more information contact the Carotas at Avenida Juárez no.28, Villa Del Carbon, Estado de Mexico 54300.

INTERNATIONAL

Ecumenical Development Cooperative Society (EDCS)
475 Riverside Drive, Room 1003
New York, NY 10115
(212) 870-2665

Founded: 1974, operational in 1977
Purpose: To provide long-term, low-interest loans to cooperatively owned businesses being started by the poor around the world, particularly in developing nations. The Ecumenical Development Cooperative Society (EDCS) is an international organization headquartered in the Netherlands. Founded by the World Council of Churches, it has primarily church membership

and sees one of its major goals as "challenging" churches in developed and developing nations to make below-market-rate investments in projects that have a "social return along with a yearly dividend."

Size and Record: EDCS is currently capitalized at over $14.5 million. Since 1981, it has lent over $7.5 million to forty projects with only one loan write-off.

Investment Opportunities: Individuals can invest in EDCS subvention certificates. These pay an annual dividend that varies at EDCS's discretion but cannot exceed 6 percent. Dividends in 1981, 1982, and 1984 were 2 percent; no dividends were paid in 1983 or 1985.

Examples of Projects: EDCS is entering its second decade. Since June 1978, forty projects have been approved to receive loans. *Sierra Leone*—A $20,000 loan to organize the production process and provide a crop-marketing network was approved for the Sowopondi Subsistence Farmers Association in 1985. The thirty farm-families comprising the association will repay the loan at 8 percent interest over five years. *Bangladesh*—In 1986, a charitable trust providing medical care and services to the poor received a loan of $250,000 at 9 percent interest. The loan will be used to expand the operation of Gonoshasthaya Pharmaceuticals, Ltd., to include a plant for manufacturing intravenous fluid for local use. *Thailand*—The Foundation of the Promised Land will use a 1986 loan of $57,000 (9 percent interest, ten-year repayment schedule) to purchase land and construct a school for the children of the Udornthani slum. The school is aimed at increasing the income-generating potential of the students through vocational education and small-scale agricultural enterprises.

Habitat for Humanity
Habitat and Church Streets
Americus, GA 31709
(912) 924-6935

Founded: 1976
*Purpose:*To work in partnership with the poor to help them improve destitute living conditions. Habitat is an ecumenical Christian housing ministry that builds or renovates houses using mostly volunteer labor. It sells the houses at no profit and no interest. Mortgage payments, usually made over a period of fifteen to twenty-five years, are put in a revolving Fund for Humanity and are used to build more houses.

Size and Record: Habitat has grown to 171 affiliate projects in the U.S. and Canada and 34 sponsored projects in seventeen other countries including Zaire, Uganda, Nicaragua, and Papua New Guinea. In 1985, it was involved in about $5 million of housing construction. The fund receives over 10 percent of its capitalization from no-interest loans.

Investment Opportunities: Individuals may lend the fund a minimum of $100 at no interest. Habitat also welcomes donations of housing materials and labor, along with financial support. Donations can be directed to specific projects or specific countries.

Examples of Projects: New projects were approved in communities in three new countries—Gitega, Burundi; Lilongwe, Malawi; and Kasulu, Tanzania. Two projects (Juilaca, Peru, and Matagalpa, Nicaragua) were approved in countries where Habitat already works. Additionally, the Kabuyu Island, Zambia, project was enlarged to include more houses in the neighboring villages of Pancasan and Luis Andino of Tomala. The Khammam, India, project was also expanded.

Women's World Banking
104 East 40th Street, Suite 607
New York, NY 10016
(212) 953-2390

Founded: 1979

Purpose: Guarantees loans to women entrepreneurs around the world, particularly in low-income regions and to women who have not had access to financial marketplaces. Women's World Banking (WWB) works with locally established affiliates. It now has affiliates in twenty-eight countries, with twenty-six more in formation; the affiliates review loan applications and select recipients. WWB guarantees up to 50 percent of the loans, the affiliates 25 percent, and a local financial institution must provide 25 percent of the financing.

Size and Record: WWB's capital stands at approximately $5 million. The fund is capitalized through grants, loans, and deposits. It has participated in about twelve hundred loans with no defaults.

Investment Opportunities: Until June 1986, WWB was issuing debentures paying 8 percent. By January 1987, WWB accepted deposits paying 6 percent or donations.

OTHER

Jubilee Partners Paul and Silas Revolving Bail Fund
Box 68
Comer, GA 30629
(404) 783-5131

Founded: 1979

Purpose: To free Central American refugees from Immigration and Naturalization Service (INS) prisons, especially those who were in imminent danger of being killed or tortured in their homelands. Freed refugees are prepared for North American culture and assisted with applications for asylum in Canada or elsewhere. When the refugee leaves the United States, the bail money is returned to be used to free someone else.

Size and Record: The fund is capitalized at about $64,000.

Investment Opportunities: This is a no-interest loan fund. There is no minimum amount of money that can be loaned and investors are repaid as they wish. As little as $1,000 can purchase the freedom of up to three people per year and then be returned intact, with rich interest in human lives. Smaller loans add up to accomplish the same thing. All operating expenses are covered by contributions and volunteer labor.

Examples of Projects: About fifty-five people have been bonded out in the last three years, with fifty resettled in Canada.

6.6 Local Employment Trading System (LETS)

Landsman Community Services, Ltd.
375 Johnston Avenue
Courtenay, BC V9N 2Y2
CANADA

LETS is one of the most innovative methods for tapping community-based capital. Capital is essentially stored labor, and LETS allows members to tap their community's labor without using federal currency. LETS allows its members to create an economy that avoids inflation, unemployment, underemployment, or any of the other factors that affect the health of our economies. In LETS, no actual currency changes hands. Instead, LETS is an economic network of members who trade goods and services with each other and track their transactions either by computer or in writing. LETS is essentially an information system that resembles a credit union. Members receive monthly statements of their transactions and their positive or negative balance, and they exchange information about goods and services offered by the members for a members' price in "green" dollars.

Here is how LETS works. Joe cuts firewood, and Peter is a welder who wants wood but has no money. But Joe does not want any welding. In a barter system or using traditional currency, that is where it stops. However, if Joe and Peter are members of LETS, when Joe delivers the wood, Peter picks up the phone, dials the LETS office, and says into the machine there, "This is Peter, No. 48, please acknowledge Joe, No. 83, $75 for firewood." Joe's account balance increases by $75 (since he provided the service) and Peter's decreases by $75 (since he used the service). In turn, Joe employs a carpenter, the carpenter gets a haircut from a barber, has some clothes made, and buys food from a farmer. The farmer now has a way to pay for a welder, so Peter gets to work again. And so it goes. The unit of exchange, the green dollar, remains where it is generated, providing a continually available source of liquidity. The ultimate resource of the community, the productive time of its members, is never limited by lack of money.

In traditional economic systems, individuals are hindered by their lack of cash. If there are few jobs in a community and little opportunity to earn money, poverty and deprivation result. In a LETS system, as long as people are able and willing to work, opportunities abound. Skills that may not be traditionally valued by employers can be used by members in exchange for other services and goods. It is amazing what skills we all have that our economy will not or cannot pay us for in cash. These skills have value, whether it is "officially" recognized or not, and LETS helps communities capture this value. Since a healthy economy is one with few leaks, and since green dollars can only be spent among members, LETS is an invaluable tool for creating a healthier community. LETS also gives members real control over their lives and their economies. Michael Linton, the founder of LETS, writes: "Next time you spend a dollar bill, put your initials on it and see when you next see it. Even if you live in a small community, it is unlikely that you will ever see it again, and inevitable that it will soon be out of town and gone forever. Try it and see. Green money stays in circulation in your own community until you earn it back. In a LETSystem, it is absolutely true that you can spend yourself into employment."

For businesses that trade within LETS, the procedure is similar. All or any part of the cost of goods or services can be in green dollars, with the balance paid in federal dollars. It is up to the merchant and the customer to come up with an equitable arrangement. This brings up two valuable assets of LETS: LETS encourages the merchant and customer to negotiate a fair price; and the amount of federal money participants in a LETSystem need is an indicator of imports into the community. A local craftsperson or farmer may be able to take all or most of his or her money in green dollars, whereas the person who owns a gas station may not be able to take any green dollars at all. LETS is a valuable tool for making community inventories to assess what we have, what we need, and how we can begin to generate more ourselves.

One of the most frequently asked questions about the practical operation of a successful LETSystem is "What about a person who spends heavily in the system and then is unable or unwilling to repay?" Since this situation occurs all the time in the traditional economy, it is natural to assume that it would happen within LETS as well. In an article in the summer 1987 issue of the *Whole Earth Review*, Michael Linton and Thomas Greco, Jr., write: "It generally seems to have escaped notice that money today is essentially a mere promise that value will be given. We are willing to trade in such promises when they derive from governments, one of the least reliable of institutions, but it seems that people are unwilling to go very far in trusting each other as individuals. At the root of the matter lie two fundamental causes—(1) the isolation of the individual from an integral local community; and (2) the failure to take personal responsibility and to assume risk." A debt in a LETSystem is considered a commitment to the community of members. It is not owed to any particular member. Michael states:

> The simple willingness to undertake a commitment to provide fair value to another member of the community at some later date ensures that anyone who acts in good faith can spend as they need. Of course, a person who consistently fails to redeem their promises will thereby lose this opportunity, but at least the situation is of their own making. Most people who have no money are poor through no fault of their own. People suffer because they are so dependent on things beyond their control, like the export market, the bank rate, general consumer demand, commodity speculation, etc. Every transaction in a LETSystem is a matter of mutual consent. Who needs a green dollar? Nobody needs a green dollar, so they earn them because they wish

to. It is pleasant to live in a community where the process of commerce is the mutual recognition of gifts, of service, of value.

LETS is a self-contained system—all accounts start at zero, members can use green dollars only with other members, and the system is always exactly balanced between those in credit and those in debit. The money cannot leave the system. This eliminates the fear of scarcity so prevalent in our current economy and serves as a basis for trust between community members.

An extremely important benefit of LETS is the real sense of community that develops among members. People begin to know each other and to value each other for their skills, talents, and gifts. As community members begin to value each other, they begin to value themselves more, too. They begin to see that, although they may not have what are traditionally considered marketable skills, they do have valuable skills that are essential and important to their community. Community members begin to see each other as inherently valuable, rather than as commodities to be bought and sold. Members of the Comox Valley (British Columbia) LETSystem write:

> I feel that I am valued in the community for the work that I provide. I like the exposure of my small children to this alternate money system. I have met many new people through the LETSystem and feel that our sense of community in the Comox Valley has greatly increased. I also have found that people have skills that they haven't used or thought about in years, and it is all being drawn out and interest rekindled. People have started to value themselves differently and come alive. (Joy Dryburgh)

> The quality and variety of work LETS members offer to do is inspirational. I've bought mittens, edible mushrooms, lamp shades made to order, firewood, had the windows washed, children cared for, haircuts, been on field trips, taken t'ai chi lessons. To hold up my end of the account, I hosted a LETS garage sale, paid $25/month federal towards office rent, cared for children and made frozen casseroles to order. My husband traded some of his salmon catch. To feel active in a creatively interacting community has been a wonderful experience. My image of self-worth has increased—trust and respect of others growing accordingly. The biggest gift of all has been the realization that even though the general economy is in a recession, my family is alive and functioning with a flair. (Margaret Pattinson)

LETS has been growing rapidly since 1985. Michael Linton has developed a game, "LETS Play," and a videotape to introduce new communities to LETS. He offers the system on diskettes and has developed material to help people implement LETS wherever the desire and commitment exist. For more information about LETS, current systems functioning in Canada and the United States, and the products available, send $1 to Michael at LETS' address.

6.7 Energy, Resources, and "Waste"

These three issues are closely related to each other and to a community's economy. Cutting energy consumption saves resources and reduces waste, whether the issue is home heating or industrial production. The Rocky Mountain Institute estimates that a full 10 to 20 percent of a community's money is spent on energy, most of which is imported. Waste and garbage are becoming our nation's number one environmental problem. We generate more garbage than we can possibly responsibly dispose of.

To develop our communities appropriately, we must recognize these realities. Ideal industries create ways of reducing their wastes by using fewer resources to begin with, and by recycling waste products. Since one organization's "waste" may be another's raw material, firms can sell or donate their waste, which is actually a "natural resource" just like water, minerals, and forest products!

To have healthy economies and a healthy Earth, we must begin to solve our waste dilemma *now*, lest we literally suffocate in our garbage.

Resources from Waste and Self-Reliant Investment
—Larry Martin

Waste is a state of mind, not a state of matter.

"Waste to Resources" is not a headline often seen in newspapers. We don't usually treat waste as a valuable resource or product. But doing so is central to an ecologically sustainable economic system and is an important strategy for economic development. Headlines read, "Garbage Disposal Crisis," but what we really face is a crisis of leadership and local power. (The perspective I advocate for dealing with waste is equally useful for dealing with energy. Not coincidentally, efficient energy use means much less waste.)

Our current economic system virtually foists wastefulness upon the public by rewarding with quick profits a linear, open flow of materials out of the earth and into the landfill. The costs of this exploitation, waste and pollution, are externalized as huge accounts, payable against the health of the Earth, which go unbalanced and, so far, mostly uncollected.

One popular analysis of our waste crisis is Hardin's "tragedy of the commons." The tragedy is that by trying to maximize our individual interests, we overtax the capacity of the ecosystems. This analysis implies that humans are inherently opportunistic and irresponsible and that ecological ruin is the manifestation of a flawed social contract.

I believe another perspective is more accurate and more useful. Yes, the tragedy is due to self-interest superceding the common good, and, yes, our sociopolitical conditions are such that irresponsible opportunism is rewarded in the short term. But most people also agree that our view tends to be shortsighted and exploitive; this suggests we *can* learn. We can improve our understanding of how natural systems work and integrate human endeavors into the existing matrix of natural energy and material cycling so that efficiency and diversity are maintained. We can learn that the Earth is not a mere resource to be exploited but a living, functioning organism with which we are participants in a dynamic relationship.

As with any relationship, this view introduces responsibility. We have the responsibility to one another and to all life that our considered actions be mutually beneficial. Creating waste is disrespectful; it implies our disdain for the other living beings that must wallow in our waste.

Our label "waste" is anthropocentric. When we see a lion leave a half-eaten zebra carcass, we might call the lion wasteful. What we don't see, or what we ignore, are that given the scale of the savannah the lion's leavings are inconsequential and easily absorbed by the natural systems there, *and* that the energy value of the carcass is available for other animals and the community of single-celled decomposing organisms. Our wastefulness is on a totally different scale. We now create so much waste—and of such odd sorts—that Earth's natural recycling systems are overwhelmed. Human wastefulness is unnatural, and waste as a material is an abstraction. Our waste either cycles in harmony with natural systems (and thus helps support the web of life) or it wreaks havoc. Separating our discards from our desired commodities does not work. They must be seen as reverse sides of a coin—a cycle and a recycle.

The solution to our waste problem is to examine how natural systems cycle and so prevent waste. The simplest analysis of sustainability dictates that linear, open flows of materials be made cyclic, or into a closed loop.

The cyclical, closed-loop resource strategy is only common (natural) sense. Just as the cycling of resources is a critical part of a natural community's energy and adaptability, a cyclic, closed-loop resource strategy can enhance the internal economy of a community. (Most simply, the community's internal economy is the wealth or value that accrues to residents of a community, or a commonly held community infrastructure, from the community's commerce.) The implementation of the closed-loop strategy is a key element in the application of local self-reliance theory. Though cities are not necessarily more wasteful than small towns and rural areas, the U.S. is predominantly urban, and so I focus the following discussion of self-reliance on cities.

The Institute for Local Self-Reliance

The Institute for Local Self-Reliance (ILSR) is a nonprofit organization that provides tools to communities, cities, states, and industries to optimize the use of local resources, carry out socially and environmentally responsible economic development, and manage materials efficiently—"common-sense economic development." ILSR has built upon the work of many social theorists to fashion a praxis of materials-use efficiency for the "locality" that more fully integrates available resources with the local economy. This praxis empowers local inhabitants and gives primacy to their lives, including the oft-neglected nonhuman community. Central to ILSR's work is recapturing the resource value of waste.

ILSR began in an inner-city ghetto about fifteen years ago, and offers a premise of self-reliant cities and production built on the values of social and ecological responsibility. Whether working initially with a mayor, city council, or neighborhood group, one of ILSR's key strategies has been to build local coalitions and raise awareness that local self-reliance requires a new kind of cooperation, a new kind of economics, and an understanding of how to direct change. To do things like manage waste effectively, individuals and the community must work together to craft policy. Whether trying to elect politicians responsible to proper Earth-resources stewardship or taking personal responsibility for consumption patterns compatible with natural systems, individuals and communities are the nursery beds for the emerging appropriate technologies and strategies for materials use.

Local Self-Reliance Theory

Self-reliance in socioeconomic systems has its analogue in natural systems. As a general rule of natural process, energy (and subsequent action) are captured or expended as close to the point of origin as possible. The diversity of ecosystems is a reflection of the diversity of local conditions and ways of responding to them. Our built systems often impose homogeneity upon highly diverse natural systems. This results in dislocations of materials and disruption of system dynamics, leaving us with what we call waste and pollution.

Local self-reliance does not mean isolation, either in natural or built systems. It means creating an organizational system that enhances the internal economy and cohesiveness of a place, reduces entropy, and provides the base for import/export relationships with other communities. It is an integrative process that links the consumer sector of the local economy with the producer sector and through the relationship strengthens both.

Import Substitution, Invention, and Efficiency: The Keys to Local Self-Reliance

One way to enhance the self-reliance of a community is to identify the imports and, where possible, substitute local products. Import substitution can dramatically improve the "balance of payments," but its real value lies in creating momentum. As communities organize to find substitutes for imports, they begin to think consciously about self-reliance—and this releases a certain inventiveness and drive for efficiency. Inventiveness and efficiency help a community reduce imports still more, but they also allow the community to develop exports—and in our information-laced society, ingenuity itself is exportable.

With the help of David Morris, Director of ILSR's Energy and Economic Development Program, the city of Saint Paul, Minnesota, developed a "Homegrown Economy." While much of the plan focused on economics, technology, and systems analysis, a critical part of the plan was to promote an awareness among the people that they are the local economy. The key to the home-grown economy is to provide inspiration and opportunity for people to use their own ingenuity to develop ways of doing things that strengthen the community while generating and distributing wealth locally. Saint Paul initiated programs to promote inventions among high school kids and city employees.

Mixing applied efficiency and invention can create both material wealth and emotional well-being. The two are essential for designing built systems that are in harmony with, and in fact enhance, the local ecosystem. But even inventiveness and applied efficiency will fail us if we do not begin with humble but keen observation of the local ecosystem in which we are trying to fit. Built systems that are fully integrated into local ecosystems and natural cycles are sustainable systems.

Case Studies of Waste Reduction and Recycling

Consider the opportunity vested in the office paper discarded daily by the city of Washington. It is equivalent to a good-sized stand of timber. San Francisco discards more aluminum annually than is produced by a small bauxite mine. All communities with sewage treatment plants dispose of enough plant nutrients to significantly contribute to the pollution of our waterways and estuaries. Instead they could be manufacturing plant nutrients and compost.

Recycling or reusing easily discarded resources provides a double savings for the community. The recycled or reused material can either be used locally or exported while at the same time reducing the amount of waste to be disposed of (at increasing prices). This avoided cost is a big piece of change. In New York, some towns are paying more for their waste disposal than for their fire or police protection. Instead, these costs can be converted to investments in environmentally sustaining economic development projects. The dividend is not only a dollar in return on investment, but an improved environment and jobs. Studies show that recycling enterprises create one job for approximately every 250 tons of material recycled. A city of 110,000 generates about that much waste daily. Recycle half of it and nearly two hundred jobs will be created. Use the materials to make new products and more jobs will be created.

A mixture of private and public initiatives to recycle and to recover the resource value of waste has been implemented in communities throughout the United States. Here are some examples. As an accolade to the distinctive spirit of the "recycler," the first example looks at the career of Jay Eaton.

Jay Eaton—A Recycling Entrepreneur

Jay Eaton operates the Portage Recycling Center in Portage, Michigan. He has sifted through the discards of Portage for twenty-seven years, recycling newspaper, glass, cans, engine parts, motors, flowerpots, metals, cameras, books, wood, appliances, furniture, toys, tires, tools, and much more. Eaton shows how large a difference one person can make.

Eaton has set up barter systems in which he gives old lawnmowers to a senior citizen who fixes them for resale, while broken appliances go to another fix-it shop. He reuses some lumber and gives other pieces to an elderly gentleman who pulls the nails and uses it for firewood. In most of his exchanges, Eaton provides local substitutes for imports and creates "employment opportunities" for people in Portage. By recycling cans and bottles, he is also creating an export from the city. Eaton's efforts were directly responsible for adding seven years to the life of the Portage landfill and for adding a recycling center to the Portage dump so that the dump now salvages 20 percent of the discards brought to it.

Eaton supports his family and several enterprises that have grown up to use the resources he recovers. Asked about his work, he just shakes his head and says, "I thought it was really dumb to throw all that stuff away."

Eaton's perspective contrasts with the view sold to us by the purveyors of our economy who encourage us to think of our resources as disposable. We are constantly encouraged to buy the new and throw away the old. Indeed, we are told that the choice between products is the very foundation of freedom. Economic planners like disposable products too, because the more disposal, the more consumption. It all leads to our gross national (waste) product. A significant number of the products we use are disposable or unfixable—and we hardly even notice the tons of paper, plastics, glass, and metals disposed of each day in our towns! As the cost of waste disposal rises, and as trash periodically backs up onto streets or barges, we are gradually waking up to the consequences of our chronic waste habit.

Recycling Saves Town's Money

Recycling centers do not attract the traffic that convenience stores do, but Palo Alto, California's, experience suggests that this may only be a matter of public awareness and education. Palo Alto has achieved a comparatively high participation rate in its recycling efforts, begun in 1980. The city began its recycling program with a $150,000 grant from the state, but the program has since become more economical than traditional trash disposal. By fall 1985 an estimated 65 percent of the city's residents were recycling at least twice a month. Half the recyclables are collected at curbside and then prepared for sale at a central facility, while the other half is brought into drop-off centers. An estimated $7,000 was saved through avoided management costs. The entire program cost $302,000 in the 1984 fiscal year. Profits from the sale of materials netted $270,000, for an approximate program cost of $25,000. The cost per recycled ton was only $4.06, compared to $60 per ton for waste picked up for disposal. The city has since become more sophisticated in its cost accounting for the recycling program and has recognized substantially higher savings in avoided costs. In fiscal year 1985–86, indirect benefits included the savings of twenty days' landfill capacity, $87,000 in avoided disposal costs, and $70,000 in avoided collection costs.

Peterborough, New Hampshire, also has a good municipal solid waste (MSW) recycling record. The citizens of Peterborough pulled together a recycling program that recovers 43 percent of the waste stream. John Isham at Peterborough's town hall indicated that if the public's attitude toward recycling improved, an even higher percentage of waste could be recycled. The population of Peterborough is 5,103, and the total waste generated annually is 1,100 tons. The city-run recycling drop-off center recycled 473 tons for a revenue of $16,830 in 1985. Total operating and maintenance costs for the program were $29,440; to this add debt service on capital at 10.5 percent interest, for a total cost per diverted ton of $35. Though this net cost is significant, it is lower than the cost for disposal.

New Jersey is testimony to this. In spring 1987, it became the first state to pass comprehensive mandatory recycling legislation. The law requires each county to recycle 15 percent of its trash the first year and 25 percent the second year. State officials are optimistic; in the words of George Klenk, a spokesperson for the state's Department of Environmental Protection, "I think if they [the counties] develop a good education program and indicate to people how this will save money in the municipal budget by reducing disposal costs, they could be pleasantly surprised by how people will cooperate."

Disposal costs for MSW are a significant driving force in New Jersey. Between 1981 and 1987, the cost of disposing of unprocessed waste rose 662 percent. One regional authority requested an annual budget increase of 50 percent to ensure disposal of its 155,000 yearly tons of trash. A spokesperson for the authority estimated that if residents recycle 20 percent of their trash they could cut the $15 million disposal bill by $3 million. This would more than pay for any recycling program.

There is of course an additional savings from recycling: the conservation of good environmental quality. Through an obvious flaw in our economic accounting, we never include the full cost of environmental quality in our cost/benefit equations. Recycling not only reduces the energy used for and pollution resulting from waste disposal, it also reduces the energy used for and pollution resulting from the extraction and processing of raw materials.

The achilles heel of recycling is supposed to be the market for the recycled materials. But one of the greatest opportunities for economic development is in recycled-material processing and utilization. As economic need drives increases in the amount of recycling, the growing supply of recycled materials should spur the development of industries to use them. The challenge for local communities is finding ways to use recycled materials or at least upgrade them to increase their value as exports.

A Self-Reliant Basis for Economic Development

Communities that recover materials from the trash stream and use them as resources for local production will realize the full potential of waste recycling as a tool for economic development. Colonized nations often point out that colonizers extract raw materials cheaply, refine them at home, and then sell them back to the colonized countries for a large profit. U.S. cities are like colonized countries in that they export what little recylced material they do collect. The two leading exports from the port of New York are scrap metal and paper. Other countries are importing these materials, processing them, and then often exporting them back to the U.S. For example, Japan imports scrap paper from us and turns it into boxes for exports.

A new breed of "ecopreneurs" is entering the market with processing technologies and end-use strategies for recycled material which capture the resource value of waste. Recycled paper and metals already feed growing industries. The American Paper Institute reports that twenty-four million tons of waste paper was reprocessed in 1987, with about 5 percent of it exported for processing overseas. Though a terrific figure, this is still only a 27 percent recycling rate. Steel mills using "scrap" recycled metals are, economically, the healthiest mills in the United States. Aluminum recycling is the best established (33 billion cans are recycled yearly) because recycled aluminum is so much cheaper to process than virgin ore. Paper, metal, and glass recycling industries can all be oriented to regional markets. But let us look at the waste stream that has best characterized the throwaway society and see what opportunities exist for the recycling of plastic.

Recycling Plastic

One of the largest fractions of plastic going into landfills is HDPE (milk-jug plastic), and the amount is increasing. Midwest Plastics is confident that they could process and resell forty to fifty million pounds of HDPE annually (the markets they presently manufacture for consume over four hundred million pounds of HDPE yearly). The point is that there is a very large market for well-cleaned HDPE, which could be tapped by communities across the country. Midwest Plastics just happens to have perfected a high-speed method of removing paper from post-consumer discards of HDPE. This allows the cleaned plastic to be ground and processed into a high-grade HDPE pellet for use in manufacturing. While Midwest remains interested in buying HDPE from recycling programs, such programs can also clean and regrind HDPE themselves.

Eaglebrook Plastics is a competing HDPE recycler. They actively solicit local recyclers to recover antifreeze, detergent, oil, and milk containers from the waste stream. On the average, one person consumes three pounds of dairy containers each year. In a community of ten thousand people, fifteen tons of HDPE could be recovered from dairy usage alone, and as much as forty tons could be recovered in all. Eaglebrook looks for communities that can grind the plastic down to three-eighths-inch mesh, package it in standard gaylord boxes, and collect it for thirty-five-thousand-pound truckloads.

St. Jude (the patron saint of lost causes) Polymer, Inc., processes about ten million pounds of polyethylene terephthalate (PET) soda pop bottles a year. They pay five to ten cents per pound for recycled bottles, depending on their degree of preparation. President Steve Babinchak says his product is essentially the same as virgin material.

Recycloplast, Inc., offers a comprehensive turnkey facility for anyone interested in starting a plastics recycling and product manufacturing business. The marketing brochure offers a promising technology: "It produces a re-usable, high-quality new material from all kinds of unsorted and contaminated waste plastic." The Recycloplast process "atomizes" the mixed recycled plastics and entrains them in the bulk plasticizer (which itself can be a recycled, but pure, plastic). The end products depend on the ratio of mixed plastics to purer plasticizer. The output can be simply granulated for sale as a raw plastic, or it can be turned into rough, simple products with thick walls or large volume such as plastic lumber, road-fastening slabs, sewers, and workshop floors. Or the output can be refined to greater density and relatively smooth surfaces for such products as garden furniture, flooring, and the like.

This is a small sample of the dynamic markets and industries that are evolving to close the loop in resource use. Clearly, technology and economics are not limiting factors. But venture capital is still hard to come by, because recycling is stigmatized by the perception that it is something scouts do for fundraising. This points to the highest barrier we face in realizing greater efficiency in our resource use: public perception. We have the better part of a generation to go before U.S. citizens will be socialized to think of recycling as a natural function.

Beyond Recycling to Waste Reduction

Recycling will always be necessary for some things like food scraps. Although much packaging cannot be reused, it can be recycled. But we should ask ourselves if we even need it. Recycling is important in closing the loop, but efficiency dictates we apply invention as close as possible to the beginning of our use strategy. It is time we reassessed the utility of products in light of their complete cost—including their recycling and disposal costs. It is better to design and buy a container that can be used again and again at the store than to discard it, separate it from the other discards, and recycle it into another container.

This perspective also holds true for industry, which is beginning to see waste reduction as the premier cost-effective strategy for waste management. Major corporations claim to have made great progress in waste reduction. "3M's world reputation for innovation is no better demonstrated than in its renowned Pollution Prevention Pays (3P) program." Begun in 1975, 3P is, after ten years, responsible for annually eliminating 100,000 tons of water pollutants, 150,000 tons of sludge and solid waste, and 1.5 billion gallons of waste water. Its advanced technology has strengthened 3M's competitive position in world markets and saved $235 million. Other major polluters such as Dow, Dupont, and American Cyanamid, have realized significant reductions in certain waste streams, reporting the elimination of 50 to 100 percent of their hazardous wastes.

The progress in industrial waste elimination is not uniform; in fact, the net amount of hazardous industrial waste is still increasing yearly. There is much yet to be done by both citizens and corporate managers. Education is the key. Inventiveness and efficiency can be learned and must be taught. In the Midwest, the Institute for Local Self-Reliance is working with citizens, business, government, and education through the Midwestern Waste Minimization Council to provide educational programs and services to industry that encourage and promote waste reduction. ILSR provides background information and technical assistance to promote a hierarchy of waste-reduction strategies. They are, in (somewhat) ascending order of complexity: improved housekeeping, waste-stream segregation, "waste exchange," on- and off-site recycling, waste audits, product reformulation and material substitution, and process modification. Literature describing industrial waste-reduction strategies for individuals and businesses is available from ILSR.

Industrial waste meets residential waste in many sewer systems, resulting in one of the worst but most easily preventable conditions for resource management. When waste streams are arbitrarily mixed, the difficulty of reclaiming the resources from the glop increases exponentially. The tragedy is that industrial wastes, heavy metals in particular, contaminate the rich organic "sludge" recovered from sewage at the treatment plant. Without industrial waste, this sludge is an excellent soil nutrient that can help rebuild the organic content of soils damaged by overuse of agricultural chemicals. In order to recover the resource value of our sewage, industry must recover its metal and organic wastes at the source.

Arcata, a town of fifteen thousand about 280 miles north of San Francisco, designed a marshland which it feeds with sewage. After primary treatment, the sewage is sent to a ninety-four-acre salt-

and fresh-water marsh for secondary and tertiary treatment. The marsh not only cleans the town's sewage better than any tertiary treatment, it also provides for a salmon ranch and a public park teeming with bird life, as well as a potential source of renewable energy. Arcata's integration of its built infrastructure with the local ecological system enhanced the quality of life in the city, the quality of the surrounding environment, and the strength of the city's internal economy. This kind of efficiency is the antithesis of waste and the basis of community economics. It is only partly a matter of more widgets per unit invested; it is much more a matter of more fully integrating our endeavors so that they are in harmony with those of others and with the natural cycle of Earth's systems. The first and hardest step is to commit to this path, curb our ego and quest to conquer, and start.

When a community takes responsibility for local conditions, it can begin to use local resources cooperatively to enhance the quality of life. Getting a community to take collective responsibility is often difficult, but, given the opportunity, most people will act to improve their immediate environment. Once we begin to act, we need to widen our vision beyond our special interests until it includes the whole community and is as integrated as the Earth. Organizing for local self-reliance—examining the relationship between the economy, energy, waste, food production, housing, and the quality of the environment—can provide this vision and opportunity.

Waste is in the public eye and can be an excellent tool to organize for self-reliance. Once there was the "oil crisis," now there's the "garbage crisis." In Chinese, *crisis* is defined as equal parts opportunity and danger. The "garbage crisis" offers us the opportunity for enhanced self-reliance and the danger of deadly pollution.

Already, the same people who championed nuclear power are advocating the disposal of "waste" in incinerators. It is critical that waste management be removed from a disposal context; the issue is resource utilization. Do we use our resources efficiently—or do we waste them?

Larry Martin is a senior associate at the Institute for Local Self-Reliance (ILSR) in Washington, D.C., working in solid and hazardous waste reduction. He is coauthor of Proven Profits from Pollution Prevention *(see Books) and is currently coordinating the Midwestern Waste Minimization Council, a public partnership between citizen groups, business, government, and academia.*

Economics as If the Earth Really Mattered

Institute for Local Self-Reliance, 2425 18th Street, NW, Washington, D.C. 20009.

Sunflower Recycling Cooperative
S.E. Grand at Division Street
PO Box 42466
Portland, OR 97214
(503) 238-1640

Sunflower Recycling (SR) was started in the fall of 1973 as a volunteer recycling effort in northeast Portland. The collection equipment consisted of a donated pushcart that served for all types of recyclables, including organics and rummage. The disastrous crash of the international paper market the next year—the worst in recent memory—provided the impetus for Sunflower to enter the garbage business.

Portland is the largest city in the nation with a free-enterprise garbage system. Sunflower's combined garbage and multimaterial recycling collection service was a first for the city and the nation. By providing garbage service SR guaranteed itself sustained growth and a sure profit center independent of market prices for recyclables. By 1979, SR had grown to nearly five hundred paying garbage/recycling customers. In 1984, SR became the first enterprise to offer free curbside recycling service to everyone in its service area regardless of who collected their garbage. The business currently serves twenty-five hundred households on its recycling routes and about nine hundred households with garbage service. In addition, SR operates a twenty-four-hour recycling drop-off center, a recycling buy-back center, a yard debris collection route, and recyclable collection for about two hundred small businesses, offices, and apartments.

On the recycling routes Sunflower picks up newspapers, glass bottles, cardboard, high-grade office paper, waste oil, and various metals. SR accepts these materials and mixed scrap paper at the drop-off. Newspaper, high-grade office paper, and aluminum cans are bought. The recycling collection averages eighty-five tons per month, the drop-off fifty-five tons, and the buy-back sixty tons, for a total of about two hundred tons. These three services complement each other and provide convenient recycling opportunities to inner southeast Portland. The use of recycled rather than raw materials provides energy savings, causes less pollution, reduces depletion of natural resources, and contributes to longer landfill life. It also saves customers money.

At this time SR does not reuse the materials it collects, but sells them to brokers. SR has no control over the prices it receives, and they vary from year to year.

Compared to the rest of the nation, Portland is in good shape for recycling. Local industries recycle newsprint, cardboard, glass, and steel, and recent state legislation has strengthened secondary markets. The largest user of old newsprint in the West is located nearby, and their large demand virtually guarantees a market for newspapers. Indeed, their purchases account for two-thirds of SR's recycling income. Portland is also an export center for paper and metal.

At first, the garbage disposal industry offered very little competition for recyclables. Today, most garbage haulers in the area offer recycling services. The 1983 Oregon legislature passed the "Recycling Opportunity Act," requiring every city of at least four thousand people to guarantee every household curbside recycling service, and the City of Portland has recently required that each garbage hauler collect recyclables.

The recycling act also requires extensive education and promotion of recycling. SR runs a clean, efficient drop-off with no competition. Since this has meant an increase in business nearby, SR also recently bought a baler, which makes buying back cardboard profitable. The diverse nature of SR's operation provides strength and security. There is a symbiosis between the recycling, garbage, and yard-debris services. People call up for one and also sign up for another. SR's garbage service is consistently profitable and growing quickly. Sunflower's gross monthly income has grown from $6,000 five years ago to over $20,000 today.

SR owns six vehicles: a forklift, two garbage trucks, and three recycling trucks. In addition, they have twenty-three 1- and 2-cubic-yard containers for garbage and six 14- to 38-cubic-yard drop boxes for storing and hauling recyclables. They also have two 6-cubic-yard composters (converted cement mixers), a four-ton digital scale, thirty wooden newspaper drop-off boxes, two recycling shelters, and eight metal bins for recycling drop-off. They purchase older vehicles to upgrade by designing and fabricating special containers adapted to their needs.

SR's biggest problem has been lack of capital, and they have often bought equipment by deferring wages. People at Sunflower earn a much lower wage ($4) than usual ($8). Through the years they have steadily increased the efficiency of their operation in order to handle more material with less labor. They hope to improve wages as they find longer-term financing for their vehicles and as the markets for recyclables reflect more accurately the value of the material collected.

Initially a nonprofit corporation, Sunflower became a cooperative in August 1984. The membership fee is $4,500 and can be paid with either money or labor (individuals pay at least 10 percent of their earnings toward membership). There are now fifteen workers, twelve of whom are members of the co-op. Most of the work is physically demanding, and workers try to balance routes with office work and other less strenuous tasks. SR provides on-the-job training for all facets of the business. As new workers gain experience, they become more autonomous.

SR makes all decisions by consensus at weekly meetings of all workers. When consensus does not work, they vote (only three times in the past six years). About once a year members meet for a weekend of long-term planning and in-depth sharing of information. Since 1984, Sunflower has had an elected management team to coordinate activities and implement the membership's decisions.

There are five voting members with a total of thirty years' experience at Sunflower. People who would not otherwise have the opportunity are managing and operating a growing business (income has tripled in five years) that is challenging the status quo in Portland's garbage industry. The workers are committed to both recycling and a healthy work environment.

Citizens Clearinghouse for Hazardous Wastes, Inc.
PO Box 926
Arlington, VA 22216
(703) 276-7070

Citizens Clearinghouse for Hazardous Wastes, Inc. (CCHW), is a national resource and crisis center that helps local environmental leaders in their fight for solutions to hazardous waste problems. It was founded in 1981 by Lois Marie Gibbs, the housewife who in 1978 started and lead the successful homeowners' fight over Hooker Chemical/Occidental Petroleum's Love Canal hazardous waste dump in Niagara Falls, New York.

CCHW has six full-time staff members and assists over seven hundred local environmental groups across the country with outreach, community organizing, technical assistance, leadership development and networking, roundtable discussions, and publications, such as their two newsletters, *Everyone's Backyard* and *Action Bulletin*.

In addition to its general organizing and informational work, CCHW also conducts such special programs as the Southern Leadership Campaign, which focuses on stopping the use of low-income, minority, rural communities as dumping grounds; Project HOPE, an outreach campaign to the Hispanic community; and the Children and Family Stress Project, which helps local activists and their families reduce the stress suffered as they fight to protect their communities from environmental pollution.

The organization's Scientific and Technical Assistance Program provides several services: technical reviews of engineering reports, analytical data, testing design, and proposed remedial cleanup action; a technical working group consisting of scientific, technical, and legal professionals and a community organizer that evaluates particular hazardous waste problems and then provides local people with information and options for action; a referral registry of experts in toxicology, law, groundwater hydrology, epidemiology, biostatistics, risk assessment, community organizing, and toxic substances management; a library covering all areas of hazardous waste, with toxicity data and profiles on over 350 chemical substances; and a speakers' bureau, available to discuss regulations affecting waste disposal, remedial cleanup alternatives, how to conduct a health survey, disposal options, levels of toxicity, and the dimensions of the environmental and public health risks that communities face.

As part of its cosponsorship of the National Campaign Against Toxic Hazards, CCHW distributes a People's Bill of Rights, which asserts everyone's right to live "free from harm imposed by toxic substances," the right "to clean air, clean water, uncontaminated food, and safe places to live, work, and play," and the right "to require our government to be accountable and industry to be responsible."

This is not mere idealism. CCHW has been very successful in providing local groups with the practical tools they need to win their fights against toxic waste pollution. One of the tools has been the newsletters, which are crisply written and stuffed with immediately useful and often astounding information about the hazardous waste problem in the United States. The newsletters carry unflinching coverage of the complicity of big business, government, and organized crime in illegal hazardous waste dumping and equally ambitious reporting of the "Actions and Victories" of local environmental groups.

In spite of its persistent and justified criticism of corporate and governmental misdeeds surrounding environmental pollution,

CCHW places ultimate responsibility for these problems and their solutions on all of us. The following excerpt from *Everyone's Backyard* says it best:

> Like it or not, America depends on its chemicals. Many we can do without, but so many of the products and goods vital to our quality of life produce harmful wastes as by-products. While there are irresponsible industries that hold public safety in contempt, we cannot place the blame for the chemical waste problem solely on the shoulders of outlaw companies. The consumers who use these products must also accept responsibility for managing hazardous waste. . . .
>
> Our environment is indeed everyone's backyard. . . . It's just like voting; if you don't participate, you usually get the government you deserve. Let's make the environment we deserve one we can live with.

6.8 Building Strong Economies from the Bottom Up

This section describes three pilot projects that are pulling together the strands of community reinvestment.

Rocky Mountain Institute: The Economic Renewal Project

Economic Renewal is a project of the Rocky Mountain Institute (RMI), an organization founded by Amory and Hunter Lovins in 1982. The institute has two overarching themes, resource efficiency and real security. It is located in a beautiful home designed by Amory and Hunter that requires no conventional energy. The house is heated entirely by passive solar and includes one-gallon flush toilets, a passive solar clothes dryer, and extremely water-efficient showers. It was designed, in Hunter's words, "so that the wife of a corporate executive could walk in and say, 'Gee, I'd like to live in a place like this.' " RMI has programs in energy, water, and land—all designed to reach people where they are, not where we might like them to be.

The institute believes that security cannot be provided by the Pentagon from the top down, but must be created from the bottom up. They argue that people feel secure to the extent that their basic needs are met and to the extent that they live in a sustainable economy under a legitimate government. Further, the more secure your neighbors are, the *more* secure you become, because your neighbors are unlikely to want to take what you have. Finally, they believe that this sense of security can be gained much more cheaply and directly than through a large standing army.

The Economic Renewal Project is a practical program designed to address real community needs, build the economy from the bottom up, and thereby create *real* security. The staff of RMI facilitates the process in communities, but their goal is to help each community take charge of its own economic destiny. The program's four main objectives are as follows.

1. *Plugging the Leaks* —A healthy economy is one in which money circulates within the community rather than pouring out. The project helps community members examine how and why money leaves and then begin to explore to what extent they can provide more of their needs themselves. Although commerce from outside our community provides us with a variety of products and services that add substantially to the quality and vitality of our lives, there is no doubt that local communities can provide for more of their necessities. RMI states, "In every town, many goods and services which are purchased out of town are, or could be, produced and/or marketed locally. Such greater self-reliance means more than saving money. Without a strong local economy, there is little basis for strong regional, and ultimately national, commerce. In this sense, a lasting recovery on Wall Street must begin on Main Street."

RMI's research indicates that the amount of money a typical town spends on energy purchased from outside is equivalent to the payroll of 10 percent of its population! For example, in Osage, Iowa, a weatherization program sponsored by the local utility saves $1.6 million each year— $1,000 per household.

2. *Investing in Yourself* —This means supporting a community's existing businesses. Most new jobs are created by small businesses, not large industries. Encouraging existing businesses to run more efficiently and to expand provides a stronger, more sustainable foundation for healthy economies. As RMI says, "A program of supporting a community's existing economic base flows logically from our first objective. Once you identify the items now purchased outside of town which could be produced locally, community businesses can move to fill those market opportunities." In Eugene, Oregon, a program called Oregon Marketplace helps local firms obtain contracts previously awarded to out-of-state firms. In its first year, nearly one hundred new jobs, over $2 million in local

contracts, and more than $1.5 million in capital investments were created.

3. *Encouraging New Enterprise* —As some businesses die and others emerge, communities can encourage new firms that build on local strengths like the existing labor force, infrastructure, and resources. For example, apple growers can process their apples into juice and sauce locally, rather than shipping them elsewhere, and businesses can turn recycled materials into locally useful products. These sorts of choices provide jobs and much needed capital and also make it unnecessary for people to import substitutes. For example, in Delta County, Colorado, a local community development corporation helped start a business that uses waste paper and local coal to make "heat bricks," a heating fuel half the price of firewood. The same CDC helped set up a mill that processes alfalfa and hay into pellets, thereby making it possible for local farmers to make money while putting fallow land back into production.

4. *Recruiting Business* —The idea here is to select particular industries that will build on underutilized resources and meet needs not being met by existing businesses. New enterprises can bring in more capital, technical expertise, the economies of scale, and participation in national and international networks. If these complement local resources, the new company will help revitalize the economy. RMI has developed a Targeted Industries Survey to improve the chances that a recruited company will enhance, not detract from, a healthy economic base.

It is essential that community members ask themselves many questions before inviting new industries to locate in their town. They must sort out future goals for the community and be sure new arrivals advance these goals. Will the new company bring in its own employees? Will it utilize community resources only to export its profits? What of air and water pollution? What are the chances that the industry will pack up and leave after it has taken maximum advantage of community members and resources? RMI advocates a cautious approach to the recruitment of new business and industry, believing that by targeting the most promising and appropriate businesses, communities will be able to make best use of resources and time.

> A community which has plugged its leaks won't be desperate for any economic activity, regardless of whether it fits local conditions. With a vibrant economy, your community will be an attractive place for businesses to locate, without the

need for expensive inducements. Responsible industry also feels more confident moving to a community where values and goals are clearly stated, and where the public and private sectors act together to achieve those goals.

Economic renewal is most effective when all sectors of the community participate. The point of the project is for community residents themselves to determine how they want their community to grow and develop. The Economic Renewal Project helps community residents, who may have no knowledge of how to proceed, to analyze their economy and develop their own solutions to its problems. This process is less expensive than traditional consulting, *and* it gives community members real ownership of the results. RMI's process is both educational and action oriented; it leaves people with a much better idea of the workings of their economy.

The first step is to contact local people from all walks of life. The leadership of each identifiable faction and interest is approached and the purpose and procedure of the project explained. RMI staff helps with these initial contacts if a community so desires. The procedure, as outlined below, then takes between ten and fifteen weeks.

1. A community meeting is held to introduce the project and the work of RMI. Participants list what they love about their community and what they would like to change. RMI staff facilitates this meeting and provides an introductory text and worksheets for exercises. This event usually takes about two hours.

2. The following week a longer session is held, usually an evening followed by a day-long meeting. The goals of this session include developing a common purpose among participants, identifying the economic problems that affect each person attending, and recruiting volunteers to work in the various resource groups. During the meeting, the group also discusses and develops the "Preferred Future." Beginning with a brief community history, the group identifies threats to the viability of the local economy and, in small groups, begins to identify what their community should be in the future. A representative of each group then reports back to the assembly and consensus is used to settle on the values, characteristics, ideas, descriptions, feelings, and goals that comprise the "preferred future" for the community. After this, the participants sign up for work in a resource area—energy, food and agriculture, health, housing, money, waste management, or water. Although this session may go smoothly, old issues and differences often surface. Good facilitators are useful.

3. Committees and resource groups are formed. The committees include a criteria committee (that develops a list of criteria, based on the preferred future and practical business and financial considerations, used to evaluate the programs developed by the resource groups), a business opportunities group, and an organization committee consisting of representatives from each resource group and the business opportunity group. This committee meets with representatives from various community associations, matching programs with appropriate organizations. The various groups and committees meet about three times over a month to develop ideas that will strengthen the economy, as well as ways to implement proposed programs and to present the ideas to the community at large. As always, RMI staff's role is to facilitate the process and provide expertise where necessary.

At the beginning of the fourth month the most promising ideas are proposed to the community, and additional volunteers are recruited to sponsor and implement the programs. Following this meeting, the implementation of agreed-upon projects is begun with the support of RMI, which provides action-plan outlines based on its research and experience.

The Economic Renewal Project has a "revolving door" policy, meaning that participants may leave or enter the process at any point. People are able to commit to what feels comfortable, knowing it is acceptable to leave as well as to become involved later in the process.

Much of the important work is conducted in the resource groups. By working in these small groups, participants develop a real understanding of how the local economy is affected by their chosen resource areas. They read case studies with an eye toward finding examples that might work in their particular town, they design new programs to fit unique community needs, and they consider such factors as costs, leakage, labor, finance, and local businesses. The process is not easy, and can require much resolution of old disputes and bridging of factions in a community, but a pilot project in Carbondale, Colorado, offers hope. By early 1987 the community had seen the following progress:

   –a business support team to provide advice and a resource
    library in an effort to keep existing businesses viable
   –a public/private business incentive program to invest in
    potential new businesses
   –a farmers' market
   –a buy-local campaign

184

–low-cost bank loans for energy efficiency projects
–an up-to-date and widely distributed list of local health
resources
–research on a newspaper recycling project

Associated benefits include:

–A public/private rapid assistance team, formed to respond to
business inquiries, scored its first victory—a new coffee-
processing plant.
–The local chamber of commerce increased its membership
fourfold after hiring its first full-time director.
–Former adversaries now work together on programs of mutual
benefit. For example, although the farmers' market was
organized by newcomers, they integrated it into the annual
harvest celebration, a tradition of the oldtimers.
–The local grocer began to distinctively label and sell locally
grown produce.
–People began moving their savings from large city banks into
the local bank, despite the loss of one-half point of interest.

RMI is quick to point out that any success is due to the
community members' commitment and action. But the project does
provide a flexible outline for community members to fill in
according to local conditions and their own preferences. Moreover,
the outline builds on success; one success generates others. And
the analysis and project development skills the community
develops will continue to safeguard the vitality of the community.

Although still in its infancy, the Economic Renewal Project is
clearly an extremely valuable process for developing healthy, self-
reliant communities that can respond to local, regional, and global
conditions. And RMI is clearly an exemplary consulting group: it
offers a flexible model and technical support, helping the local
community develop *its own* programs.

Burlington, Vermont

Burlington provides a wonderful example of what the combination
of progressive politics and community involvement can do. The
1983 election of socialist Bernie Sanders as mayor catalyzed the
revitalization of the city and the empowerment of many previously
disenfranchised citizens. Sanders ran on a platform of affordable
housing, economic democracy and opportunity, and the promise

of active citizen involvement in city policy making and squeaked into office thanks to the undaunted efforts of his campaign volunteers (called "Sanderistas" by their opposition) who registered hundreds of poor people. In March 1987 he was reelected to a third consecutive term by a substantial majority in a three-candidate race.

Bernie has become quite well known for his outspoken candor. He told me, "Basically, being a third party and having already taken on the entire establishment and having engendered the hatred of everybody who's about to hate us, there's nothing more we have to worry about."

The coalition that supports Sanders includes the elderly, the poor, single mothers, students, and unemployed young people. Despite relatively little money, they have come up with many different programs and ideas and Burlington feels vital and creative, though it is far from perfect.

Despite its low unemployment, the vast majority of jobs in Burlington are in the service sector and pay little more than the minimum wage. With skyrocketing rents (when there are rentals available) and rampant gentrification, housing, especially new housing, is increasingly difficult for the average Burlington resident to afford.

Affordable housing has therefore been one of the major priorities of the Sanders administration. The city was the first in the country to fund a community land trust to remove housing from the speculative market. Sanders told me,

> The land trust is one intelligent approach for taking property out of the speculative market. We can also pressure private developers to build affordable housing along with the other types of housing they build, and we do that. We hustle for federal grants to build subsidized housing. But ultimately the bold step is to say, private developers aren't going to do it. We'll get as much out of them as we can. Then we'll do it ourselves on a nonprofit basis. Right now we're searching for the proper model to handle that.

This search for new ideas is typical of how his administration handles problems. And their ability to face problems head on, no matter how unpopular they may be, is also typical. When I asked Sanders how he was able to attract and keep this staff, he replied,

> There is a tremendous hunger out there in the community on the part of the very bright, energetic men and women

who would like to use their intelligence and their energy in a socially useful way. One of the tragedies of our society is that there are very few opportunities for those people. People have to earn a living, often doing things that aren't particularly socially useful. I think what we have done is to essentially put up a sign saying we want the brightest and most energetic people to help us do things that are socially useful. And once they are on board, we give people, within reason, a great deal of freedom to develop their ideas. We have highly motivated people and they stay. We are willing to look at any idea. We're not afraid. We look at a problem and try to solve the problem. Sometimes we go in a conservative direction, sometimes we go in a very bold direction, but the goal is to solve the problem. Our feeling is if it's a good idea let's do it!

Another example of Burlington's innovative approach to problems is its contract with the Industrial Cooperative Association (ICA) for help in creating an overall plan for the city's economic development, with a focus on worker-ownership. From the ICA partnership came the Local Ownership Development Project, which consists of a report (*Jobs and People: A Strategic Analysis of the Greater Burlington Economy*), educational outreach, and hands-on technical assistance to companies wanting to become worker owned. Burlington has also established a revolving loan program that funds such worker-owned businesses as Wild Oats (see page 192). "Bringing local industry under local control is very important. It's an example for the future and the principle is worth an investment of money. We are one of the few cities in America actively promoting worker ownership. Usually it is a reaction to a crisis. Here in Burlington, we are being pro-active."

Chris Mackin of ICA has said, "There's no question but that, in terms of understanding and commitment, Burlington is on the frontier of the local ownership movement." And Peter Clavelle, director of the city's Community and Economic Development Office, states, "Burlington residents . . . find themselves in a trend toward low skill, service employment. Particular groups, specifically female heads of households and working-class youth, are not sharing in the prosperity of the region. Our challenge is to create quality, stable jobs." Bruce Seifer, city hall's economic development specialist, affirms that "the primary objective is to create a healthier, more stable and diverse economy by restructuring the system toward a more home-grown and -developed approach."[10]

Economics as If the Earth Really Mattered

City hall takes a very active role in traditional development projects as well, encouraging citizens to participate in public hearings and in meetings of neighborhood planning assemblies, much to the chagrin and frustration of developers. Sanders believes that if a developer is going to benefit from locating in Burlington, then Burlington residents—all of them, not just the wealthy or the business community—must also benefit. The administration also works with other organizations, such as the Burlington Peace and Justice Center, the Burlington Central American Solidarity Association, and the sister-city program with Puerto Cabezas, a Miskito Indian town in Nicaragua. Last year, Sanders actually visited Nicaragua, one of the few mayors to have done so. He told me, "Think globally, act locally is something I believe is, to a significant degree, part of what we are trying to do. We take very seriously what is happening in Nicaragua, for example, and we see that as a local issue."

Some of the other programs that have been implemented in the past four years include a day care center, a teen center, a tree-planting program, and a recycling project. Though sometimes criticized for his seeming lack of environmental concern or awareness, Sanders has some perspective.

> There are values we are willing to subsidize even if they aren't cost-effective. Let's face it, if someone could get rich by taking used newspaper, believe me, they'd have done it by now. You wouldn't be able to find an old copy of the *Free Press* anywhere in the city. Clearly, the idea and the vision of recycling—making people conscious of the issue of reusability of things rather than simply producing garbage—is a principle that I think is worth supporting. And perhaps the time will come when these things will be cost-effective in hard economic terms, especially if you raise people's consciousnesses enough to make government do the right thing with regard to the environment.

Sanders, and those who work closely with him, have a vision that extends beyond the city limits. Perhaps this is one of the things that not only attracts but energizes the "Sanderistas" in the face of persistent adversaries like Homeowners Against the Land Trust (HALT) and criticism of Sanders's rhetoric, lack of ecological concern, and occasional antifeminist perspective. Sanders describes the vision this way:

Burlington is not a world unto itself. What we can primarily do is develop and implement ideas. Many of the things we can do are models. It's amazing how many ideas are being picked up nationally. The vision is to create a democratic society, which means the involvement of as many people in the process as possible and using the resources of government to help those people who are at the bottom of the economic ladder. To give people who normally don't have power access to government.

Sanders and his supporters have proven that rhetoric can be followed by real action and real change. It is time more cities took notice.

The Burlington Community Land Trust

Burlington is one of the most recent communities to embrace the land trust model. Burlington is home to Vermont's largest academic, banking, real estate, medical, and other professional communities. With an unemployment rate of 2.9 percent and over $350 million in development proposals moving through the city's approval processes, Burlington's economy is booming. Enrollment in the city's academic institutions brings over 10,000 out-of-town students and their purchasing power to the area each school year. On the surface it would appear that all is well in Vermont's largest city. On closer inspection, however, the impact of such rapid and concentrated growth is taking its toll on long-term, working-class residents of the city.

As development continues, the resulting gentrification, commercial encroachment, and skyrocketing land values, along with increasing pressure from students seeking off-campus housing, have given rise to the most severe affordable-housing crisis in the city's history. The vacancy rate for Burlington rentals is less than 1 percent. Fair-market monthly rents range from $425 for a one-bedroom apartment to $700 for four bedrooms. Rents doubled between 1970 and 1980, and have doubled again in the last seven years. The average cost of a newly constructed home in Burlington is $78,278; that of an existing house is only slightly less.

The vast majority of Burlington wage earners are of low to moderate income, and their incomes are not keeping pace with their housing costs. Home ownership, the benchmark of a stable community, is a foregone dream for Burlington's working class. Of the fifteen hundred new jobs being created in Burlington, nearly all will provide only minimum-wage, service-type employment. Of the new housing units currently being built or proposed, only a fraction are considered affordable by local standards. Most are expensive backyard expansions, or very high priced waterfront condominiums, exactly the type of home that Burlington's long-term residents need the least.

It is not surprising that local housing developers and speculators provide for a market that can afford to buy, but therein lies the problem. In fact, many of them wish dearly that it were economically feasible to provide moderately priced housing units because the demand is so high. But such are the vagaries of a market that promotes a basic necessity (shelter) as a commodity, and then scratches its head upon realizing that hardly anyone can afford it!

This situation is not unique to Burlington, of course, but the city's approach to the problem is unique. Burlington is the first community in the country to create a land trust through the allocation of seed money and technical assistance. This initiative has prompted inquiries from public officials in Florida, New Hampshire, and Massachusetts, among others, who are facing housing and development crises not unlike Burlington's. In promoting the development of the Burlington Community Land Trust (BCLT) as a private, democratically structured, nonprofit tax-exempt corporation, Burlington has demonstrated tremendous faith in the land trust model. The city has also been BCLT's largest investor thus far—allocating $200,000 from a 1983 general fund surplus for start-up acquisitions and operating costs.

Community response to the BCLT has been remarkable. A dedicated corps of volunteers (including church representatives, tenants, homeowners, contractors, bankers, realtors, lawyers, and public and private housing administrators) worked hard to develop an organizational structure to assure the long-term operational integrity of the trust. This early, broad-based support for the BCLT, combined with city financial resources, has led to an extraordinary array of accomplishments in only three years and a dramatic show of confidence from local social investors, banks, and housing developers. BCLT's successes in bringing together the human and financial resources needed to implement its innovative model led to recent awards by the United Nations and the U.S. Department of Housing and Urban Development. (For all the wrong reasons,

I might add—for example, unleashing the private sector to continue its wasteful and profit-driven ways vis-à-vis housing production.)

By 1987, the BCLT held sixteen separate land parcels—eleven single-family homes, five multifamily buildings (with fifteen residential units and two commercial units), and Burlington's Community Health Center. All in all, it has created twenty-seven perpetually affordable units. The city's initial investment of $200,000 has leveraged more than $2 million in low-cost development financing and outright subsidies, including a land donation on which six new homes were built and sold at below-market rates. BCLT has also recently initiated three housing cooperatives, one of which will house elderly and disabled Burlingtonians.

The high cost of financing is every bit the stumbling block to affordable housing that expensive land is. One of BCLT's early goals—and accomplishments—was the creation of a revolving loan fund designed to broaden the organization's mortgage financing capabilities. Personal outreach to the local religious community and to private individuals has resulted in access to over $150,000 in affordable loans for Burlington's lower- and moderate-income residents purchasing land trust homes.

Two of Burlington's religious orders have placed a total of $55,000 with BCLT for four to six years at 4 to 6 percent interest. The balance of loans is from individuals and ranges from $2,000 at 0 percent to $30,000 at 7 percent, for anywhere from two to eight years. BCLT has also been successful in securing commitments of below-market funds for both acquisitions and mortgage financing from virtually every bank in the city.

But much more is needed if Burlington Community Land Trust is to sustain its momentum and provide and maintain decent, safe, and affordable housing for Burlington's low- and moderate-income residents. Current goals are to double the size of the revolving loan fund and to aggressively seek additional public and private support to sustain the program.

The BCLT has determined that its revolving loan fund can best utilize money for a minimum term of two years. Interest rates on each investment or deposit with BCLT are generally determined on a case-by-case basis, and reflect a matching of the needs of the various projects to be financed with the needs of the investor.

Economics as If the Earth Really Mattered

Wild Oats, Inc.
19 Church Street
Burlington, VT 05401
(802) 658-0511
Contact: Andrea Miksic

When Charlene Wallace and Andrea Miksic joined forces in 1983 to purchase Wild Oats (then a custom sewing and alterations business) from its founder, who had decided to let the business fold, they had no idea that in just three years they would be accepting offers from Bloomingdale's and Saks for maternity clothes. The growth of Wild Oats from this simple partnership to a worker-owned corporation with nearly $500,000 in projected sales for 1986–87 is a wonderful example of what can happen when opportunities are recognized and acted upon.

Charlene, who had been employed as a sewer by the original Wild Oats, felt confident that she could run the firm. Andrea had her own home-based sewing business (and also sold at craft shows) but was running out of space and welcomed the opportunity to become a partner and move into Wild Oats. A loan from Vermont Job Start (a state-funded program that makes loans of up to $10,000 to small businesses) enabled them to purchase Wild Oats and set up shop.

The transition from custom sewing and alterations to maternity wear occurred in May 1984 when Andrea, then pregnant, designed some maternity clothes for herself and then received requests for copies from pregnant friends. Andrea's stylish yet simple and comfortable designs appealed to women who were not happy with most maternity fashions available in stores.

The two women decided that a mail-order catalog of maternity clothes might help supplement their business. A small line was developed and the samples sewn. Sewing services were traded for typesetting, photography, and printing costs. Andrea planned to model the fashions, but, as luck would have it, she went into labor before the photos were taken. The catalog was finished later with the help of pregnant friends and customers. The result—a sixteen-page black and white catalog featuring a sixteen-item line of maternity clothes—was finished in November 1984, and by January 1985 the orders started to arrive.

Encouraged by the success of their catalog, they decided to hit the New York City wholesale market. After many referrals, they successfully located a sales representative who agreed to take them on. Told not to expect much at first, they returned home and waited. Within four weeks they had orders for $30,000 of summer merchandise—all due in March and April.

This was a critical point in Wild Oats' history. There was no way Andrea and Charlene could handle all the work themselves; their space was much too small, and they needed machines, sewers, and fabric! Credit was difficult to get. A collateralized loan was obtained from a local bank, the partnership was changed to a corporation, and Wild Oats moved into a much larger space.

Sewers were hired and everyone worked eighty-plus-hour weeks for the next two months to meet the deadlines. They are still amazed (and proud!) that despite all the obstacles and lack of time, they did it.

Another hurdle the business overcame involved production. At first Wild Oats did all its own sewing. However, it has decided to subcontract the sewing to factories within a reasonable distance of Burlington. Factory work is extremely technical and requires attention to all details of the operation (work flow and time/motion efficiency studies on the sewers, for example). Since there was no experienced industry professional at Wild Oats guiding the process, time and money were lost while trying to do it all in-house.

Currently all design, cutting, and sample sewing are done at Wild Oats, and the sewing of orders is subcontracted to one of six companies (four in Vermont, two in New Hampshire). These companies are carefully chosen for their quality of work and promptness of delivery, as well as for their proximity (within an eighty-mile radius) to Burlington so that frequent trips can be made to monitor quality.

Eight women now work at Wild Oats (both full- and part-time)—a "sample" sewer, two cutters, bookkeepers, and a retail salesperson for their small storefront shop. Industry professionals continually express amazement that Wild Oats' cutters are women (one of whom is pregnant at this writing), since it is typically considered a "hard" job. Says Andrea, "It certainly isn't any more difficult than road construction!" Eventually, Wild Oats would like to do its own sewing once more, when it is a well-established, stable company and can finance an expansion effectively.

Wild Oats has carefully examined its market—the twenty-five to thirty-five-year-old mother-to-be with an annual income above $25,000. (She is also likely to be a first-time mother.) Since women are having fewer babies today than in previous years and waiting longer to have them, more money is spent per pregnancy than before. Although there is some competition, Wild Oats' garments "offer a better, contemporary look (not executive office, not K-Mart, not little-girl look, not highest fashion, not too elegant)" at a retail price under $100. Their line of dresses, slacks, jackets, and the like are designed by Andrea and Charlene and are all simple, fashionably cut, and comfortable. Only natural fabrics are used, and Wild Oats is becoming known for its beautiful fabrics and simple lines.

Wild Oats now has sales reps based in New York, Dallas, and San Francisco. Its clothes have been featured in *Maternity Matters* and *Maternity*, the only two trade magazines for maternity fashions. The clothes are sold in several Lady Madonna stores, Motherhood in California, Mother's Work in Stamford, Connecticut, Shirley's in the Midwest, and Burdine's in Florida, in addition to Bloomingdale's, Macy's California, and Saks. Since the clothes do not scream "maternity wear" at you (for example, Andrea and Charlene do not use stretch panels in their slacks, preferring wide stretch waistbands instead) many women who are not pregnant enjoy the loose fit and comfort as well.

Wild Oats worked with Nancy Wilson of the Industrial Cooperative Association (ICA) for over a year developing a plan for worker ownership. It is also expanding. The business is committed to its workers (currently all women), who will borrow from ICA's revolving loan fund to purchase common (voting) shares in the company. Only workers will be allowed to own common stock, and the goal is for Wild Oats to eventually become a totally worker-owned company, buying back any stock purchased by outside investors.

Although the concept of worker ownership was at first foreign to the women hired by Wild Oats, after several workshops conducted by ICA and much discussion, the idea really took hold. Andrea and Charlene have noticed workers coming up with new ideas and beginning to take a new interest in all aspects of the business. Andrea feels the key to effective worker ownership is educating people on the outcome of their decisions at *all* levels of the business.

This is an exciting company, run by women learning through experience, willing to work hard, open to new ideas and their inherent risks, *and* willing to accept the consequences of their decisions. For more information on the company and what your involvement could be, contact Andrea at the above address/phone.

6.9 For More Information on Community Reinvestment and Resources/Waste

The following list of organizations, books, and publications is provided to help you locate additional resources on the topics covered in this chapter. Use the Resource section at the end of the book to get the complete listings for the groups and written materials below.

Organizations

see also the Directory of Revolving Loan Funds in chapter 6
Brooklyn Ecumenical Cooperative
Burlington Community Land Trust
Center for Neighborhood Technology
Center for Popular Economics
Citizens Clearinghouse for Hazardous Wastes
Community Land Trust in the Southern Berkshires
Community Workshop on Economic Development
The Corporation for Enterprise Development
Dwelling House Savings and Loan
E. F. Schumacher Society
Earth Care Paper Company
Economic Renewal Project
Farallones Institute
Fund for Renewable Energy and the Environment
Gesundheit Institute
ICCR Clearinghouse of Alternative Investments
Industrial Cooperative Association
Institute for Community Economics
Institute for Food and Development Policy
Institute for Gaean Economics
Institute for Local Self-Reliance
Intermediate Technology Development Group of North America
Jobs for People
Local Employment Trading System (LETS)
National Association of Community Development Loan Funds
National Center for Employee Ownership
National Congress for Community Economic Development
National Cooperative Business Association
National Economic Development and Law Center
National Federation of Community Development Credit Unions
The Natural Choice

New Alchemy Institute
New Hampshire College
Of the People
Philadelphia Association for Cooperative Enterprise
Regeneration Project
Resource Recovery Systems
Rural Economics Alternatives Project
School of Living
Self-Help Association for a Regional Economy (SHARE)
Self-Help Credit Union
South Atlanta Land Trust
Southern Cooperative Development Fund
Sunflower Recycling Cooperative
Trusteeship Institute
Turtle Island Earth Stewards
Wild Oats
Women's Institute for Housing and Economic Development
Women's Technical Assistance Project
Worker Owned Network

Books

Center for Popular Economics, *Economic Report of the People*
Church Investments in Minority-Owned Banks and S&Ls
Dennis Clark and Merry Guben, *Future Bread*
The Community Land Trust Handbook
An Environmental Review of Incineration Technologies
Garbage Disposal Economics: A Statistical Snapshot
Peter Jan Honigsberg, Bernard Karmoroff, and Jim Beatty, *We Own It: Starting and Managing Co-ops, Collectives, and Employee Owned Ventures*
Robert Jackall and Henry M. Levin, *Worker-Cooperatives in America*
Jane Jacobs, *Cities and the Wealth of Nations*
Michael Kilcullen, *Directory of Alternative Investments*
Frank Lindenfield and Joyce Rothschild-Whitt, *Workplace Democracy and Social Change*
David Morris, *The New City-States*
Michael Phillips, *Transaction Based Economics*
Shann Turnbull, *Democratising the Wealth of Nations*
Andrew Von Sonn, *The Money Rebellion*

Publications

CATALYST: Investing in Social Change
Changing Work
Community Jobs
Compost Patch
Dollars and Sense
The Human Economy Newsletter
Network News
Workplace Democracy
see also the publications of the following organizations:
Center for Neighborhood Technology, Citizens Clearinghouse for Hazardous Wastes, Co-op America, Fund for Renewable Energy and the Environment, Institute for Community Economics, Institute for Food and Development Policy, National Center for Employee Ownership, National Congress for Community Economic Development, New Alchemy Institute, Regeneration Project, School of Living

Notes

1. Chuck Matthei, "Land Reform Begins at Home," *Building Economic Alternatives*, Winter 1986.
2. Ibid.
3. Robert Swann, "The Community Land Trust: An Alternative," *Whole Earth Papers*, no. 17.
4. Ibid.
5. *Catalyst*, vol. 1, no. 1.
6. Institute for Community Economics, *The Community Landtrust Handbook*.
7. *Cooperative Enterprise*, vol. 1, no. 1, Winter 1987.
8. Quotations are taken from *The Other Side*, July/August 1987.
9. *Community Loans*, March 1987.
10. The quotes in this paragraph are from *Building Economic Alternatives*, Winter 1987.

CHAPTER SEVEN

The Economics of Culture and Place

The projects in chapter 6 all concern creating healthy, self-reliant, *local* economies. These projects are not only exciting because they offer the possibility for newly vibrant communities, but also because they fit into the unique culture of their location. It is essential for any economic activity to be in the context of its place. The projects in this section have that as their goal.

Our dominant economy ignores local culture and place. This is most easily seen in our attitude toward Third World development. Typically, economic development aims to eliminate poverty and "raise the standard of living" of people in impoverished countries. But the standards and means used are Western; seldom do they fit the local culture and ecology *at all*. Instead of growing from the locality, such development is imposed. Instead of working *with* the people, development "officers" dictate to them.

Indeed, the very intent of such development agencies as the United States Agency for International Development (USAID), the World Bank, and the International Monetary Fund (IMF) are questionable. Most projects they sponsor are focused on increasing *export* production—even at the expense of providing food and other necessities at home. The rationale is that Third World countries need exports to pay off their massive debts. But the debts are the direct result of colonialization, failed (often large-scale) environmentally disastrous development efforts, and militarization—often magnified by corruption. Brazilian priest Father José Almire summarizes: "An international financial system has been created that robs the poor to pay the rich. It takes money from the poor to feed and comfort the rich—and to nourish an arms race that may bring a nuclear holocaust that will be the end of all humanity."[1]

As an example of the tragic folly of ignoring local conditions, let us look at one of the World Bank's projects, the Polonoroeste Project in the Brazilian Amazon. The World Bank and the Inter-American Development Bank (IDB) have been supporting the Brazilian government's attempt to relocate peasant farmers into the rain forest. The axis of the project is a two-lane paved road that extends deep into the rain forest and provides access to the area for thousands of landless people.

The problems with the scheme are manifold—and disastrous. The lush rain forest is an extremely fragile environment with soil that, once cleared, is too poor to support farming for more than a few years. Once the soil gives out, the farmers must move on, back to the cities or deeper into the rain forest—in either case to hopeless, backbreaking labor.

The land is then often bought by cattle ranchers (sometimes the same families who made the peasants landless in the first place), whose cattle proceed to wreck the land beyond repair. (Jack in the Box, Roy Rogers', and Bob's Big Boy all import beef produced on rain-forest land. A recent nationwide boycott of Burger King to force that company to abandon such practices was successful.) Once cleared, the rain forest takes hundreds of years to regenerate itself; once grazed, the forest may *never* recover.

The loss is indescribable. Rain forests are home to nearly half the species of life on the Earth. (More species of fish live in the Amazon River than in the entire Atlantic Ocean!) Such diversity is the pool evolution draws from. In addition, rain forests absorb much of the world's carbon dioxide and create much of its oxygen—they are in a sense the lungs of the Earth. Some scientists even predict that if we release the carbon dioxide stored by the forests (by destroying them), the atmosphere might trap enough heat to begin melting the polar ice caps.[2] In one way or another, loss of the rain forests would be disastrous for all life on the planet.

In addition, rain forests protect the watershed of the land used by 40 percent of the farmers in the world. When the forests are destroyed, erosion occurs and the resulting silt fills lakes and reservoirs, causing damaging floods. Rain forests are also home to many peoples who have lived there for thousands of years and have developed sustainable ways of living in their tropical forest homes. These peoples and their unique cultures are destroyed when the forest is destroyed—and when outsiders come, bringing their deadly diseases.

The Polonoroeste Project is decimating the rain forest and indigenous peoples, and it is hardly helping the peasants. Indeed, it only seems to help the banks and the companies that own the mineral rights (and lobby against what token protection there is for aboriginal peoples).

In the case of Polonoroeste, the World Bank has at last recognized that it made a mistake, thanks to the growing pressure being applied by environmentalists, anthropologists, and the general public as awareness of the importance of native peoples and of the rain forests increases. But it admits that attempts to monitor development and remove settlers, using a satellite warning system and visiting the area with helicopters, is not working very well. And, while the World Bank may be attempting damage control, the IDB has decided to continue its role and extend the road another three hundred miles. According to the IDB, "Environmental factors are being taken into account from the start."[3]

The plight of Third World peoples and lands is shared by Native Americans on their reservations here in the United States. Poverty and lack of opportunity are combined with extreme prejudice to contribute to unemployment rates far exceeding national norms (up to 85 percent in Shannon County in the Pine Ridge Reservation in South Dakota, for example). Native Americans have been repeatedly forced off their lands as the government and corporations extracted oil, coal, and other minerals. Mineral leases have been the cause of disputes and have even been used by the government and corporations to pit Indian Nation against Indian Nation. Mineral leases are the real reason behind the tragic situation at Big Mountain. "There is no dispute between the tribes," according to Big Mountain Navajo elder Pauline Whitesinger. "We're caught in the middle between the energy companies and the U.S. government."[4]

Indians here and peasants abroad are often the victims of major corporate disasters that go virtually unnoticed. For example, in 1979 United Nuclear Corporation's uranium mill in Church Rock, New Mexico spilled ninety-four million gallons of highly contaminated effluent into the Rio Puerco, contaminating surface- and groundwater as far away as Holbrook, Arizona, 115 miles downstream. This, not Three Mile Island, was the largest release of radioactive waste in U.S. history. Flora Naylor, a Navajo who was unaware of the spill, walked in the contaminated water while tending her family's sheep the morning of the accident. She died four months later. Sheep drank the water and lambs were born deformed. "When you touched the nose, it fell off. It left a hole on each side," Flora's family said. Only ten of that year's lambs survived. Before the spill, the family had 155 sheep; all but 60 have died.[5]

More recently, in January 1986 a young Cherokee working at Kerr-McGee's Sequoyah Fuels plant in Oklahoma was killed when a cylinder overfilled with uranium hexafluoride exploded. Thirty-two workers and sixty nearby residents had to be hospitalized. At this plant, milled uranium is processed into uranium hexafluoride, which is then shipped to other plants to be made into fuel and weapons-grade material. There is only one other plant in the U.S. that does this. The waste—uranium, radium, thorium, arsenic, lead, molybdenum, selenium, and other heavy metals—is kept in open ponds that overflow during the rainy season. Sequoyah Fuels also dumps waste into the Illinois River. In addition, Kerr-McGee is spraying an "experimental fertilizer" containing heavy metals and nuclear wastes on up to two thousand acres of land.[6]

The litany of wrongs goes on and on. It is clear that traditional models of development neither work nor are appropriate to local conditions. Indeed, more often than not they increase exploitation of both people and resources. Healthy local economies, ones that take local conditions into account, require local control. And, paradoxically, strong local economies benefit the whole by maintaining diversity and providing bases for trade among equals. To build local economies, we need to respect local communities. It is time we began listening.

To find out what, if any, sort of development might be appropriate, I asked traditional Native Americans at Seventh Generation Fund's economic development conference, "Investing in Our People and Land," what they feel and what projects they see as workable. And I went searching through Third World contacts, especially in Central America, in search of projects working *with* the people—not *"for"* them. Some of these projects are described in more detail below.

José Barreiro has been extremely active in Native American affairs, is editor-in-chief of the *Northeast Indian Quarterly* (see Resources) and is a director of the Indigenous Press Network (IPN) and Associated Indigenous Communications (AICom). He distinguishes between Third World and Fourth World peoples.

> Fourth World identifies peoples from tribal communities across the various hemispheres, people from aboriginal or indigenous cultures, who still have a memory of their culture, language, and religion, and a sense of the history of their relationships to particular places of the Earth. People whose ways of living are primarily in relationship to the natural world that surrounds them.
>
> These people have cultures that are just emerging in the postindustrial consciousness of the world. These people organize their systems of human habitation on the logic of the ecological systems they live in, in order to keep the balance. Their main needs as human beings—shelter, food,

and so on—are met within one or two ecosystems. There is an awareness they are going to be there for a long time, have been there a long time.

These people, whom you call "tribal" or "aboriginal," and who have been called Native Americans in the Western hemisphere, form a common basis of an understanding for humanity that it is also full of diversity. There is more of a recognition in Native culture than in Western cultures of other systems, other peoples, and the other species that surround the human being. Ecosystemic living—the ecological principles of the cultures—these are things that are common across the Native world. One can see unity of principle among Native people. This is what we refer to as the Fourth World. It includes the Inuit of the northern Arctic, the Mayan in the jungle valleys of Central America, the peoples in the jungles of the Amazon: millions of people around the world.

These peoples are beginning to recognize each other and communicate directly with each other, to exchange information and delegations and so forth. Numerous meetings have taken place on an international level, from the late 1960s and early 1970s, that were unique in human history. First steps were taken to break down the barriers between these Indigenous peoples. And some lasting friendships were made, like between the Mayan people and Iroquois people. They are beginning to create common ground and common definitions.

These definitions are based on the concept of the Fourth World—the "other side of the Third World"—which hasn't been totally colonized culturally. The Third World can be defined more as the people who have been colonized so thoroughly culturally that what is recognized now are the economic oppressions on these people who are trying to be more like the Second and First World people. The Fourth World is saying, "We want to be left alone. You are all wrong, come this way."

The Fourth World offers the circle. In the First and Second World you have conflict, antagonism, materialism. In the Fourth World you have the circle. You have the harmonious concept.

The Fourth World is the basis. That's what was here. The First World is missing a true ethic of human inhabitation in the Earth. It has forgotten the first lesson. The Fourth World has a memory yet—a memory most of mankind no longer has. This ethic of human inhabitation cannot be remade. It has already been made. (There is no greater complexity than the complexity of the living Mother Earth.) In the natural world systems of humanity, tribal peoples are the elders of the human family. There is a cosmology that is the very basis of many of the native religions and cultures, as well as a symbology that transfers. The most common of these symbols is the bisected circle—the circle divided in four by the four directions.

When asked, "How can people in the First World help in a culturally appropriate way?" José responded:

It's important to see the way Native peoples greet each other themselves. The immediate recognition is one of respect for the ancient knowledge, respect for the locality of the people who are coming in from the outside and respect for the local people who are living on their ground. There is the recognition of one as a guest and the recognition that one is not going to understand, no matter how much learning one brings with oneself, the culture in a day or a year or even in twenty years. So relax. You need to be guided and you need to bring a sense of understanding about who is important in a community—not by the outward manifestations but by the real manifestations of the culture you're in. You do this by looking at the things Native peoples pay attention to among themselves.

Among the most important elements is respect for specificity. Respect for the situation *as it comes to be seen in a community*. This includes the specifics of language and of place. These are deeply ingrained in tribal cultures. They have their roots in the specific awe and respect given to the nature of the place—of a specific waterfall or riverbed or mountain range—and the powers that this may have to the people and the meanings that it may have to the people. It is one of the first things destroyed in the mind of the cultures of the Native peoples by the West, by Christianity, and by the belief, often held by those trained in First World values, that there is no specific spiritual quality to places. That this quality resides somewhere else. This is at the root of some of the misunderstandings between the cultures. These principles make their way through everything you try to do between a mind that does not see this reality and a mind that works from this reality.

This ability to understand *place*—the energy or spirit of a specific place—is critical, I feel, to creating new relationships and learning how to reinhabit the Earth. What is appropriate in one place may not be in another. And this has as much to do with the spirit of the place as it does with the physical limitations of the land and climate and the culture of the people living there. As José observes, we First Worlders are just *beginning* to emerge, and the people who have the most to teach us (for we are new here) are dying. It is time, past time, to listen and to learn.

At the "Investing in Our People and Land" conference, "making people whole again," empowerment, and appropriate development were the major issues. The purpose of the conference was to develop ways of building economic self-reliance for Native Americans living on their lands. The vast majority of participants were already working on their reservations on projects of various sorts, ranging from agriculture to small-business development to dealing with the intricate relationships and failed communication between Native Americans, their tribal councils, the Bureau of Indian Affairs (BIA), and the federal government. Most participants recognized that the solutions will not come from the U.S. government, the BIA, "experts," non-Indian consultants, or corporate America. These routes have already been tried and have usually failed miserably. Instead, the participants focused on developing systems and models that work with traditional culture and spirituality. "Our values are the foundations of our economies. If we are guided by spirituality, then as individuals we carry that: we walk with a clear mind, in honesty, compassion, and respect. The economic systems we build will reflect this."

Some of the obstacles to dealing with the major issues of "making whole again," empowerment, and appropriate development were identified as:

- materialism and the values exemplified by materialism
- the belief in outside experts
- activists who "tend to influence people without looking inward to their own honesty and spirituality"
- oppression, racism, and control of information and resources by such "external forces" as government laws, policies, and technical people
- internalized oppression ("We have internalized this oppression and become our own worst enemies. . . . We fail to build our own positive vision of the future or to build ways to resolve our own internal conflicts.")

The participants' solutions to these obstacles began with "establishing the wholeness of ourselves" and "extending that wholeness out in our relationship to the Earth," and continued backward and forward to "where we are coming from, who we are, and where we wish to go as a people—distinct from our feelings of being victims of oppression." The whole focus was on reaffirming connections with the land, history, and the community and then using that base to develop critical thinking, draw from local assets, and begin small, appropriate-scale projects. In many ways, the process outlined by the participants is akin to that being developed by the Rocky Mountain Institute. "This process starts with problem solving . . . and includes recognizing and identifying our own skills, knowledge and capacities . . . our local resources of all kinds—and determining how we can help ourselves and each other to meet our basic needs for self-reliant, meaningful, diverse and enriching lives . . . this process is inherently respectful of the earth and all our relatives. . . . "

The best projects we can support with our time and money are those that come from the people themselves. The people who should make the major decisions and seek the needed financial and technical assistance are the people affected by the project. Although money is essential, and often even small amounts are difficult to obtain—especially for the kinds of grassroots projects described in this book—some of the best work happens, not because of money, but because of commitment, patience, and untold hours of hard work of all kinds. These are the guarantees that money will be used wisely.

At the conference, Rose Auger, a Woodland Cree healer from Alberta, Canada, remarked, "I think the Creator sent that man [Jesus] here not to save Christians, but to show us humans our powers. We are all common people, the commonness is the Creator." And she went on to tell this story (as recorded in notes by Antoine Seronde):

> A long time ago, Whites and Indians were put together to see what sort of world they would create. We were all given Original Instructions, but in different ways we all pulled away from these. We began warring with others, and this created an imbalance in the world. Now we've all been thrown together again by the Creator. Black, White, Yellow, and Red people, all of us, so we can change this. We can decide how to work out the imbalances. Each of us has that capacity. Everyone has it in himself to know what's wrong and what's right, but we have to learn these "natural laws." This is a knowledge that comes from wholeness, from being connected with the Creator. So we must begin with wholeness in ourselves before we can translate this to others. When you are whole, you can see clearly.

We are called to "see clearly" and to think clearly. When we ask "What can we do to help?" we need this clarity.

7.1 Fourth World Examples

One World Trading Company/Artisanos Mayas
PO Box 310
Summertown, TN 38483
(615) 964-2334
Contact: Edward Sierra

One World Trading Company is a nonprofit alternative trading organization formed in 1984 as a project of PLENTY USA. Since its inception in 1974, PLENTY has had a strong commitment to save the most endangered of human species—the Native Americans. PLENTY has worked with Lakotas, Crees, Mohawks, and Mayans, always to support native self-sufficiency through community development projects. PLENTY sent volunteers to Guatemala after the massive earthquake in 1976. They were moved by the patience and dignity of the Mayan people and by their perseverence and determination. And they were awed by the grace with which they work their land, produce their weavings, and raise their families, despite poverty and hardship.

In 1980, PLENTY was forced to remove its volunteers from Guatemala because of the increasing violence. "From 1978 to the present, 50,000 to 70,000 people were murdered; 200,000 refugees were created; approximately 35,000 women were widowed; 200,000 children were orphaned; and nearly 440 villages were burned to the ground."[7]

PLENTY established its Refugee Fund in 1983. This fund has channelled over $100,000 to projects serving Mayan refugees. Then, in 1984, One World Trading Company was created to provide marketing, mail order, logistical support, and market feedback to Mayan artisans (see "The Eternal Mayas," below).

A growing line of natural-fabric, long-lasting clothes and gift items is being developed that incorporates the beauty of Mayan woven cloth into useful and practical styles. Thanks to grants from such organizations as Oxfam Mexico, the Seva Foundation, Onaway Trust, and Cultural Survival, they have produced two color catalogs, supported some operating costs, and researched the market.

Sales are growing, especially among such alternative networks of socially conscious consumers as Co-op America. One World

Trading also hopes to sell their products in gift shops, boutiques, and select clothing stores. In 1986, sales increased by 40 percent over 1985, and the organization hopes that growth will continue. Since the goal of One World Trading is to be the important link between the Artisanos Mayas and their market outside of Guatemala, more capital is needed for the growth and development necessary to lead to self-sufficiency.

The Eternal Mayas

(Edited from an article written by a representative of Artisanos Mayas)

Prior to 1524, the land south and east of Mexico, the country of Guatemala, and the eastern parts of Honduras and El Salvador were all lands of the Mayas, part of the great Mayan civilization, the "Eternal Mayas," whom we proudly represent. The history of five hundred years, when calculated from the date of our origin until now, is a short time, but has seen the complete dismemberment of our lands and the erosion of the values that sustain us.

We do not enter into this discourse to analyze the causes and motives that are behind who we are today—this is better left to the conscience of the civilized nations.

The Maya have been divided, and some of our nations (many choose to call them tribes) have been split up into four countries: Mexico, Guatemala, Honduras, and El Salvador. Those of us presenting this proposal are Mayan from Guatemala, a country that is largely agricultural, with coffee, cotton, and sugar among the principal export products. Land for such production is held in the hands of a few non-Indians.

The little land that remains to us is nearly impossible to cultivate, for it is located on mountainsides or is composed of sandy and rocky soil, which all works to diminish our harvest yields of corn and beans, which in turn affects our livelihood and our religious practice. We say that the first man came from corn, which is to say we cannot live without it.

Besides working the earth, we are also weavers, and this has been another of the things that sustain us, both in dress and in commerce. The women have ancient designs and new ones, and in order to help make a living they combine weaving with the agriculture of their husbands to raise their family income.

Economics as If the Earth Really Mattered

The concept of weaving is widespread, and our tribes have all developed their own ways of weaving. In ceremonial garments, for example, ancient cultural features are seen to differ from one place to another. The visitor, when he takes one of the garments, whatever it may be . . . is receiving a unique gift, because it is also a reflection of the Maya culture. . . .

Some garments are made by hand on a backstrap loom by the women, and they signify, not the material worth of the product, but a weaving continuity to what we call the "Mystic Maya," a way of living and a worldview, a penetrating insight into the person who did the weaving, thoughtfulness converted into the weaving itself.

With this in mind, we are trying to supply some of our indigenous products to other countries. . . . Presently, the beneficiaries are eighty families (totaling 480 people) who live in the tribal nations of Kekchi, Quiche, Cakchiquel, Pocomchi, and Tzutujil of Guatemala. They represent a growing network of producers.

In Guatemala various enterprises lend money with interest, but to avail oneself of them one has to meet many prerequisites, among them the need to offer collateral equal to the amount requested. This, for us, is exceedingly difficult, because our few lands, which we would willingly offer to back up our loan, are of insufficient value. It is poor mountainous land with rocks and sand. In some cases, we have neither land nor inventory to serve as collateral. Furthermore, the interest on loans is high, actually 12 percent annually, and we suspect that most of our "profit" would go to interest payments.

Artisanos Mayas began work in 1983. It started with one of us supporting some artisans who left us their handiwork on consignment. By the end of that year ten families were involved; the next year fifteen more joined the circle; in 1985, another twenty-five; and in 1986 an additional thirty; giving us a total of eighty families.

Artisanos Mayas (the core group representing several tribes) lent money to buy materials and supplies to the small producers (in the manner of capitalizing a small cottage industry) and bought their finished weaving. As a result of their cottage industry, two of the families have bought a quarter-acre plot of land from their earnings; another family bought a simple sewing machine; a couple of families have studied stitching and sewing; and five people are learning how to produce clothing. Our workshop is available to them and to another five people who make shirts and vests.

We also offer producers the following services:

—education and training
—moral and economic support for orphaned families
—commercial consulting to small home producers (to enable them to become independent and self-sufficient small businesses)
—market feedback

In our four years, we have become experienced with the national commercial traders, and in the last two years we have initiated a small but important trade with foreign countries.

From the moment we were deprived of our lands, especially the rich ones, we saw the need to plant in poor soil and resigned ourselves to a life locked into poverty. About twenty years ago our weaving began to take on economic value because of an influx of visitors from abroad, which, we felt, gave our villages an opportunity to better their lives and livelihoods. Then the non-Mayan middlemen arose and made themselves the greater beneficiaries of our work.

It was not until 1983 that we initiated a new approach to solving our problems of uprooted families, need for living quarters, and lack of lands. *We found our way by means of a business enterprise that would parcel out our profits among the producers and that would help us get our home production going and offer some training.*

We want to emphasize that it was not until 1983 that we saw things with real clarity. The sociopolitical situation in the country gives us little ground on which to set up a direct connection to the marketplace abroad. Thus, we have set up a mechanism for marketing outside the country and a network of small home-based producers within the country. What is lacking is capital.

Our general objective is to . . . strengthen the wherewithal of eighty families (within two years, two hundred families) enough to allow them to provide shelter, education, land, and medicine for themselves. The business is legally set up (with appropriate commercial and export licenses and certifications) as an export shop based in Guatemala City, which for four years has been marketing indigenous goods internationally.

We wish to assure that each family becomes owner of their particular business, while establishing and assuring a market for their goods that compensates them sufficiently for their time and effort. Through the ongoing production of traditional weavings, we expect to help the young people retain their ancestral customs

209

and the ancient symbology wherein each figure in their work signifies cultural roots to the "Eternal Mayas."

Seventh Generation Fund
PO Box 10
Forestville, CA 95436
(707) 887-1559

The Seventh Generation Fund (SGF), a nonprofit organization providing financial, technical, and management support to projects initiated and controlled by Native Americans, was founded in 1977 upon the Haudenosaunee (Six Nations) principle of considering the impact of decisions on the next seven generations. The fund was created from the vision of Daniel Bomberry, a Cayuga-Salish whose grandfather was a *condoled* Cayuga chief of the Haudenosaunee (Iroquois) Grand Council at the turn of the century. Bomberry was an activist who believed that traditional principles would be the means of survival of Native American people.

SGF supports projects that spring from grassroots Indian communities—projects created by the people themselves based on *their* needs, not on the preconceived ideas of outside "experts." The Fund believes that self-reliant economies are absolutely essential for the survival of traditional Native Americans. These economies will be human scale and will depend on local renewable resources and the skills of members of the community. The fund believes, further, that traditional Native American principles can provide others with a "framework of living with each other and the earth which is harmonious and not destructive."

The fund provides seed grants and helps projects to raise additional money on their own. A wide range of technical assistance is available, including lawyers, researchers, consultants in marketing, media, and the like. All of the field staff have backgrounds in Native American organizing. Networking is vital in connecting projects facing similar circumstances.

The fund has four main goals:

(1) developing self-reliant economies;
(2) supporting indigenous ways of life (indigenous political organizations and community systems) and applying traditional thought to contemporary issues;
(3) supporting efforts to reclaim and live on aboriginal lands, and protecting tribal lands, resources, environments, and sovereignty; and

(4) supporting efforts begun by Native American women to promote the spiritual, cultural, and physical well-being of the native family consistent with Indian values and ethics.

SGF regularly publishes *Native Self-Sufficiency,* an excellent newsletter containing articles on "current news and emerging trends in native rights." The newsletter contains the best in traditional Native American thinking on contemporary topics and provides information on events and projects in the United States, Canada, and Latin America. Subscriptions are $8 per year ($15 for contributing subscribers); the newsletter is published quarterly.

A few SGF projects, demonstrating the diversity of its program, are briefly described below:

Akwesasne Freedom School—A community-controlled school (grades 1–7) founded in 1980 to serve the Akwesasne Mohawk territory, the school was built by students, parents, and teachers, most of whom are Mohawks. Students are taught in the Mohawk language. The school believes that "it is up to us to turn this around, to educate our own children, to prepare them that they will endure, that our Nation will flourish once again." The Freedom School is a victim of General Motors' PCB contamination, and funds are being raised to buy a new twenty-four-acre site.

Kaho'olawe/Pele Defense Project—This project aims to halt the development of a large geothermal power facility within the middle-east rift zone of the Kilauea volcano. Native Hawaiians' daily spiritual life and physical activities are influenced by the goddess Pele, and it is essential that she exist in her pure form and environment. The project will use the legal defense of the native people's right to free exercise of Pele religion.

Native Self-Sufficiency Center—The center was established by several Mohawk families to demonstrate self-reliant ways of living using traditional native ways blended with small-scale appropriate technologies. The center aims to develop alternatives to consumerism by providing examples of inexpensive ways to build homes, produce energy, and grow food. It is their hope that the quality of life and the balance achieved between themselves and the Earth will help awaken Mohawks abandoning traditional ways to their value and relevance in today's world.

Pyramid Lake Project—Local, state, and county agencies, as well as corporations, seek control of water from the Sierra Nevada that feeds Pyramid Lake, the homeland of the Cui-up Dicatta Paiutes. The federal government is being pressured to enact legislation that will undermine the tribe's present water rights. This project, organized by Paiute community members, informed the community of the implications of accepting a settlement offered to the tribe by the U.S. and presented an indigenous analysis of the proposal and alternative positions.

Iroquois Midwives Project—A native women's health program of the Iroquois Confederacy founded in 1976 by young expectant women rediscovering traditional birthing practices and reaffirming their identities within their culture. Goals include expanding the number of trained midwives; empowering midwives to become active leaders in birth and children's health in general; and establishing a facility to train midwives, as well as a birthing facility.

Newe Elders Project—The elders and other Western Shoshone are working to maintain and strengthen traditional ways of living. The principles and values of Shoshone culture are used as the foundation for addressing issues and problems facing their communities. Since the elders are the primary repository of this knowledge, the project seeks to cultivate supportive working relationships between elders and youth. It assists in conducting traditional activities and in reawakening awareness of the viability of an indigenous way of life at the grassroots level. "The project will help ensure the continuation of the Shoshone people at this critical time in their existence."

> And each generation was to raise its chiefs and to look out for the welfare of the seventh generation to come. We were to understand the principles of living together; we were to protect the life that surrounds us; and we were to give what we had to the elders and to the children. (Oren Lyons, in a talk at the Cathedral of St. John the Divine, 24 May 1978.)

First Nations Financial Project
Route 14, Box 74
Falmouth, VA 22405
(703) 371-5615

Rebecca Adamson, president of First Nations, states,

> We cannot educate our children, we cannot preserve their health, we cannot protect their well-being, we cannot promote their mental development if our livelihood is dependent on others. Without the capacity to control the economic future of their reservation, tribes will remain in their current cycle of social disintegration.

First Nations Financial Project (FNFP) was founded in 1979 as a nonprofit organization to help tribes gain control of their resources and develop healthy economies on their reservations consistent with traditional values and culture. The project combines direct on-site work with the tribes and Native American organizations with national policy development and advocacy. It works with the existing skills, resources, and talents on the reservations and helps its clients use them to the fullest.

The project aims to reduce tribal dependence on federal funds and to build business and development capacity into the reservations. "To understand the First Nations Financial Project, you must realize that we are a national strategy for moving reservation development forward. The synergism for such a strategic approach is quite significant," explains Vice President Sherry Salway. The components of the strategy include technical assistance, a research and data bank, a marketing program, the national policy and advocacy arm, and the Tribal Commerce and Enterprise Program. FNFP's technical assistance program provides hands-on work at development sites; the other components provide information, capital, marketing expertise, training, and education and assistance, including legal work on sensitive national policy issues. The project's Oweesta Fund provides planning and development money and technical assistance to tribes in order to establish such ways of increasing capital for tribal businesses as revolving loan funds, cooperative financial institutions, and community development funds.

These components enable FNFP to assist and guide a business or project from its inception to self-sufficiency. And they work *with* their clients during the process. "We don't ask the Tribes to come to D.C. to tell us their problems; rather, we go to where the problems are, roll up our sleeves, and work with the tribes to meet that need or solve that problem," states Chuck Jacobs, field specialist for the project. FNFP also expects tribes or organizations to provide at least one staff person to work with First Nations' field staff to ensure that the knowledge and skills demonstrated are transferred to the tribe. The tribe or organization must agree to share what they have learned with other Native American groups working in similar areas.

First Nations provided the technical assistance necessary for the Upper Skagit people to implement a program allowing them to control their economy. Since they live in a timber-rich area, most of the nation's ventures focus on wood products. FNFP first helped the Upper Skagits obtain a $90,000 BIA loan guarantee to purchase equipment and provide operating capital for a mini-sawmill. This created seven jobs and the potential for more. The project then helped develop a plan for marketing carved cedar products incorporating traditional Pacific Northwest Coast designs; a woodshop was later added. In addition, the Upper Skagits have been assisted in establishing a mail-order smoked-salmon business; of course, the fish are sold packed in the tribe's cedar boxes.

First Nations began working with Ramah Rug Weavers in 1985, before they were formally organized. After the formation of the Ramah Navajo Weavers Association, research was begun into marketing outlets and ways of diversifying their products to include pillows, handbags, and other woven goods. One goal of the project is to increase income from the weavers' work by improving the conduct of the business and eliminating middlemen. An equally important goal is to prove that such traditional skills as rug weaving are commercially viable and can provide work and livelihood that ensures the survival of traditional ways.   FNFP has introduced the weavers to the spinning wheel (more efficient than the hand spindle) but leaves it to the weavers to decide whether it threatens traditional values. They have also begun breeding the old Navajo-Churro sheep back into the flocks to improve the quality of the wool.

The number of women in the association has more than doubled since 1985 and production has increased accordingly. This project has also been assisted by the Seventh Generation Fund, as was First Nations itself.

The Saginaw Chippewa of Michigan have implemented a tribal investment plan to overcome federal dependency and to create viable options for self-sufficiency. The Indian Land Claims Commission awarded them money as compensation for lands improperly taken. The first award ($16 million) was paid out by the BIA as per capita grants to tribal members and "descendents," many of whom had no present-day connection to the reservation. The Saginaw Chippewa now have nothing to show for that settlement. For two years the nation struggled for the right to control and invest a subsequent award of $10 million in a manner that enhances the economic self-reliance of the reservation by generating internal capital.

The tribe voted to reject the BIA's per-capita plan and, instead, use all of the trust fund award for long-term development, despite the 40 percent rate of unemployment on the reservation. They were the first Native American nation in the U.S. to reject the BIA's plan. In order to gain control of their money, it was necessary to legally circumvent BIA's authority over it. First Nations helped with the documentation of economic conditions and other data instrumental in the federal administration's reversal of its previous opposition to tribal control. Outside financial experts worked with tribal leaders in developing a long-term tribal investment plan that deploys 90 percent of the fund's earnings into the tribe's social/ economic program and returns 10 percent to the principal.

First Nations also worked with the Saginaw Chippewa to develop investment criteria (low-risk, socially sensitive, maximum impact for local development). Staff gave workshops for the tribal council on interviewing, evaluating, and selecting a money manager and provided a list of investment advisors within the state. FNFP will work with the tribe to help them set priorities and budget their social and economic programs, which include membership health insurance, assistance for the elderly, business development and investment, tribal education, legal services, juvenile homes, land acquisition, recreation programs, and burial benefits. The project will also assist in developing an organizational capacity to meet the increased demands on the tribal administration.

As a result of its experience with the Saginaw Investment Plan, First Nations is working on formulating policy that grants Native American nations the right to use their trust funds for economic development on reservations. This might circumvent the need for having to push for special legislation—an expensive and time-consuming process. The policy could have great impact on the economic health of reservations, since the BIA currently holds over $1.8 billion in trust funds for about one hundred tribes. With the exception of the Saginaw Chippewa, no tribes derive any direct benefit from the current law demanding that these monies be deposited in commercial banks or securities unconditionally guaranteed by the United States. (No doubt much of this money is invested in T-bills that finance the production of nuclear weapons and components and in other investments equally abhorrent.) With the models that First Nations is developing in business, marketing, and finance, the implications of tribes gaining direct control over their money are incredible!

First Nations also works to unravel land-tenure problems, helping nations gain access to resources on their own lands. They are identifying problems requiring solutions at the federal level, including BIA regulation changes. Since the problems are identified at the grass roots, their definition will emerge from the field, not from Washington. Since 1985, FNFP has also published

Business Alert, a Native American business and economic affairs bulletin.

In March [1987], the Chairman of the Senate Committee on Indian Affairs, Senator Daniel K. Inouye, introduced the American Indian Development Finance Corporation (AIDFC) Act, S.721. This bill seeks to provide for the economic development of Indian tribes by furnishing capital, financial services, and technical assistance to Indian-owned business enterprises. These goals would be accomplished by establishing a federally chartered, mixed ownership Development Finance Institution which would be authorized to provide a broad range of financial intermediary services, including equity capital, direct loans, loan guarantees, and business management assistance. The Corporation proposed in the legislation would be designed to operate on the same level as the private market.[8]

The Lakota Fund
See page 154 for complete information on this revolving loan fund.

Associated Indigenous Communications/Indigenous Press Network (AICom/IPN)
CrowFlying, Inc.
Crow's Hill Farm
RD 1 136D'226 Blackman Hill
Berkshire, NY 13736-9801
(607) 657-8413 or 657-8414 or 255-1923
Contact: José Barreiro

—Arthur Stone

Associated Indigenous Communications (AICom) is a for-profit computer network service for all native people, those interested in matters that concern indigenous peoples, and businesses in general.

AICom's extensive computer services include a confidential electronic mailbox that allows instant communication with other subscribers and computer system designs tailor-made for businesses. It is accessible from most parts of the world via a local telephone call.

Connected with AICom is the Indigenous Press Network (IPN), a nonprofit information service that supplies AICom subscribers with a weekly report of national and international Indian news items. This service is also available as a newsletter.

Beyond its range of information and computer services, what makes AICom/IPN such an important and exciting venture is the people behind it. John Mohawk, a lecturer in American Indian studies at SUNY/Buffalo and former editor of *Akwesasne Notes*, is information director for IPN and president of CrowFlying, Inc., the parent company of AICom.

José Barreiro, former managing editor of *Akwesasne Notes*, is managing director of information for IPN and the key contact person for AICom. Barreiro is also editor-in-chief of the *Northeast Indian Quarterly*, the journal of the Indigenous Communications Resource Center (ICRC) at Cornell University.

Both Mohawk and Barreiro have extensive journalistic and academic backgrounds and have been active for years in Native American issues. In 1985, their quick action and in-depth investigation prevented four hundred K'anjobal Indians from being deported to Guatemala and almost certain death.[9] AICom was able to prove to U.S. authorities that the K'anjobals had been fleeing persecution by the Guatemalan army, and thus allowed the Indians to apply for asylum.

The two other AICom partners are Robert Stiles, a Maryland-based filmmaker and computer expert, and Ronald LaFrance, an educational administrator who is an Extension Associate in the American Indian Program at Cornell University and past director of the Akwesasne Freedom School, Mohawk Nation, at Akwesasne. LaFrance has done extensive consulting work for public schools, colleges, and universities.

Stiles, who is vice president of CrowFlying, Inc., and managing partner of Stiles-Akin Films, has made several documentary films, including *Haudenosaunee: Way of the Longhouse*, which won the Maryland Filmmaker Award at the 1981 Baltimore Film Festival, and *AKWESASNE: Another Point of View*, with John Mohawk.

AICom began in mid 1985 with capitalization of $150,000 from a private investor. Most of this funding has underwritten the purchase of computer equipment and services, minimum salaries, operating costs, and assistance to Indian groups to help them hook up to the network.

So far, seventy-two organizations have subscribed, including newspapers, magazines, radio stations, human rights groups, journalists, university Indian studies programs, cultural centers, legal resource centers, Congressional liaison groups, tribal offices, and community, religious, and environmental groups.

AICom would like to get all 250 Indian tribes in North America on line, as well as many of those in other countries. They are already linked with native groups in North, Central, and South America, as well as in Australia and the Philippines. According to *The Progressive*, this makes AICom the "first Native American 'global' wire service."

7.2 Third World Examples

In addition to projects initiated and controlled by indigenous (Fourth World) peoples, there are other worthwhile efforts committed to serving people in the Third World. The best of these are small, always work at the grass-roots level, and involve person-to-person connections. There are many such efforts under way to help the people of Nicaragua. The Capp Street Foundation and the Aprovecho Institute can provide information on many small-scale initiatives.

As social investors, we must always remember that we are working with people from different cultures and often with people who have been displaced from their ancestral lands and are being forced to learn a new way of life in a new place. We must respect their traditions and skills and integrate them into any work we do to help with income production, food production, and living situations.

As Margaret and Bill Ellis of TRANET (see Resources) wrote in *Resurgence:*

> We need to understand other cultures so that we can understand and reform our own culture. We need to analyze our concepts of health, resource conservation, ownership, family, clan, universe, person, etc., from a non-Euro/ American viewpoint. . . . Anthropologists have generally studied other cultures as guinea pigs, not for self-criticism. There is much in other cultures that fits well with our current attempts to design a better future for ourselves. There are 'new era' concepts already conceived and still practiced by various peoples around the world which we need to understand.

Bill Ellis tells the story of his 1983 visit to an appropriate technology center in Papua New Guinea. The center's work focuses around designing small-scale technologies and cottage industries in remote villages.

But the day I arrived, the native director of the center was back in his jungle village because a number of his relatives had died under somewhat suspicious circumstances. The story which later unfolded is that the relatives had been killed by the local witch doctor at the urging of the village elders. Those disposed of had become successful entrepreneurs, building small businesses and gaining personal wealth. One was sending shredded coconut to Port Moresby, one was exporting caned furniture, another solar-dried tropical fruits, and another was selling hemp rope. But the village elders saw only that A.T. was creating individualism. The "successful" individuals were no longer contributing to the common good. This Papua New Guinea society was based on community and cooperation. The newly introduced economic system was based on individualism and competition.

Some of the most well-intentioned projects and programs can thus actually destroy ways of life based on concepts like respect, harmony and balance, and relationship that we are at last beginning to realize are vital to the re-creation of our society.

Earl Martin, who works with the East Asian Mennonite Central Committee and has spent over ten years doing volunteer work in Vietnam and the Philippines, asks in his article "Are Volunteers Unwitting Imperialists?":

Despite all our good intentions and solid humanitarian work, is it possible that we volunteers around the world play into dehumanizing and oppressive structures of power? . . . Is it possible that North American volunteer agencies can be the sugar coating on a larger American pill laced with the cyanide of economic and military manipulation? If outgoing volunteers are not aware of and disturbed by such questions, it is dangerous to send them. [10]

He offers the following suggestions for volunteers in Third World countries: "Go to listen . . . a humble attitude of seeking to learn from local people goes a long way toward avoiding some arrogant pitfalls. Join with the weak . . . our wisest teachers . . . the sick, the homeless, the imprisoned. Be aware of the violence of structures. Give voice to the voiceless. Be prepared to write and speak upon your return to tell the real story of what is going on."

These guidelines can help in evaluating projects we are interested in supporting with our money or volunteer time.

Having a Positive Impact in Latin America: Developing Worker-Owned Cooperatives
—Estelle and Mario Carota

We raised a very large family in California, but left the United States in 1969 to live in Prince Edward Island, Canada, when the local draft board refused to give some of our sons conscientious objector status for the Vietnam War. We had been professional consultants in community development and public participation in development plans. About twenty-five years ago we went to Mexico with our children to work on some projects with the poor so that we could be of service and at the same time provide our children with the opportunity to learn about Latin America.

In 1983, we were invited back to Mexico to work with some prayer groups to develop a program to assist the poor and the unemployed. Since we had finished raising our family, except for our two teenaged boys, we decided to spend our "golden years" working once again with the people of Mexico. We are committed to organizing worker cooperatives that create self-employment for young campesinos. We had always been members of consumer cooperatives and credit unions and we felt that organizing new forms of worker cooperatives would be the most valuable contribution we could make to the people of the Third World.

The key generation in Latin America is the new baby-boom generation of young parents who have been raised in rural areas. It is this generation of young mothers and fathers who must find ways to sustain their families.

In addition to the economic problems of caring for two, three, and four young children, such parents, still in their twenties, are faced with awesome cultural pressures. As children, they were raised with the simple values of large close families, a relevant religious life, and the true pastoral culture of living on the land. Now these new parents must carry out their vocation in a world that tells them that they must have North American–like families. The religious faith of their childhood is becoming increasingly irrelevant in today's economic and political environment. The skills that they learned as part of a very poor but very self-sufficient rural family must often be abandoned, since there is no more land left to cultivate for themselves. And now, because of the worldwide economic situation, there is virtually no use looking for a job in the cities.

What makes it extremely difficult for these young rural couples is that they must cope with these rapid and drastic adjustments with little or no help from the church, the government, or the private sector. The church has all it can do to take care of its people in the cities. The governments, spending over one-third of their budgets on interest payments for their huge North American debts, have no funds for job creation programs for the unemployed—especially those in rural areas. The private sector, faced with ever-decreasing sales of its products, is too concerned about its own problems to worry about the situation of the unseen poor.

The greatest problem facing the planet today is the poverty of the Third World, especially in comparison to the wealth of the First World. And now IMF and World Bank austerity programs have been imposed on the poor of Latin America so that their countries can pay the debts accumulated by the rich.

As we work with the poor daily and see how this situation directly affects them, it is very disturbing to realize that this amounts to compulsory poverty. The tragedy is that, because of the growing inability of the countries to retire their debts, it is going to be compulsory poverty without end. Although there are frequent crisis conferences of borrowers and lenders, these meetings are only held to refinance the debts and to find ways to get the interest paid. The solutions for retiring the debts have yet to be addressed.

Everyone wants peace and tranquillity in Latin America, and many North American groups are working toward that end. But there can be no peace until there is justice. And there can be no justice until this new generation of young parents has a way to sustain its families. It is certain that the fathers of these families will not sit and watch their children starve. Their reservoir of stoicism from their old culture is draining away rapidly. That is the enormous reality facing all of the affluent people of Latin and North America.

Many programs in Latin America focus on women and children. It is our belief that new programs and forms of assistance are essential to help young fathers, who are often left out on the fringes. These young men have no land to cultivate, no unemployment insurance, no welfare, and no jobs.

We feel that worker and producer cooperatives could fill this gap. We believe that the campesinos can take their natural resources, however limited, and, through a cooperative effort, turn them into marketable products that will earn the income needed to support their families.

Despite the difficulty of establishing successful worker cooperatives, there are an increasing number of examples that prove cooperatives can be successful in creating jobs for the poor.

221

There is, of course, the very successful cooperative movement in Mondragon, Spain. There, the Basques, long victims of prejudice and geographical isolation, have created twenty-two thousand new worker-owned jobs in the past thirty years. Quietly, but in a very revolutionary way, they have created their own schools and university, consumer co-ops, financing institutions, a research center, and a social security system that is better than that of the central government of Spain. The amazing thing is that they did this, not in a utopian vacuum, but in the harsh competitive world of socialism and capitalism.

Closer to home, in Ciudad Juárez, Mexico, there is an excellent example of a successful cooperative created by the very poorest of the poor—the garbage pickers. It took four or five years, but they now own and operate the concession that profitably recycles paper, rags, metal, and glass in a manner that supports almost three thousand men, women, and children. People who literally lived in the utmost form of poverty now live in their own homes, away from the dump.

Many factors motivate the establishment of successful cooperatives. That the workers are the owners of their own enterprise and are thus motivated to produce quality products in a more efficient way is undoubtedly important. That all workers share equally in the profits, and that workers build up a substantial equity for their future, are others. In addition, a loving, not adversarial, relationship between workers and owners is built up within a co-op and is a very important factor.

Driven by this knowledge and our desire to be of service, we began work in Mexico with an effort to organize a tanning cooperative in a community on the edge of Mexico City. The plan was to tan sheepskins and from them make sheepskin jackets. However, we did not want to live in that huge, polluted city. Fortunately, through the kindness of a friend who had a weekend home in the beautiful rural village of Villa del Carbon, we were able to enjoy rural life and commute to the new cooperative in Los Reyes, La Paz. Villa del Carbon is a kind of county seat in a rural area containing about thirty poor communities. This location enabled us to reach out to the rural poor, who were in even greater need than the unemployed on the fringes of Mexico City.

We started by going to two communities of about sixty or seventy families, San Salvador de la Laguna and San Isidro del Bosque. Although introduced to the leaders of the communities by government agricultural field workers, we had a very difficult time gaining the people's confidence, especially in San Isidro. We traveled up the road from Villa del Carbon to San Isidro eight different times before we had our first meeting.

Winning the confidence of the poor, however challenging, is the vital first step without which nothing can be done. This is a concept that is much, much easier to understand than to bring to life.

After four centuries of exploitation by the Spanish conquerors and settlers, and centuries of slavery before that in indigenous cultures, it is understandable that the poor of the Third World have so little confidence in strangers "wanting to help them." Add to this the many broken promises of today's corrupt Third World governments about new and wonderful programs to help the people, and one can get a small idea of why the poor lack confidence in outsiders. The real tragedy is that all of this has served to undermine not only their confidence in their governing elites but, sadly, in themselves as well.

This is what we faced as we tried to organize the young men of San Isidro into the completely foreign and unknown concept of worker cooperatives. To make matters even harder for them, we were working with them as unpaid volunteers and living on our own savings. When we told them that we were there as such and with no idea of getting anything out of them, it was only natural that they found this hard to believe. But with a great deal of patience, consistency, perseverance, and little proofs of sincerity, we were finally able to win their confidence and work together to take the first steps toward organizing a production cooperative.

The sawmill cooperative now owned and operated by the young men of San Isidro is a good example because of its dramatic "before and after." We started out to organize another tanning cooperative because of the community's agricultural resource of sheep. The men even took a course in tanning at a nearby government sheep development center. Then, out of the blue, we were offered a portable sawmill as a gift by an organization in the United States. San Isidro is a mountain community surrounded by forests; and a sawmill would make it possible to create work for its people through its own natural and renewable resources.

This gift was just what was needed for the liberation of the campesinos from their exploitation by the para-governmental monopoly that was making huge profits from the community's own forest. True, the men were able to get work from the monopoly, and this did help them to sustain their families. However, the wages were pitifully low (one to two dollars per day), and the work was seasonal. If the families, sometimes with as many as four children, did not have their, or their parents', corn patch, they would have literally starved. To give a clearer meaning to this, the men needed to work half a day in order to buy a couple of pounds of beans. Is it any wonder these fathers head for the city to find work and the means to support their growing families? The tragedy is that they fully realize that the countryside is a far better place to raise their families.

That is why we are so intent on organizing production cooperatives for the rural poor.

Miraculously, we were able to get the sawmill across the border without proper papers (and, better yet, without having to pay the normal bribe). After that, it did not take long to learn how to operate the sawmill and produce much-needed lumber. Fortunately, the cooperative does not have any problem marketing the lumber. Although there are plenty of trees around, no one else has the tools and equipment to produce nicely sawn boards and timbers. The cooperative had it made—after it went through one long, excruciating year to obtain the federal government's permission to cut down trees.

Nevertheless, now a small group of young men own and operate their own enterprise. A short time ago they were exploited workers at the mercy of a huge lumber monopoly. The source of their liberation was the control and ownership of the tools of production. The power that brought about their liberation was their organization into a cooperative—a cooperative in which all workers are owners and all owners are workers.

We now have a revolving loan fund that makes interest-free loans to existing co-ops or groups wanting to organize a co-op. We are using the Mondragon cooperative movement in Spain as a model, and the fund committee has decided that any loan is made on the condition that the borrowing co-op must agree to lend back 10 percent of its annual profits to the fund so that it can grow and help other cooperatives. There are now twelve fragile production cooperatives (some examples are Los Reyes—pants, El Ranchito—chickens, San Salvador—embroidered goods and sheepskin products, San Isidro—lumber, Guadalupita—sweaters and handwoven woolen fabric, Pueblo Nuevo—corn mill, Tenancingo—furniture, Tlultenango—handwoven woolen goods and fabric), seven tiny consumer cooperatives, and four weak credit unions.

The revolving fund is working with the Federation of Christian Cooperatives to develop markets for the products of the co-ops. A catalog is in production, featuring blankets, belts, tote bags, tablecloths, sweaters, vests, rugs, and other handcrafted items.

The revolving loan fund is supported through the social investment of our friends and people in the United States, Canada, and Mexico. These people ask for no return on their investment and enable us to make interest-free loans to form cooperatives and buy the tools and materials necessary to begin production.

We realize that there is risk involved in all this, but we know from personal experience that it is possible to have a positive impact in the lives of the poor. And we believe in the people's ability to become self-employed, self-sufficient, and self-supporting. We feel fortunate to be able to participate in this kind of work. And we are personal witnesses as people obtain their well-deserved dignity through the management of their own enterprises and carry out a nonviolent revolution. Worker cooperatives place the tools of production in the hands of the people without violence. This is why we are so dedicated to the creation of cooperatives as one of the great hopes for the poor young families of the Third World.

Capp Street Foundation
211 Gough Street, 3rd Floor
San Francisco, CA 94102
(415) 552-0860
Contact: James P. Garret, Executive Director

The Capp Street Foundation (CSF) was established in 1973 to support grass-roots projects in the United States and Latin America that were too controversial or innovative to be supported by most other organizations at the time. Some CSF projects include the Leonard Peltier Defense Fund (Peltier, by the way, was awarded the 1986 International Human Rights Prize by the Human Rights Commission of Spain because he "defended the rights of his people to hold onto their land; and . . . the culture of the American Indian people"), Big Mountain Support Group, the Africa Fund, AIDS/KS Foundation, and the Women's Economic Agenda Project.

In 1983, CSF decided that fundraising for projects in Central America should be a major activity. "By addressing the real needs of Central Americans for economic self-sufficiency and social services, CSF could help to create model development projects, alleviate suffering, and contribute to a just peace in the region." Their Central America Program is directed by Father José Alas, a Salvadoran who has worked with the poor in Central America for over thirty years. In 1983 CSF opened an office in Managua, Nicaragua (Apartado Postal A175, Telcor Altamire, Managua, Nicaragua), to provide technical assistance to projects there. Since the beginning of their Central America Program, nearly $2 million has been channeled to projects in those countries. For example:

> $182,000 to assist nine cooperatives in Rio San Juan, one of the poorest regions of Nicaragua, enabling them to purchase herds of cattle, construct sheds, and buy equipment and feed. Technical training in herd management and disease control was also provided.

> $40,000 to enable a Salvadoran refugee camp in Costa Rica to buy tools, seeds, and fertilizer for a new farming project.

> $20,000 to work with Lenca Indians in Honduras on the use, production, and distribution of traditional herbal medicines.

Three times a year (November, February, and June) CSF offers people the opportunity to visit the Capp Street House in Managua and tour their projects in the region. In addition, CSF also has a Partnership Program, which sets up relationships between specific cooperatives in Central America and churches, schools, and community groups in the U.S. They hope to expand this program into other regions. CSF has also been meeting with Native American leaders and communities to explore more effective working relationships with such groups. It hopes to help establish international funding programs for Africa, the Caribbean, and the Philippines in the future.

CSF's work is mostly funded by donations from individuals in the U.S. They also will channel donations toward specific projects at the donor's request, and they guarantee that funds are being used responsibly and well.

One example of their many current projects is the Nicaragua Windmill Repair Project. Another is their assistance in fundraising for CONFENIAE, a confederation of Indian communities in eastern Ecuador, devastated by an earthquake on 12 March 1987. Two thousand to thirty-five hundred people are missing and presumed dead and a number of communities simply disappeared, including Cascabel, where over five hundred persons lived. According to Cristobal Naikiai, president of CONFENIAE, infectious disease is spreading and Ecuadoran government relief is not reaching the Indian villages. An earthquake relief fund has been organized by the South and Central American Indian Information Center (SCAIIC—PO Box 7550, Berkeley, CA 94707 [415] 452-1235) and the Capp Street Foundation is channelling the funds. For more information, contact either

SCAIIC or CSF. Make checks for any donations payable to the Capp Street Foundation.

Nicaragua Windmill Repair Project
1531 Oregon Drive
Sacramento, CA 95822
(916) 457-5212
Contact: Jay Singer

Although windpumps are widely distributed throughout southwestern Nicaragua in mostly rural locations, an estimated 50 percent of them are totally out of service because they are broken, and another 40 percent are in poor condition and require major repairs. These windpumps were installed in the thousands by the landed elite to open more pastures and increase their export livestock production. Since the redistribution of these lands to small farmers and cooperatives, the windpumps are being used increasingly for gardening, though their primary use is still for beef production. However, most campesinos do not have the expertise to repair the windmills. And those who do have the knowledge lack the tools.

The Nicaragua Windmill Repair Project (NWRP) was founded to improve the rural water supply, develop resources within the country to enable Nicaraguans to manufacture spare parts for the windpumps, train the people in all aspects of proper maintenance and repair, set up shop facilities with tools to leave with the Nicaraguans when the training is completed, make the operation financially self-sufficient, and help the students organize into a self-supporting, cooperative service group.

There are people currently on location in Nicaragua, and a machine-tool shop was recently donated and was making its way there earlier this year. Bruce Morse, a volunteer with the project who returned to the States in December, writes that the windmills, in several fan diameters, are mostly Chicago Aeromotor waterpumps built between 1915 and 1978, most being thirty to forty years old. They are mounted on steel towers. He estimates that there are at least two hundred windmills within range of their shop, most in need of repair.

NWRP is seeking volunteers with the necessary skills to actually live on site for six to twelve months, training and working with the other volunteers and the Nicaraguans. A reliable four-wheel-drive work vehicle, other supplies and tools, and financial support are also needed. The project is affiliated with UNAG—the National

Economics as If the Earth Really Mattered

Union of Small Farmers and Ranchers in Nicaragua. If you are interested in helping in some way, contact Jay at the above address. It only takes $300 to rebuild a windpump, about one-tenth the cost of a new one, and this will provide many years of service to the campesinos who need it most.

The Technical Support Project for a
New Nicaragua (TECNICA)
2727 College Avenue
Berkeley, CA 94705
(415) 848-0292
Contact: Michael Uhrman or David Creighton
—Susan Suchman

The current situation in Central America has created a unique relationship between the citizens of First World countries and citizens of Nicaragua. At the same time that the United States is enforcing a crippling embargo on the economy of that country and providing arms to antigovernment forces, individuals from Europe, Australia, Canada, and the United States are living and working inside Nicaragua. Between one thousand and two thousand internationals have been working there at any given point in the last five years.

TECNICA, the Technical Support Project for a New Nicaragua, is a tax-exempt, nonprofit, volunteer-based organization working to increase this international effort by providing person-to-person technical aid to Nicaragua. Each month TECNICA sends a delegation of fifteen to twenty-five Americans to Nicaragua, composed of technical professionals who "contribute" their vacations and expertise by working on projects, teaching Nicaraguans, and solving critical technical problems. Assisted by TECNICA personnel in Berkeley, California, and Managua, Nicaragua, volunteers are placed in two-week work assignments that range from computer repair to welding and architectural design. In this way, Americans have the unique opportunity of providing aid while learning at first hand how the Nicaraguan people feel about the changes that are taking place in their country.

"Most TECNICA volunteers are not political activists," a staff member explained. "They are professionals who like the idea of being needed by technology-hungry Nicaragua. They're not particularly involved in Nicaragua before they go, but we often find that when they come back they're very supportive of

Nicaragua. They like the fact that they're welcomed by the Nicaraguan people. The Nicaraguans really do need our help."

TECNICA volunteers thus return to the United States with a stronger understanding of what it means to be a citizen of a Third World country and with a need to talk about it. They learn to appreciate the delicate balance between international political and economic pressure and the effort of a people to improve life on a small scale.

Following the revolution's victory in 1979, almost half of the qualified professionals in the Nicaraguan work force left Nicaragua for safer, better-paying jobs. In response to this "brain drain," TECNICA has sent over three hundred volunteers since its founding in late 1983. The response, in Nicaragua and among the volunteers, has been enthusiastic. Successful work projects have been completed in areas as diverse as mechanical and electrical engineering, statistics, chemistry, computer programming, hydraulics, commercial laundry repair, and welding.

Converting these experiences into dollars and cents is also interesting. It is estimated that the work contributed by TECNICA volunteers (over twenty-five thousand hours) can be valued at over $3 million. This makes TECNICA the single largest nongovernmental source of technical assistance to the Nicaraguan people. Most important, because of the nature of the expertise of the volunteers, critical work and crucial repairs would go undone without their assistance.

For example: The International Division of the Central Bank is responsible for holding and allocating all foreign currency—the scarcest resource in Nicaragua. The calculations and record keeping for this essential activity depended upon a cumbersome, chronically late, manual card system. In her two-week visit, TECNICA volunteer Debra Tarnapol trained the Nicaraguans at the bank in the use of Lotus 1-2-3 and helped them set up a currency conversion and record-keeping system on the computer. Most important, Debra replaced need with knowledge, and now the Nicaraguans are able to continue the work on their own.

"It's a wonderful counterpoint to the use of computers in a repressive or destructive capacity," Debra commented.

And the "profits" from TECNICA do not stop in Nicaragua. When TECNICA volunteers return to the United States, they are informed, articulate ambassadors for a country that is poorly understood here. They participate in talks, slide shows, discussion forums, church meetings, and innumerable informal gatherings. Michael Uhrman, TECNICA's founder, estimates that returned volunteers have reached over thirty thousand people in the United States and England. His estimate must be conservative—as every TECNICA volunteer can tell you, there is no way to estimate the number of times any one individual is able to respond to the question "What is going on in Nicaragua?"

TECNICA is currently seeking funds for program administration. Total expenses for the offices in Berkeley and Managua (offices critical to the effective placement of short-term workers) were $129,000 in 1986. In 1987, TECNICA would like to expand the program to include more workers in the skilled trades. Requests from Nicaragua for such assistance are already being considered, but additional staff with expertise in these areas are needed in Managua and Berkeley. The estimated cost of this expansion is $23,000.

Funds for the support of TECNICA in 1986 were raised from volunteer program fees ($30,000), individual contributions ($50,000), foundation grants ($34,000), and restricted projects ($7,000). In addition to administrative fees, volunteers pay their own air fare and act as staff for the local chapters.

Individuals interested in going to Nicaragua as volunteers are also needed. "TECNICA: At Work in Nicaragua," a twenty-minute videotape about the program, is available through the national office or local chapters. If you are interested, call or write the Berkeley office, or contact one of the following local groups: New York City, Lou Project, (212) 426-0634; Amherst, Massachusetts, Joe Boland, (413) 549-1458; Chicago, (312) 524-0198.

"I don't think most Americans have the chance to do something really useful in the life of another country," Al Woodhill, a returned volunteer commented. "TECNICA gives you that chance."

7.3 Bioregionalism

Learning more about indigenous cultures helps us see the role culture plays in shaping our relationships with each other and with the Earth. Increasingly, we North Americans living here in Turtle Island are feeling the need to re-create our culture. I do not believe we are culturally destitute, but we have forgotten much; many generations separate us from personal cultural memories. The human potential movement is growing stronger every day because of our need to fill this emptiness. Traditional peoples have answers to the timeless questions "Who am I? Why am I here? Where have I come from?" We do not.

Re-creating our culture is essential if we are to shape an economy for the living Earth. Economics is culturally defined. Isolated groups have always developed methods of trade and exchange that work for them. Outside influences affect these methods, but the changes incorporated are determined as much by the culture as by the influences—so long as local communities make the changes. Traditional peoples look to their beliefs and values when faced with change, and, as we have seen, this is beginning to have a powerful positive impact on the well-being of Native American communities.

One of the most outstanding commonalities among native cultures is their relationship to the Earth. Whether it be desert, plain, tundra, or jungle, native people know, intimately, the place where they live. They know the animals, plants, smells, sounds; they even know when change is afoot, or something is wrong, before there is any noticeable physical sign. The process of this knowing can be a combination of myth, oral tradition, education, and ritual practice. Whatever the process involves, it, too, is culturally determined and influenced by the spirit of the place itself.

Re-creating our culture is not easy or painless. It is absolutely vital that we create from what is within us. We cannot borrow or adopt another culture's traditions. Culture, I believe, is something intrinsic in each of us. It connects us with each other in meaningful ways and helps us develop relationships with life that make sense. It is therefore essential to know ourselves and to really trust our perceptions of the world. The best place to begin this process is where we live—home.

There is a small, but strong and growing, "movement" called bioregionalism that is, in essence, about re-creating our culture by knowing home. Not just how to get from one place to another, but intimately knowing the soil, the rocks, the trees and plants, the animals, birds, and insects, as well as the history of a place and the culture of the people who lived there before. Who were they? How did they live? How did they relate to the Earth here? To each other? What was important to them? What has changed over the years and why?

A bioregion is not defined by political borders; rather, it is defined naturally by mountain ranges, rivers, watersheds, the climate, and the people living there. Since the goal is to create self-reliant, ecologically sustainable communities able to provide opportunity and creativity for members, a bioregional perspective includes all aspects of society.

Economics as If the Earth Really Mattered

Bioregionalists would agree, I believe, on the sacredness and value of all life. Today, humanity is challenged to wrestle with this very issue. Assigning varying degrees of value, usually determined by usefulness to humans, has gotten us to where we are now—a time when the whole of life itself is threatened. In the words of Thomas Berry:

> So now we experience a moment when a change of vast dimension is demanded . . . a period of change from the mechanistic to the organic, from an oppressive human tyranny over the planet to the rule of the earth community itself, the community of all the living and non-living components of the planet, that neither the nation states nor western civilization has ever seen before.

Bioregionalists would also agree that the basic sustaining, self-organizing laws of nature can be applied to such human systems as agriculture, technology, energy and resource use, economics, land issues, health, education, and politics. David Haenke wrote in *Ecological Politics and Bioregionalism*:

> The power of natural law runs the Earth, and nothing on this planet exists outside of its ultimate control. The Earth is organized, controlled, and governed bioregionally, whether we choose to acknowledge it or not. However, to accept this direction, and to work within this knowledge, is an extraordinarily powerful thing.

Observing how nature's law plays itself out in natural systems, reflecting on the meaning this has, and discovering ways to apply what we learn to our lives is an incredible challenge and opportunity. We have tried "figuring out" nature, finding ways of taming her to suit our needs. We have looked upon the Earth as a warehouse full of goodies for the taking. And for quite some time we have been assuming that somehow our knowledge and technology will solve our problems in time to save us. This kind of thinking (or nonthinking) has gotten us here.

It is time now to become students of the Earth, to plant our feet firmly on the surface of the planet and pay attention to what she has to say. The Earth speaks in many languages—as many as there are people to hear. She speaks the language of color, scent, touch, pattern, sound. And she gives generously of her gifts.

Bioregionalists have made the choice to pay attention to what the Earth is saying. Each of us, in our own place, has made the commitment to begin to know our home. We start where we are and we go from there. We have land, plants, animals, rivers, lakes, and oceans. We have families, neighbors, friends, our community. We even have traditions indigenous to our region when we take the time to seek them out.

The qualities of diversity, cooperation, appropriate scale, and self-reliance are the foundation of bioregional thinking. And they influence the projects implemented in our regions, whether they be in agriculture, housing, finance, education, health, or resource use.

There is no one "official" national organization of bioregionalists. There are, however, a number of bioregional organizations. And in 1984, bioregionalists gathered together for the first time at the North American Bioregional Congress (NABC). A second congress took place in 1986. *Congress* here is a verb. Participants formed committees in such areas of interest as economics, health, feminism, education, water, agriculture, forests, green cities, culture, and arts. Statements and proposals were drafted that groups could approve, amend, or rewrite entirely. (This principle continues to apply to proposals adopted at previous Congresses.) At the end of much discussion and hard work, each committee submitted its statement and proposals to the whole Congress. Using pure consensus (one person can block the passage of a committee's proposal), all participants worked together to create, in the words of Alexandra Hart, "the most cogent current statement of the bioregional movement *as a whole* that exists."

The consensus process is challenging, time consuming, sometimes painful—but always worth it. We learn patience, respect, how to listen, and that we each do, indeed, have a piece of the truth, but not the whole picture.

NABC celebrates and acknowledges our place in the web of life. We come together to support each other in our commitment to work for the healing of the Earth. We share music, quiet talks, dancing, silence, the sunset, sacred sweats, healthy food, stimulating discussions, games, and ourselves. Each Congress publishes a daily newsletter, *The Voice of the Turtle*. A dedicated (and by the end of the week, tired) crew (Alexandra Hart, whose words I used above, is the editor) stays up until the wee hours printing the events of the day, reports on workshops, the work of committees, notices of events, musings of participants, and highlights of the event in general.

We are consciously creating our history as a movement by documenting the Congress gatherings and publishing the

233

proceedings. (See Resources for how to obtain a copy of the 1986 proceedings; a fourth Congress is scheduled for 1990.) We respect the wisdom and truth in native traditions and are beginning to listen to the "small, still voice" within. We are aware of the importance of traditions and rituals and their role in bringing people—a people—together. We are neophyte seekers, "babes in the forest," re-learning, re-membering, re-creating our culture. T. S. Eliot says it very well in "Little Gidding":

> We shall not cease from exploration
> And the end of all our exploring
> Will be to arrive where we started
> And know the place for the first time.

Join us!

7.4 For More Information on Culture and Place

The following list of organizations, books, and publications is provided to help you locate additional resources on the topics covered in this chapter. Use the Resource section at the end of the book to get the complete listings for the groups and written materials below.

Organizations

AICom/IPN
American Friends Service Committee
Amnesty International
Aprovecho Institute
Big Mountain Legal Defense/Offense Committee
Buffalo Robe Lodge
Capp Street Foundation
Center for Indian Economic Development
Central America Resource Center
Charlie Soap/Cherokee Nation
Clergy and Laity Concerned
CoMadres
Cultural Survival
Elfin Permaculture
Enfoprensa
Environmental Project on Central America

Federation of Christian Cooperatives
First Nations Financial Project
Friends of the Third World
Global Education Associates
Granados del Valle
Humanitas International
Ikwe Marketing Cooperative
Indigenous World Association
Institute for Food and Development Policy
Institute for Social Ecology
Jobs with Peace Campaign
Jubilee Crafts
Ladakh Project
Little Colorado Project
MADRE
Medical Aid for El Salvador
Native Self-Sufficiency Center
The Natural Rights Center
Navajo Coal Commission
Network for Native Futures
New Life Farm
Newe Elders Project
Nicaragua Network
Nicaragua Windmill Repair Project
North American Bioregional Congress III
Oglala Lakota Fund
One World Trading Company/Artisanos Mayas
Oxfam America
People of the Earth
Permaculture Institute of North America
Planet Drum Foundation
Pueblo to People
Rainforest Information Centre
Ramah Navajo Weavers
San Juan Pueblo
Seventh Generation Fund
Sirius Community
Survival International
TECNICA
Tets'ugeh Traditional Housing Project
Third World Resources
Traidcraft

TRANET
Zuni Craftsmen Cooperative

Books

Tom Barry and Deb Preusch, *The Central America Fact Book*
Basic Call to Conscience
Directory of Central America Organizations
Gary Habhan, *The Desert Smells Like Rain*
Joan M. Jensen, *With These Hands: Women Working on the Land*
Sean McDonagh, *To Care for the Earth: A Call to a New Theology*
Corinne McLaughlin and Gordon Davidson, *Builders of the Dawn*
Gerald and Patricia Mische, *Toward a Human World Order*
Kirkpatrick Sale, *Dwellers in the Land: The Bioregional Vision*
Charlene Spretnak, *The Spiritual Dimension of Green Politics*
Charlene Spretnak and Fritjof Capra, *Green Politics: The Global Promise*
Paul A. W. Wallace, *The White Roots of Peace*
Women in Development: A Resource Guide for Organization and Action

Publications

Akwesasne Notes
The Alliance
Cultural Survival Quarterly
Daybreak
Katuah
Native Self-Sufficiency
The New Catalyst
North American Bioregional Congress Proceedings
Northeast Indian Quarterly
The Other Side
Parabola
Plenty Bulletin
Siskiyou Journal
Toward Freedom
TRANET
Woman of Power
World Rainforest Report

Notes

1. *Facts for Action*, no. 16.
2. *Multinational Monitor*, June 1987.
3. Ibid.
4. *Big Mountain News*, Fall 1985.
5. *High Country News*, 1/19/87.
6. *Native Self-Sufficiency*, vol. 8, no. 4.
7. Guatemala Church in Exile.
8. *Business Alert*, vol. 2, 1st quarter, 1987.
9. *The Progressive*, August 1985.
10. *The Other Side*, May 1987.

PART IV

Resources

Introduction

As extensive as this resource list may appear at first glance, it must be noted that many excellent organizations are not included, the reasons being a lack of space and my own inability to know about them all. In the years that I have been publishing *CATALYST,* I have discovered many groups and organizations committed to social change, human rights, and ecological awareness. In addition, there are many, many wonderful books and publications. The ones listed here are those I know personally. In addition, especially in the Third World section, I have tried to include only nationally based organizations, although hundreds of regional and local groups are working for peace and solidarity with the people of Latin America. Many of the national organizations (such as the American Friends Service Committee and Clergy and Laity Concerned) have local chapters. Write to the organizations to find the address of the chapter nearest you. For a comprehensive listing of groups working in and for Central America, I highly recommend *Directory of Central America Organizations,* third edition (1987) published by the Central America Resource Center in Austin, Texas (see listing). The book includes over one thousand organizations listed by state and is available for $15, postpaid.

The section on social/alternative investing is the most complete listing in the book, since this is the area in which I have focused much of my energy over the past five years. I have chosen not to include individual investment counselors, planners, and brokers because the field is expanding so rapidly that there is no way to include everyone. For the names of people near you, contact the Social Investment Forum (see listing for address).

The listing of books and periodicals (with the possible exception of the investment section) has an obvious personal bias. There are many other wonderful books that could be included, many that you may think are obvious oversights on my part. I apologize for the gaps in the list and invite you to send me information (c/o

Resources

New Society Publishers, 4527 Springfield Avenue, Philadelphia, PA 19143) on anything you think I should know about that is not included. And bear in mind that the minute this list is printed it is, by definition, out of date. But it should get you started and, if nothing else, provide some inspiration and awe at the vast amount of good work being carried on by caring, committed individuals around the country.

CHAPTER EIGHT

Organizations

Affirmative Investments, Inc.
59 Temple Place, Suite 408
Boston, MA 02111
(617) 350-0250

Registered investment advisory firm specializing in advising individuals and institutions on privately placed, direct investments in socially positive enterprises. Investments may be in the form of loans, equity investments, privately placed bonds, and real-estate limited partnership interests. Minimum investment is usually $5,000.

AICom/IPN (Associated Indigenous Communications/ Indigenous Press Network)
PO Box 98
Highland, MD 20777

The American Committee on Africa
198 Broadway
New York, NY 10038
(212) 962-1210

American Friends Service Committee (AFSC)
1501 Cherry Street
Philadelphia, PA 19102
(215) 241-7000 or 241-7168

AFSC sponsors programs of refugee assistance and development in Central America. The organization has networks around the country; activities include supporting human rights, providing refugee care and support, education, audiovisual media, publications, direct assistance, and research. AFSC also publishes the *United States Anti-Apartheid Newsletter* ($10/year), has material-aid campaigns under way, and is involved in many other activities relating to apartheid and peace and justice issues.

Resources

Amnesty International
322 Eighth Avenue
New York, NY 10001
(212) 807-8400

Human rights advocacy; works for the release of political prisoners and against torture and execution. Activities include research, education, publications, and speaking tours.

Anawim Fund of the Midwest
1145 W. Wilson Avenue, Suite 2424
Chicago, IL 60646

The Aprovecho Institute
80574 Hazelton Road
Cottage Grove, OR 97424
(503) 942-9434

Aprovecho ("I make the best use of" in Spanish) is a nonprofit organization committed to helping people in Third World countries take charge of their lives using technologies appropriate to their skills and resources. Researches and develops innovative techniques for housing, heating, and small-scale food production, with a special emphasis on cookstoves. Works in Third World countries and provides opportunities for internships on their land in Oregon. Excellent resource for person-to-person projects in the Third World, especially Central America. Regular newsletter. Membership is $15/year, additional contributions most welcome.

ARABLE (Association for Regional Agriculture Building the Local Economy)
PO Box 5230
Eugene, OR 97405

Bank for Socially Responsible Lending
PO Box 404920
Brooklyn, NY 11240
(718) 768-9344

Ben & Jerry's Homemade, Inc.
Route 100, PO Box 133
Waterbury, VT 05676
(802) 244-5641

Big Mountain Legal Defense/Offense Committee
2501 N. 4th Street, Suites 18-19
Flagstaff, AZ 86001
(602) 774-5233 or 779-2587

Information and updates on the Navajo-Hopi land "settlement" and relocation.

Bioregional Project (North American Bioregional Congress)
Turtle Island Office
c/o Jacinta McKoy
1333 Overhulse Road NE
Olympia, WA 98502
(206) 866-1046

Publications and information about bioregionalism. Can put you in touch with bioregional groups in your area. Proceedings for the North American Bioregional Congress III are available for $7. Make checks payable to Seth Zuckerman, PO Box 159, Petrolia, CA 95558.

Boston Community Loan Fund, Inc.
25 West Street, 2nd Floor
Boston, MA 02111

Brooklyn Ecumenical Cooperative
562 Atlantic Avenue
Brooklyn, NY 11217

Housing for low-income families, including ownership.

Buffalo Robe Lodge
Box 31
Faust, Alberta T0G 0X0
CANADA

Burlington Community Land Trust
PO Box 523
Burlington, VT 05402
(802) 862-6244

Burlington Revolving Loan Program
Community and Economic Development Office
City Hall, Room 32
Burlington, VT 05401
(802) 862-6244

Calvert Social Investment Fund
1700 Pennsylvania Avenue, NW
Washington, DC 20006
(800) 368-2748

Calvert offers a managed-growth portfolio (mutual fund) and a
money-market portfolio. The fund avoids investments in nuclear
power, defense contractors, and companies doing business in or with
South Africa. Its investments support companies delivering safe
products and services that have participatory management, negotiate
fairly with workers, create a safe working environment, have equal
opportunities for women and minorities, and have good community
relations. The minimum initial investment is $1,000.

Capital District Community Loan Fund
33 Clinton Avenue
Albany, NY 12207

Capp Street Foundation
211 Gough Street, 3rd Floor
San Francisco, CA 94102
(415) 552-0860

Supports grassroots projects in the U.S. and Latin America.
Implemented Central American Program in 1983 to help create
"model development projects, alleviate suffering and contribute to a
just peace in the region." Also has office in Managua, Nicaragua.

Catherine McAuley Housing Foundation
1601 Milwaukee Street
Denver, CO 80206
(303) 393-3806

Catskill Mountain Housing Revolving Loan Fund
PO Box 473
Catskill, NY 12414
(518) 943-6700

Center for Indian Economic Development
1442A Walnut Street, Suite 266
Berkeley, CA 94709

Helps tribes start projects within the capacity of the tribe to direct and manage, which expand as experience and competence are gained. Emphasizes short-term, low-capital business start-ups.

Center for Neighborhood Technology
2129 W. North Avenue
Chicago, IL 60647
(312) 278-4800

Seeks affordable, locally controlled ways for city residents to meet needs for food, shelter, energy, jobs, and a healthy environment. Provides services to neighborhood organizations in those areas and produces *The Neighborhood Works,* an excellent monthly publication on "resources for urban communities." $18/year.

Center for Popular Economics
Box 785
Amherst, MA 01004

Nonprofit organization that teaches "people-oriented economics." The Center addresses the needs and concerns of social-change activists, community groups, and churches, educating them about how the economy works in order to help their work be most effective. Offers Summer Institutes, workshops, and excellent publications.

Central America Resource Center
PO Box 2327
Austin, TX 78768
(512) 476-9841

Provides information on Central America—publishes *The Central America NewsPak,* a biweekly compilation of current news on events in Central America, and the excellent *Directory of Central American Organizations*. The third edition (1987) lists over 1,000 by state.

Charlie Soap
Director of Community Development
Cherokee Nation
Tahlequah, OK 74464

Chrysalis Money Consultants
21 Linwood Street
Arlington, MA 02174
(617) 648-0776

Offers financial counselling and education, particularly on psychological and social issues linked to money.

Citizens Clearinghouse for Hazardous Wastes, Inc.
PO Box 926
Arlington, VA 22216
(703) 276-7070

National nonprofit organization helping local environmental activists fight for solutions to hazardous waste problems. Provides general organizing information, publishes papers, books, and reports, plus two newsletters—*Everyone's Backyard* and *Action Bulletin*. Organizations they have assisted have very often succeeded in their efforts. Membership is $15/year.

Clergy and Laity Concerned
198 Broadway
New York, NY 10038

Action-oriented interfaith network of fifty-three chapters and action groups in thirty-one states, working for a just society and a peaceful world. Activities include political organizing, education, providing refugee sanctuary, organizing trips, and supporting human rights.

CoMadres
PO Box 21299
Washington, DC 20009

A support group for families of Salvadoran disappeared, political prisoners, and assassinated.

Community Land Trust in the Southern Berkshires
195 Main Street
PO Box 276
Great Barrington, MA 01230
(413) 528-1737

Community Workshop on Economic Development (CWED)
100 South Morgan Street
Chicago, IL 60607
(312) 243-0249

A coalition of forty-two community-based organizations that promote community economic development. Includes a variety of organizations from youth services to housing.

Conscious Investments
93 Saturn Street
San Francisco, CA 94114
(415) 621-6414

Offers workshops and seminars for those interested in social investing.

Consumers United Group
2100 M Street, NW
Suite 207
Washington, DC 20063
(202) 872-5709

International holding company that provides services to members of associations and cooperatives. Products include health care insurance, supplements, and term life.

Co-op America
2100 M Street, NW
Suite 310
Washington, DC 20063
(800) 424-2667 or (202) 872-5307

America's alternative marketplace. Membership nonprofit organization of cooperative, democratically managed, responsible businesses and individuals who support those principles. Publishes catalog of members' products (crafts, clothing, Third World products, publications, herbal products, etc.) and *Building Economic Alternatives;* access to health insurance. Membership is **$15 for** individuals, $50 for organizations (includes listing in directory sent to all members).

Cooperative Fund of New England
108 Kenyon Street
Hartford, CT 06105

Cornerstone Loan Fund
PO Box 8974
Cincinnati, OH 45208
(513) 871-3899

The Corporation for Enterprise Development
1725 K Street, NW
Suite 1401
Washington, DC 20006
(202) 293-7963

Specializes in designing economic development policy for low-income communities and populations.

Council on Economic Priorities
30 Irving Place
New York, NY 10003
(212) 420-1133

Research organization that publishes a monthly newsletter and other publications of interest to social investors, which focus on various subjects related to corporate responsibility. $25/year.

Covenant for a World Free of Nuclear Weapons
2406 Geddes Avenue
Ann Arbor, MI 48105

Cultural Survival
11 Divinity Avenue
Cambridge, MA 02138
(617) 495-2526

Human-rights organization focusing on indigenous peoples and ethnic minorities. Activities include research, education, direct assistance and speaking tours. Publishes the excellent *Cultural Survival Quarterly.*

Data Center
464 19th Street
Oakland, CA 94612
(415) 835-4692

Subscription, research, and clipping service on corporations, industries, labor, plant shutdowns, Central America, etc.

Delaware Valley Community Reinvestment Fund
924 Cherry Street, 2nd Floor
Philadelphia, PA 19107
(215) 725-1130

Dreyfus Third Century Fund
600 Madison Avenue
New York, NY 10022
(800) 645-6561

Dreyfus is a mutual fund that invests in companies with "best-of-industry" records in such areas as safety and environmental impact. Beginning in 1986, Dreyfus decided to avoid companies operating in South Africa, but there is no screen for weapons production or nuclear power. The minimum investment is $2,500.

Dwelling House Savings and Loan
501 Herron Avenue
Pittsburgh, PA 15219
(412) 683-5116

Earth Care Paper Co.
325 Beech Lane
Harbor Springs, MI 49740
(616) 526-7003

Excellent source of recycled paper, notecards, stationery, etc. Bulk suppliers of various grades, colors, and sizes of recycled paper and envelopes. Provides useful information on recycling and organizing community recycling programs. Send for catalog.

Economic Renewal Project
Rocky Mountain Institute
Drawer 248
Old Snowmass, CO 81654

Ecumenical Development Cooperative Society (EDCS)
475 Riverside Drive, Room 1003
New York, NY 10115
(212) 870-2665

E. F. Schumacher Society
Box 76, RD 3
Great Barrington, MA 01230
(413) 528-1737

Promotes community land trusts, alternative economics (including SHARE and an alternative currency project using "berkshares"), small business using local resources and serving local needs, and appropriate technology.

Elfin Permaculture
40A Brooks Street
Worcester, MA 01606

Offers workshops, design courses, and access to many other permaculture resources.

Enfoprensa
PO Box 53048
Washington, DC 20009

Collects, prepares, and distributes news and information about Guatemala.

Environmental Project on Central America
Earth Island Institute
13 Columbus Avenue
San Francisco, CA 94111
(415) 788-3666

Focus is on environmental issues and situations in Central America. Publishes *Green Papers* on these issues (excellent!). The goal is to bring the environmental and anti-intervention movements together to work for common goals.

Estelle and Mario Carota
Avenida Juárez No. 28
Villa del Carbon
MEXICO 54300

Farallones Institute
15290 Coleman Valley Road
Occidental, CA 95465

Concerned with agriculture, environment, and appropriate technology. Provides educational programs and publications.

Federation of Christian Cooperatives
Estelle and Mario Carota
Apartado 1205
Toluca
MEXICO 50000

See "Having a Positive Impact in Latin America" (page 220) for more information on this group of worker-owned cooperatives in Mexico. Products include blankets, tote bags, tablecloths, belts, sweaters, vests, skirts, blouses, shawls, rugs, etc. All handcrafted.

Financial Alternatives
1514 McGee Street
Berkeley, CA 94703

First Nations Financial Project
Route 14, Box 74
Falmouth, VA 22405
(703) 371-5616

Friends of the Third World
611 Wayne Street
Fort Wayne, IN 46802
(219) 422-1650

Begun by a group of students in 1970, the objectives of Friends of the Third World are to "demonstrate the existence and viability of an alternative system of trade as an effective way to address problems of poverty and unemployment; to sell products at or near cost so that producers retain a larger portion of the selling price; and to promote the understanding that by purchasing an article, one is taking direct action to reverse a major inequity in the world." Provides marketing, development, and technical assistance. Offers wonderful selection of crafts, food products, and many books (Whole World Books) on countries (nations of Asia, Africa, Latin America, the Middle East) and subjects (economics, hunger, population, socialism, etc.).

Fund for an OPEN Society
311 S. Juniper Street, Suite 400
Philadelphia, PA 19107

Fund for Renewable Energy and the Environment (FREE)
1001 Connecticut Avenue, NW
No. 638
Washington, DC 20036
(202) 466-6880

Formerly the Solar Lobby; addresses renewable energy, recycling, and conservation through research, public education, and direct action. Publishes catalog and newsletter.

Funding Exchange
666 Broadway, 5th Floor
New York, NY 10012
(212) 260-8500

National organization of fourteen community-based public foundations, established to fund grass-roots and activist organizations addressing such social issues as race and sex discrimination, nuclear proliferation, and economic injustice. Also sponsors conferences on socially responsible investing and publishes the *Directory of Socially Responsible Investments* ($7).

Gesundheit Institute
404 N. Nelson Street
Arlington, VA 22203

Loving, holistic medical care and prevention. Dr. Patch Adams is the founder. The institute is committed to providing free medical care and using the healing power of laughter and fun.

Global Education Associates (GEA)
475 Riverside Drive, Room 570
New York, NY 10115
(212) 870-3290

Founded by Gerald and Patricia Mische, GEA works to create a more human world order. Focuses efforts on education, research, and working for human rights globally. Publishes regular newsletter and "Whole Earth Papers." All publications are excellent and their work is among the best of its kind.

Granados del Valle
PO Box 118
Los Ojos, NM 87551

Agricultural development corporation founded by livestock growers and artisans with the goal of demonstrating that traditional people can revitalize their cultural and land-based resources with modern agricultural and business practices. Provides management and marketing assistance as well as loan capital to help growers cut costs and increase income.

Grassroots International
South Africa Freedom Fund
PO Box 321
Cambridge, MA 02139
(617) 479-9180

Habitat for Humanity
Habitat and Church Streets
Americus, GA 31709
(912) 924-6935

Haymarket People's Fund
25 West Street, 5th Floor
Boston, MA 02111

Information and resources for people with inherited wealth; funds projects working for social change.

Humanitas International
PO Box 818
Menlo Park, CA 94026

Works to increase awareness of human rights violations, to aid those whose rights have been violated, and to encourage the use of nonviolent action to work for social change.

Ikwe Marketing Cooperative
Route 1, Box 206
Osage, MN 56570

Markets wild rice and traditional crafts created by women. "We are skilled people...we believe that our traditional skills—maple sugar harvest, wild rice harvest, traditional crafts—are highly valuable skills

252

that others do not possess. These skills, combined with our resources, are a viable basis for economic development. This form of economic development is our best chance of changing the conditions of our community in the long term." (Winona LaDuke, founder and staff member of the Cooperative.)

Indigenous World Association
275 Grand View Avenue, No. 103
San Francisco, CA 94114

Specializes in the problems of displaced and refugee Indians in Central America. Received nongovernmental consultative status in the United Nations in 1985.

Industrial Cooperative Association
249 Elm Street
Somerville, MA 02114
(617) 628-7330

Nonprofit organization committed to working with worker-owned companies; provides technical and educational assistance to communities and businesses wanting to convert to (or organize as) worker-owned. Also has a revolving loan fund for worker cooperatives.

INFACT
256 Hanover Street
Boston, MA 02113
(617) 742-4582

Nonprofit organization committed to holding transnational corporations accountable. Organizers of Nestlé boycott.

Institute for Community Economics
151 Montague City Road
Greenfield, MA 01301
(413) 774-7956

Institute for Food and Development Policy
1885 Mission Street
San Francisco, CA 94103
(415) 864-8555
Works to identify the root causes of hunger and food problems around the world and educate the public and policy makers. Regular newsletter.

The Institute for Gaean Economics (IGE)
64 Main Street, 2nd Floor
Montpelier, VT 05602
(802) 223-7943

Working to shape an economy for the living earth, IGE sponsors workshops on alternative economics and alternative systems and organizations that are in harmony with the Earth's systems and cycles. Regular membership newsletter with articles on resources, business, finance, education, etc., from a Gaean (Earth) context. The Gaea Center, in Worthington, Massachusetts, is located on forty-five acres of mostly wooded land—a beautiful, relaxing place to experience Gaea as well as learn about her needs. Vegetable and herb gardens, children's programs, and educational seminars ranging from geomancy to business. Membership (includes newsletter) $50/year.

Institute for Local Self-Reliance
2425 18th Street, NW
Washington, DC 20009
(202) 232-4108

Promotes healthy local economies, the concept of "waste as resource," and appropriate technology. Provides research, education, and direct technical assistance to cities and towns. Many publications available.

Institute for Social Ecology
PO Box 348
Rochester, VT 05767

Founded by Murray Bookchin to combine practical research in alternative technologies with the study of socioeconomic problems. Regular courses and workshops, summer semester. Undergraduate credit available for most courses.

Interfaith Center on Corporate Responsibility (ICCR)
475 Riverside Drive, Room 566
New York, NY 10115
(212) 870-2995

Provides information on practices of major corporations. Shareholder actions and corporate resolutions are major activities.

Publishes *Multinational Monitor* (see Publications) and *Directory of Alternative Investments* (see Books).

Intermediate Technology Development Group of North America (ITDGNA)
PO Box 337
Croton-on-Hudson, NY 10520

Publications on such subjects as policy and economics, agriculture and forestry, building and construction, cooperatives, energy, etc., stressing appropriate technology and alternatives to traditional methods and technologies.

Investor Responsibility Research Center (IRRC)
1755 Massachusetts Avenue, NW
Washington, DC 20036
(202) 939-6500

Researches and reports on contemporary social and public policy issues as they affect corporations; publishes a range of publications on business issues of concern to social investors. Excellent resource for information on South Africa.

Jobs for People
1216 East McMillan, Room 304
Cincinnati, OH 45206
(513) 861-1155

Builds worker-owned cooperatives that employ low-income people.

Jobs with Peace Campaign
76 Summer Street
Boston, MA 02110

Jubilee Crafts
300 West Apsley Street
Philadelphia, PA 19144
(215) 849-0808

Nonprofit alternative trade organization that markets crafts of Third World peoples with the goal of educating Americans about the circumstances and conditions of those peoples and our role in the situation. "We see our work at Jubilee as a contribution to justice, not a way to make money." Offers local groups and individuals the opportunity to sell the crafts, too. Write for catalog and information on how you can become involved.

Jubilee Loan Fund
1750 Columbia Road, NW
Washington, DC 20009
(202) 332-4020

Jubilee Partners Paul and Silas Revolving Bail Fund
Box 68
Comer, GA 30629
(404) 783-5131

Koinonia Partners
Route 2
Americus, GA 31709

Ladakh Project
c/o Open Space Institute
122 E. 42nd Street, Room 1901
New York, NY 10168
(212) 949-1966

Winner of the 1986 Right Livelihood Award; a project in northern India that supports the Ladakhi culture and traditional practices and materials.

The Lakota Fund
PO Box 340
Kyle, SD 57752
(605) 455-2500

LETS (Local Employment Trading System)
375 Johnson Avenue
Courtenay, BC V9N 2Y2
CANADA

Leviticus 25:23 Alternative Fund
Mariandale Center, Box 1200
Ossining, NY 10562
(914) 941-9422

Little Colorado Project
PO Box 3245
Flagstaff, AZ 86003

First project of the Seventh Generation Fund. Four communities in the Little Colorado River Valley are working together using drip irrigation learned from an Israeli farm expert to produce good food for families and raise enough to sell, while protecting water rights and supplies. Highly successful project that has earned national attention.

The Low-Income Housing Fund
55 New Montgomery, Suite 223
San Francisco, CA 94105

MADRE
853 Broadway, No. 301
New York, NY 10003
(212) 777-6470

Mother-to-mother, people-to-people connections between the U.S. and Central America, with the goal of stopping U.S. intervention in Nicaragua, the rest of Central America, and the Caribbean.

Medical Aid for El Salvador
6030 Wilshire Boulevard, No. 200
Los Angeles, CA 90036
(213) 937-3596

National Association of Community Development Loan Funds (NACDLF)
151 Montague City Road
Greenfield, MA 01301
(413) 774-7956

Member association of community development loan funds. Provides information, networking, assistance to member funds; promotes the model of the revolving loan fund. See page 134 for more information.

National Center for Employee Ownership
426 17th Street, Suite 650
Oakland, CA 94612
(415) 272-9461

Research and outreach organization for employee stock ownership plans (ESOPs). Publishes newsletter and reports, and sponsors workshops and conferences on employee ownership.

National Congress for Community Economic Development
1612 K Street, NW
No. 510
Washington, DC 20006
(202) 659-8411

Membership organization for community-based development organizations working for economic revitalization. Provides advocacy, policy analysis, training, and technical assistance. Publishes monthly newsletter, *Resources,* that focuses on specific projects and includes articles relevant to nonprofit community organizations. $48/year.

National Cooperative Business Association
1401 New York Avenue, NW
Suite 1100
Washington, DC 20001
(202) 638-6222, ext. 210
National membership and trade association representing cooperative businesses and addressing the needs of the various industries within the community of cooperative businesses.

National Economic Development and Law Center
1950 Addison Street
Berkeley, CA 94704

National organization focusing on all aspects of community economic development. Regular publication, *Economic Development and Law Center Report,* is excellent ($20/year, quarterly).

National Federation of Community Development Credit Unions (NFCDCU)
29 John Street, Room 903
New York, NY 10038
(212) 513-7191

Provides information, technical assistance, and support to community development credit unions around the country. Can provide information on credit unions in your area and select investments in credit unions throughout the country for your portfolio.

Resources

Native Self-Sufficiency Center
PO Box 213
Coldbrook, NY 13324

Established by several Mohawk families as a demonstration site for use of appropriate technology by Native communities that provide examples of inexpensive ways of producing energy, building homes, and growing food.

The Natural Choice
LIVOS Plant Chemistry
614 Auga Fria Street
Santa Fe, NM 87501

Catalog of nontoxic home products (stains, paints, oil finishes, polishes, etc.)

The Natural Rights Center
PO Box 90
Summertown, TN 39483
(615) 964-2334

A project of PLENTY USA. Staffed by two attorneys and a number of interns, paralegal volunteers, and researchers, the Natural Rights Center commits from one-third to one-half of its resources to protecting the natural rights of other species, the land, and the water. The rest involves issues of global importance, such as toxic waste, nuclear power, and human rights. (Included as a resource in this section because indigenous peoples are in extreme danger as a direct result of our lack of acknowledgement of the "rights of nature.")

Navajo Coal Commission
PO Box 308
Window Rock, AZ 86515

Working on comprehensive plan to reclaim lands damaged by strip mining.

Network for Native Futures
Route 1, Box 235
Nedrow, NY 13120

Provides a variety of technical assistance programs that train people to become planners and developers within the context of their cultures while blending what is appropriate from non-native cultures.

New Alchemy Institute
237 Hatchville Road
East Falmouth, MA 02536

Research and educational programs on permaculture, integrated greenhouse and aquaculture systems, and other alternative technologies. Regular newsletter.

New Alternatives Fund
295 Northern Boulevard
Great Neck, NY 11021
(516) 466-0808

New Alternatives is a mutual fund that invests in solar and other environmentally sound forms of energy production as alternatives to fossil fuels and nuclear power. Investments include a diversity of companies, ranging from smaller firms devoted to photovoltaic solar cells or domestic hot-water heaters to larger firms producing insulation or energy management systems. No more than 25 percent of the fund's assets will be invested in companies not listed on the New York or American stock exchanges. The fund does not invest in defense contractors or companies producing nuclear power. Other alternatives, such as cogeneration, biomass, and hydro, are also supported by the fund. Minimum investment is $2,650.

New Hampshire College
2599 North River Road
Manchester, NH 03104
(603) 485-8415

Offers master's program and joint bachelor's/master's program in community economic development.

New Hampshire Community Loan Fund
Box 666
Concord, NH 03301
(603) 224-6669

New Life Farm
Box 3
Brixey, MO 65618

New Life Farm is a nonprofit, tax-exempt organization in the south-central Missouri Ozarks doing research and providing information on sustainable, environmentally responsible, renewable resource–based appropriate technologies, community economic development, and energy and resource conservation strategies that foster self-reliance for families, farms, communities, the Ozarks, and other bioregions.

Newe Elders Project
7895 Stillwater Road
Fallon, NY 89406

Nicaragua Network
2025 I Street, NW
No. 1117
Washington, DC 20006
(202) 223-2328

A network of over two hundred groups promoting friendship between the U.S. and Nicaragua.

Nicaragua Windmill Repair Project
1531 Oregon Drive
Sacramento, CA 95822
(916) 457-5212

North American Bioregional Congress IV
See entry under Bioregional Project.

Northern California Community Loan Fund
14 Precita Avenue
San Francisco, CA 94110
(415) 285-3909

Nuclear Free America
2521 Guilford Avenue
Baltimore, MD 21218
(301) 235-3575

Nonprofit organization advocating nuclear-free zones, divestment of city, state, and university funds from companies manufacturing nuclear weapons, and boycotts of the consumer products of weapon contractors. *The New Abolitionist* updates members on nuclear-free-zone activity and provides other related information. $10/year.

Of the People
234 North Market Street
Paxton, IL 60957

Below-market-rate loans for disadvantaged people wishing to start worker-owned co-ops.

Oglala Lakota College
PO Box 490
Kyle, SD 57752
(605) 455-2321

One World Trading Company/Artisanos Mayas
PO Box 310
Summertown, TN 38483
(615) 964-2334

Oxfam America
115 Broadway
Boston, MA 02116
(617) 482-1211

Development assistance and humanitarian aid to Latin America, Asia, and Africa. Provides education, lobbying, organizing trips, direct assistance, research, and publications.

PACE (Philadelphia Association for Cooperative Enterprise)
2100 Chestnut Street
Philadelphia, PA 19103
(215) 561-7079

Promotes worker ownership among workers, addresses concerns of unions. Provides research, education, and technical assistance. Worked with workers to create the O&O supermarkets. Project in Pittsburgh working with former employees of an Armour meatpacking plant.

Parnassus Fund
1427 Shrader Street
San Francisco, CA 94117
(415) 664-6812

The Parnassus Fund utilizes a "contrarian" investment strategy, essentially buying out-of-favor companies that have what they call "Renaissance" qualities: high-quality products and services; market-orientation that stays "close to the customer"; sensitivity to the community in which the company is located; a good relationship with its employees; and the ability to be innovative and respond well to change. Minimum investment is $5,000. (As an interesting note: some of their material is printed on recycled paper.)

Paul Terry & Associates
1269 Rhode Island Street
San Francisco, CA 94107

Pax World Fund
224 State Street
Portsmouth, NH 03801
(603) 431-8022

The oldest of the screened mutual funds, Pax World does not invest in any company engaged in the manufacture of weapons or weapon-related products. It also avoids investments in companies engaged in the liquor, tobacco, and gambling industries. It excludes companies operating in South Africa, with the exception of those providing food and medicines. Minimum investment is $250.

Peace Fleece/Soviet American Woolens
RFD 1, Box 57
Kezar Falls, ME 04047
(207) 625-4906

People of the Earth
Rainforest Action Network
466 Green Street, No. 300
San Francisco, CA 94133
(415) 788-3666

Goals are preservation of the rain forest and acting against the worldwide genocide of indigenous peoples.

Permaculture Institute of North America (PINA)
4649 Sunnyside Avenue, N
Seattle, WA 98103

Nonprofit organization that promotes permaculture. Networking, source of permaculture resources, regular newsletter, *The Permaculture Activist*.

Planet Drum Foundation
Box 31251
San Francisco, CA 94131
(415) 285-6556

Publishes biannual newspaper, *Raise the States*, and other bioregionally focused publications. Membership is $15/year.

Pueblo to People
1616 Montrose
Houston, TX 77006
(713) 523-1197

Nonprofit organization formed by people who have lived and worked in Central America. An alternative trade organization focusing efforts on craft and agricultural cooperatives of very-low-income people in Central America and the Philippines. Provides assistance to producer groups in product design, production methods, obtaining needed financing, etc. Write for catalog of products; contributions are greatly appreciated as well.

Rainforest Information Centre
PO Box 368
Lismore, New South Wales 2480
AUSTRALIA

Excellent resource on rain-forest issues worldwide. Regular newsletter with updates, political news, and reports on activities of the World Bank and other large developers relating to the rainforests. $15/year.

Ramah Navajo Weavers
PO Box 489
Pine Hill, NM 87321

The Ramah Navajo Weavers are expanding the marketing network for their products, developing a revolving loan fund, and creating a cooperative to propagate the Navajo Churro sheep, which are prized for their high-quality, long-fibered wool.

Regeneration Project
Rodale Press
33 E. Minor Street
Emmaus, PA 18049

Advocates the principle of regeneration in areas of health, the economy, agriculture, etc. Publishes quarterly newsletter ($12/year) that addresses regeneration from the personal to the community level. Specific ideas and projects, including some urban economic revitalization projects, are in each issue.

Resource Recovery Systems
PO Box 501
Old Lyme, CT 06371
(203) 434-9635

Offers "a management approach" to municipalities interested in removing a large portion of their recyclables from the solid-waste stream.

Rocky Mountain Institute
Drawer 248
Old Snowmass, CO 81654

Rural Economic Alternatives Project (REAP)
PO Box 1259, Delta Station
Stockton, CA 95291
(209) 465-4265

Nonprofit organization committed to helping family farms survive and flourish in California's Central Valley. Model program that includes a market association (the Stockton Farmers Cooperative, which is grower owned), a central receiving warehouse, a truck for local deliveries, and full-time staff. Also working with AFSC on the Small Farm Viability Project, which provides workshops, testing of new crops, development of ethnic and specialty crops, and farmer-worker training.

San Juan Pueblo
PO Box 1099
San Juan Pueblo, NM 87566

Adopting sustainable agriculture as an integral part of the Pueblo's economic development plan.

School of Living
RD 1, Box 1508 AA
Spring Grove, PA 17362

Promotes ideas of Henry George, Ralph Borsodi, and Mildred Loomis. Focus on alternative economic systems and concepts, appropriate technology and life-style, cooperation and community. Publishes *Green Revolution* quarterly for $6/year, and other material as well.

Self-Help Credit Union
413 E. Chapel Hill Street
Durham, NC 27701
(919) 683-3016

Seventh Generation Fund
PO Box 10
Forestville, CA 95436

Seventh Generation Fund, Office of Economic Development
PO Box 3245
Flagstaff, AZ 86003
(602) 774-7222

Seventh Generation Fund
Office of Native Rights/Native Women
PO Box 3035
Reno, NV 89505
(702) 322-2751

SHARE (Self-Help Association for a Regional Economy)
E. F. Schumacher Society
Box 76A, RD 3
Great Barrington, MA 02139

See page 123 for details on SHARE. The E. F. Schumacher Society is also implementing a local currency, "berkshares," in the Great Barrington area. Assists with land trusts and other locally based economic alternatives.

Resources

Sirius Community
Baker Road
Shutesbury, MA 01072

An intentional community located on ninety acres of land in the village of Shutesbury, Sirius is committed to appropriate technology, open and honest relationships, and working in harmony with the natural kingdom. They have developed beautiful and bountiful gardens, and their buildings incorporate passive solar construction and other innovative techniques. Sirius offers workshops on topics ranging from land stewardship, spirituality, politics, and developing community to "the inner side of world events." The community is committed to alternative economics, and several cooperative and worker-owned businesses (including a construction company) have been started by members. A new community center with expanded facilities for guests is currently under construction (your donations are most welcome!). Write for brochure.

Social Investment Forum
711 Atlantic Avenue
Boston, MA 02111
(617) 423-6655

National professional association of advisors, bankers, analysts, investment funds, research and community organizations, and publishers active in developing the concept and practice of socially responsible investing. Will provide a list of socially responsible investment advisors in your area upon request.

Social Responsibility Investment Group
The Chandler Building, Suite 622
127 Peachtree Street, NE
Atlanta, GA 30303
(404) 577-3635

Management of assets for socially responsible investors.

South Atlanta Land Trust
1523 Jonesboro Road
Atlanta, GA 30315
(404) 525-2683

Southeast Reinvestment Venture (SERV)
159 Ralph McGill Boulevard, NE
Room 412
Atlanta, GA 30365
(404) 659-0002, ext. 276

South Shore Bank of Chicago
Investment Fund for Housing/Rehab CD-Loan Program
7054 S. Jeffery Boulevard
Chicago, IL 60649
(312) 288-7017

Southern Cooperative Development Fund
1006 Surrey Street
PO Box 3885
Lafayette, LA 70502

Provides financial and technical assistance to eligible minority and cooperative businesses.

Spruce Mountain Design
26 State Street
Montpelier, VT 05602

Sunflower Recycling Cooperative
S.E. Grand at Division Street
PO Box 42466
Portland, OR 97214
(503) 238-1640

Survival International
2121 Decatur Place, NW
Washington, DC 20008

Serves the needs of indigenous peoples around the world by promoting and protecting their rights and supporting their efforts at self-sufficiency and self-determination.

TECNICA (Technical Support Project for a New Nicaragua)
2727 College Avenue
Berkeley, CA 94705
(415) 848-0292

Places professionals and technical persons in short-term jobs in public and private organizations in Nicaragua. These volunteers pay their own expenses and work with Nicaraguans, training them in such areas of expertise as computers, engineering, etc.

Tets'ugeh Traditional Housing Project
PO Box 596
Tesuque, NM 87574

Project restores the traditional homes at the pueblo.

Third World Resources
464 19th Street
Oakland, CA 94612

Print and audiovisual resources from and about Central America and the Third World.

Traidcraft Ltd.
Kingsway, Gateshead
NE11 CNE
UNITED KINGDOM

One of the oldest alternative trade organizations, its objective is to increase "love, justice and equity in international trade." In 1984, Traidcraft issued its first share prospectuses, which were not only rapidly purchased but were oversubscribed by 60 percent, despite the fact that investors were warned that they would be unable to make speculative gain from them. In 1986, Traidcraft once again issued more shares and investors were warned that "dividends will be low, a maximum of 6 percent before tax, and directors do not envisage a substantial appreciation in the share price." Again the shares sold out quickly. Traidcraft has over 120 employees in Britain and estimates that its trading activities, which generate a turnover of about £3 million per year, support 6,000 jobs, mostly in the poorest countries of the world.

TRANET (Transnational Network for Appropriate/ Alternative Technologies)
Box 567
Rangely, ME 04970
(207) 864-2252

A "quarterly newsletter-directory of, by and for people who are participating in transformation." TRANET was initiated in 1976 by a group of alternative technology (AT) practitioners at the U.N. Conference on Human Settlements in Vancouver, Canada. Each issue is packed full of organizations and individuals working to make the world a better, more humane place by implementing innovative techniques and ideas. TRANET also carries out special projects like the TRANET/UNESCO Mini AT Library Program, which sends the one hundred best books for a village technology library to Third World villages. Each library costs $800, and your contributions are most welcome. Membership ($30/year) includes subscription to the quarterly newsletter.

Trusteeship Institute (TI)
Baker Road
Shutesbury, MA 01072

Nonprofit organization that helps companies convert to worker ownership. Mondragon cooperatives serve as their model. TI also helps organize land trusts and promotes the concept of social investing.

Turtle Island Earth Stewards
PO Box 364
Clinton, WA 98236
(206) 321-1884

Network of land-trust communities developing models for land trusts.

Vermont Community Loan Fund
PO Box 827
Montpelier, VT 05602

This revolving loan fund was in the developmental stages at the time of this writing. Work began in 1987 and the fund expects to be operational by spring 1988. The fund will make loans to community-based development projects that increase or preserve the supply of affordable housing or support locally based economic development opportunities for lower income Vermonters. The fund will also provide technical assistance. Loans of greater than $1,000 and at rates between 0 percent and current money-market rate are sought. VCLF worked with the Institute for Community Economics and has assembled a committed core of people that have made the fund's existence possible. Write them for more timely information.

Western Massachusetts Community Loan Fund
145 State Street, Suite 500
Springfield, MA 01103
(413) 739-7233

Women's Institute for Housing and Economic Development
179 South Street
Boston, MA 02111
(617) 423-2296

Women's Technical Assistance Project
1000 Wisconsin Avenue, NW
Washington, DC 20007
(202) 342-2081

Nonprofit organization working to build and facilitate a community
of shared skills and resources among community-based women in
the Southeast and Southwest at the grass-roots level. Provides
organizational, resource, strategy, and solidarity development to
women working to create new institutions based on values and
addressing the barriers, especially of race and class, which keep
women from working together.

Women's World Banking
104 East 40th Street
New York, NY 10016

Worcester Community Loan Fund
PO Box 271, Mid-Town Mall
Worcester, MA 01614
(617) 757-5631

Worker Owned Network
50 S. Court Street
Athens, OH 45701
(614) 592-3854

Working Assets Money Fund
230 California Street
San Francisco, CA 94111
(800) 533-3863

Working Assets avoids investments in defense contractors, nuclear power, repressive regimes (e.g., South Africa), and polluters of the environment. The fund supports equal opportunity, job creation in the United States, moderate-income housing, higher education, good labor relations, and small business. Half of Working Assets' funds are in government securities (not T-bills) and commercial banks. The securities include Freddie Mac's, Fannie Mae's, and Sallie Mae's. The banks they invest in have strong records in the community. The minimum investment is $1,000. Working Assets also offers a "socially responsible" VISA card!

Zuni Craftsmen Cooperative
PO Box 426
Zuni, NM 87327
(505) 782-4425

Formed in 1967 to enable Zuni craftspeople to control the way their work is distributed and, at the same time, form a strong tribal economic base. The cooperative has more than three hundred member craftspeople, each with his or her own unique style. Jewelry is "crafted to your specific commission, without rushing or taking shortcuts." Large quantities of finished jewelry are not stockpiled, and only the highest quality silver and other natural materials are used. Send $2 for a copy of their beautiful color catalog. Prices range from $10 to $1,000, with most items under $150.

CHAPTER NINE

Bibliography

9.1 Books

Adair, Margo. *Working Inside Out: Tools for Change*. Wingbow Press.

Anzalone, Joan, ed. *Good Works: A Guide to Careers in Social Change*. Dembner Books.

Bailey, Alice A. *A Treatise on White Magic*. Lucis.

Barry, Tom, and Deb Preusch. *The Central America Fact Book*. Grove Press. U.S. and corporate roles in Central America. Excellent resource!

Basic Call to Consciousness. Akwesasne Notes (see Publications).

Berry, Wendell. *The Unsettling of America*. Avon.

Bowers, Cathy, and Alison Cooper. *U.S. and Canadian Investment in South Africa*. Investor Responsibility Research Center (see Organizations).

The Briarpatch Book: Experiences in Right Livelihood and Simple Living. New Glide/Reed.

Brown, Lester R. *State of the World*. Worldwatch Institute.

Bryant, Dorothy. *The Kin of Ata Are Waiting for You*. Moon Book/Random House.

Center for Popular Economics. *Economic Report of the People*. South End Press.

Cheatham, Annie, and Mary Clare Powell. *This Way Daybreak Comes: Women's Values and the Future*. New Society.

Church Investments in Minority-Owned Banks and S&Ls. Interfaith Center on Corporate Responsibility (see Organizations).

Clark, Dennis, and Merry Guben. *Future Bread*. Includes "A Guide to Cooperative Ownership." The story of the O&O Supermarkets. O&O Investment Fund, 119 Cuthbert Street, Philadelphia, PA 19106.

The Community Land Trust Handbook. Institute for Community Economics (see Organizations).

The Community Loan Fund Manual. Institute for Community Economics (see Organizations).

Deval, Bill, and George Sessions. *Deep Ecology: Living as if Nature Mattered*. Peregrine Books.

Directory of Central America Organizations. Central America Resource Center (see Organizations).

Directory of Socially Responsible Investments. Funding Exchange (see Organizations).

Domini, Amy, and Peter Kinder. *Ethical Investing*. Addison-Wesley.

Dooling, D. M., ed. *A Way of Working: The Spiritual Dimension of Craft*. Parabola Books.

Eggert, Jim. *What Is Economics?* Kaufmann.

Ekins, Paul, ed. *The Living Economy: A New Economics in the Making*. Routledge & Kegan Paul.

Elgin, Duane. *Voluntary Simplicity*. Bantam Books.

An Environmental Review of Incineration Technologies. Institute for Local Self-Reliance (see Organizations).

Foreign Investment in South Africa. Investor Responsibility Resource Center (see Organizations).

Garbage Disposal Economics: A Statistical Snapshot. Institute for Local Self-Reliance (see Organizations).

Gift Giving Guide. Funding Exchange (see Organizations).

Goldstein, Joseph. *The Experience of Insight*. Shambhala.

Guide to War Tax Resistance. War Resisters League, 339 Lafayette Street, New York, NY 10012.

Habhan, Gary. *The Desert Smells Like Rain*. North Point Press.

Haenke, David. *Ecological Politics and Bioregionalism*. New Life Farm (see Organizations.)

Hallman, Victor G., and Jerry S. Rosenbloom. *Personal Financial Planning*. McGraw-Hill.

Hawkin, Paul. *The Next Economy*. Holt, Rinehart & Winston.

Henderson, Hazel. *Creating Alternative Futures*. Wideview/Perigee. Available from Box 347, St. Augustine, FL 32085.

Honigsberg, Peter Jan, Bernard Kamoroff, and Jim Beatty. *We Own It: Starting and Managing Co-ops, Collectives and Employee Owned Ventures*. Bell Springs.

Inglis, Mary, and Sandra Kramer, eds. *The New Economic Agenda*. Findhorn Press.

Inherited Wealth: Your Money and Your Life. Haymarket People's Fund (see Organizations).

Invest Yourself: A Guide to Action. A catalog of volunteer opportunities. The Commission on Voluntary Service and Action, PO Box 117, New York, NY 10009.

Jackall, Robert, and Henry M. Levin, eds. *Worker-Cooperatives in America*. University of California Press.

Resources

Jackson, Wes, Wendell Berry, and Bruce Colman, eds. *Meeting the Expectations of the Land*. North Point Press.

Jacobs, Jane. *Cities and the Wealth of Nations*. Random House.

Jensen, Joan. *With These Hands: Women Working on the Land*. Feminist Press.

Kamoroff, Bernard. *Small-Time Operator*. Bell Springs.

Kanter, Rosabeth Moss. *The Change Masters*. Simon & Schuster.

Kilcullen, Michael. *Directory of Alternative Investments*. Profiles projects seeking alternative investors. Interfaith Center on Corporate Responsibility (see Organizations).

Kirsch, Charlotte. *Facing the Future: A Financial Guide for Women Left Alone*. Penguin.

Kuhn, Thomas S. *The Structure of Scientific Revolutions*. University of Chicago Press.

Lafferty, LaVedi, and Bud Hollowell. *The Eternal Dance*. Lewellyn.

Lindenfield, Frank, and Joyce Rothschild-Whitt, eds. *Workplace Democracy and Social Change*. Porter Sargent.

Lydenberg, Steven, Alice Tepper Marlin, and Sean O'Brian Strub, for the Council on Economic Priorities. *Rating America's Corporate Conscience*. Addison-Wesley.

MacLeod, Greg. *New Age Business: Community Corporations that Work*. Canadian Council on Social Development, PO Box 3505, Station C, Ottawa, Ontario K1Y 4G1 CANADA.

McLaughlin, Corinne, and Gordon Davidson. *Builders of the Dawn*. Sirius Publishing, Baker Road, Shutesbury, MA 01072.
Compendium of intentional communities exploring new ideas and technologies in education, economics, childrearing, relationships with each other and the Earth, etc.

Martin, Larry. *Proven Profits from Pollution Prevention*. Institute for Local Self-Reliance (see Organizations).

Mische, Gerald and Patricia Mische. *Toward a Human World Order*. Paulist Press.

Moran, Peg. *Invest in Yourself*. Doubleday.

Morris, David. *The New City-States*. Institute for Local Self-Reliance (see Organizations).

Moskowitz, Milton, Michael Katz, and Robert Levering, eds. *Everybody's Business: The Irreverent Guide to Corporate America*. Harper & Row.

Mungo, Raymond. *Cosmic Profit*. Atlantic-Little Brown.

Myers, Norman, ed. *Gaia: An Atlas of Planet Management*. Anchor Press/ Doubleday.

The 100 Best Companies to Work for in America. Addison-Wesley.

Ouspensky, P. D. *In Search of the Miraculous*. Harcourt Brace Jovanovich.

Peavey, Fran, with Myra Levy and Charles Varon. *Heart Politics*. New Society.

Peters, Thomas J., and Robert H. Waterman, Jr. *In Search of Excellence*. Harper & Row.

Phillips, Carole. *The Money Workbook for Women*. Arbor House. Not just for women!

Phillips, Michael. *Honest Business*. Random House.

———*The Seven Laws of Money*. Random House.

——— *Simple Living Investments for Old Age*. Clear Glass Publishing, Box 257, Bodega, CA 94922.

——— *Transaction Based Economics*. Clear Glass Publishing, Box 257, Bodega, CA 94922.

Prigogine, Ilya. *Order Out of Chaos*. Bantam Books.

Robin Hood Was Right: A Guide to Giving Your Money for Social Change. Vanguard Foundation. Order from Haymarket People's Fund (see Organizations).

Sale, Kirkpatrick. *Dwellers in the Land: The Bioregional Vision*. Sierra Club Books.

Schaefer, Christopher, and Tijno Voors. *Vision in Action: The Art of Taking and Shaping Initiatives*. Hawthorn Press, Anthroposophic Press.

Schmookler, Andrew Bard. *The Parable of the Tribes: The Problem of Power in Social Evolution*. Houghton Mifflin.

Schumacher, E. F. *A Guide for the Perplexed*. Harper & Row.

——— *Small Is Beautiful*. Harper & Row.

Shaw, Linda S., Jeffrey W. Knopf, and Kenneth A. Bertsch. *Stocking the Arsenal: A Guide to the Nation's Top Military Contractors*. Investor Responsibility Research Center (see Organizations).

Shi, David. *The Simple Life*. Oxford University Press.

Slater, Philip. *Wealth Addiction*. Dutton.

Socially Responsible Buyer's Guide. Covenant for a World Free of Nuclear Weapons (see Organizations). Handbook listing consumer products of major nuclear weapons contractors according to product category. Also lists "acceptable" alternative brand names.

Spangler, David. *Emergence: The Rebirth of the Sacred*. Dell.

Spretnak, Charlene. *The Spiritual Dimension of Green Politics*. Bear & Co.

Spretnak, Charlene, and Fritjof Capra. *Green Politics: The Global Promise*. Dutton.

Swimme, Brian. *The Universe Is a Green Dragon: A Cosmic Creation Story.* Bear & Co.

Theobald, Robert. *The Rapids of Change: Social Entrepreneurship in Turbulent Times.* Knowledge Systems.

Tobias, Michael, ed. *Deep Ecology.* Avant Books.

Turnbull, Shann. *Democratising the Wealth of Nations.* The Company Directors Association of Australia Ltd., 27 Macquarie Place, Sydney 2000 AUSTRALIA.

Van Matre, Steve, and Bill Weiler. *The Earth Speaks.* The Institute for Earth Education, PO Box 288, Warrenville, IL 60555.

Von Sonn, Andrew. *The Money Rebellion.* Mayflower Unlimited, PO Box 1136, Venice, CA 90291.

Wallace, Paul A. W. *The White Roots of Peace.* Chauncey Press.

Walsh, Roger, M.D. *Staying Alive: The Psychology of Human Survival.* Shambhala.

Women in Development: A Resource Guide for Organization and Action. New Society. ISIS Women's International Information and Communication Service.

9.2 Publications

Akwesasne Notes
PO Box 196   Mohawk Nation   via Rooseveltown, NY 13683

The Alliance
2807 Stark   Portland, OR 97214 $15/twelve issues.

CATALYST: Investing in Social Change
64 Main Street, 2nd Floor   Montpelier, VT 05602   (802) 223-7943
     Focus on small-scale, sustainable, environmentally aware enterprises working for social change. Quarterly, $20/year.

Changing Work
Institute for Corporate Studies   PO Box 261   New Town Branch
Newton, MA 02258   Quarterly, $12/year.

The Clean Yield
Fried & Fleer Investment Services, Ltd.
Box 1880   Greensboro Bend, VT 05842   (802) 533-7178
     A monthly stock-market newsletter (advisory) that focuses on publicly traded emerging growth companies. Includes updates of their "model portfolio" and "Clean Profiles." $75/year for individuals and nonprofits, $100/year for businesses.

Community Jobs
1319 18th Street, NW   Washington, DC 20036   (202) 659-5627

Lists socially responsible jobs and internships available around the country.

Compost Patch
306 Coleridge Avenue   Altoona, PA 16602   (814) 946-9291
Offers information about social investing, recycling, community revitalization. Free sample.

The Corporate Examiner
Interfaith Center on Corporate Responsibility (ICCR)
475 Riverside Drive, Rm. 566   New York, NY 10115   (212) 870-2316
Monthly newsletter examines policies and practices of major U.S. corporations with regard to South Africa, labor, minorities, foreign investment, the military, and others. Regular updates on shareholder actions and the corporations' responses. $25/year.

Cultural Survival
11 Divinity Avenue   Cambridge, MA 02138   (617) 495-2526
$20/four issues

Daybreak
PO Box 98   Highland, MD 20777
Dedicated to land, life, and the seventh generation. Publisher: Oren Lyons; Editor-in-Chief: John Mohawk. $12/twelve issues.

The Defense Monitor
Center for Defense Information   1500 Massachusetts Avenue, NW
Washington, DC 20005   (202) 862-0700
Published ten times a year, this newsletter focuses on the military, defense contractors, and all issues that involve them. Statistical information on military profits, cost overruns, the contents of our arsenal as a whole, etc. Receives no funds from government or military contractors. Subscriptions: $25/year.

Dollars and Sense
38 Union Square   Room 14   Somerville, MA 02143

Earth First!
PO Box 5871   Tucson, AZ 85703 $15/eight issues

The Ecologist
Worthyvale Manor Farm   Camelford, Cornwall PL32 9TT   U. K.
See especially vol. 15, no. 3 (1985) which includes "The Perceptual Implications of Gaia" by David Abram. $20/six issues.

Envest
Energy Investment Research, Inc.
PO Box 73   Glenville, CT 06831   (914) 937-6939
Biweekly newsletter focusing on developments and investment opportunities in companies providing products and services in cogeneration, alternative energy, energy management and conservation, environmental protection, and waste management. Features commentary, interviews, and company profiles. $225/year.

Resources

Environmental Action
1525 New Hampshire Avenue, NW   Washington, DC 20036
(202) 745-4870
  Bimonthly publication that is a great resource for individuals concerned with the environment. Although not strictly focused on corporations' activities, much that is covered is related to (and often the direct result of) corporate actions.

GOOD MONEY
PO Box 363   Worcester, VT 05682
(802) 223-3911 or (800) 535-3551
  Published since 1982, this bimonthly newsletter contains information on the ethical and social practices of publicly traded corporations. Ethical issues from animal rights to weapons production are covered regularly, as is the financial performance of socially responsible companies. GOOD MONEY also provides services to individual and institutional investors (portfolio screening) and publishes several issue papers and other reports of interest to social investors. Newsletter is $75/year.

The Human Economy Newsletter
Mankato State University   Economics Department
Box 14   Mankato, MN 56001 $15/year.

In Business
Box 323   Emmaus, PA 18049
  Small business "stories," resources for small-business owners. Bimonthly, $18/year.

In Context
PO Box 2107   Sequim, WA 98382
  A journal committed to "humane sustainable culture." Excellent publication—highly recommended! $16/quarterly.

INSIGHT
Franklin Research and Development Corporation
711 Atlantic Avenue, 5th Floor   Boston, MA 02111   (617) 432-6655
  An advisory newsletter, published quarterly. Subscription also includes monthly market update on twenty companies, fifty in-depth briefs on selected stocks, and quarterly industry reports. $87.50/year for individuals, $175/year for institutions.

Katuah
Box 683   Leicester, NC 28748 $10/four issues.

Multinational Monitor
PO Box 19405   Washington, DC 20036
  Monthly publication provides information about transnational corporations and their effects here and abroad. Excellent resource for companies in Central America and other developing regions. Issues are examined from many perspectives. Recommended. Individuals $22/year, nonprofits $25/year, businesses $35/year.

National Boycott Newsletter
6506 28th Avenue, NE   Seattle, WA 98115   (206) 523-0421

Economics as If the Earth Really Mattered

Quarterly newsletter with such categories as human rights, animal rights, the environment, peace, and labor, as well as longer articles on specific boycotts and corporate activities. $8/year first class; $5/year bulk rate.

Native Self-Sufficiency
PO Box 10   Forestville, CA 95436 $15/four issues.

Network News
National Mutual Housing Network   1012 14th Street, NW, Suite 1006
Washington, DC 20005   (202) 662-1540

The New Abolitionist
2521 Guilford Avenue   Baltimore, MD 21218   (301) 235-3575
Newsletter of Nuclear Free America, providing updates on such activities as the development of nuclear-free zones and divestment and boycott campaigns against nuclear weapons manufacturers. $10/year.

The New Catalyst
PO Box 99   Lillooet, BC V0K 1V0   CANADA $12/four issues.

New Options
PO Box 19324 · Washington, DC 20036
Edited by Mark Satin, author of *New Age Politics*. Focus is beyond left and right politics to an open-minded and (usually) realistic perspective on what is going on. Excellent! $18/twelve issues.

North American Bioregional Congress Proceedings
Hart Publishing   PO Box 1010   Forestville, CA 95436

Northeast Indian Quarterly
400 Caldwell Hall   Cornell University   Ithaca, NY 14853
$12/four issues.

Not Man Apart
Friends of the Earth   530 7th Street, SE   Washington, DC 20003
$18/six issues, $25 for membership in Friends of the Earth (includes the newspaper).

One Earth
Findhorn Publications   The Park   Forres IV36 OTZ   U. K.
Excellent publication, especially November/December 1985, "Earth: A Call to Action." $12/quarterly.

The Other Side
300 West Apsley Street   Philadelphia, PA 19144 $19.75/ten issues.

Parabola
656 Broadway   New York, NY 10012
"Myth and the Quest for Meaning." $18/four issues.

Plenty Bulletin
PO Box 90   Summertown, TN 38483
Donations accepted/published quarterly.

Resources

Resurgence
Worthyvale Manor Farm   Camelford   Cornwall PL32 9TT   U. K.
  Excellent magazine that focuses on alternatives in all areas. Articles, stories, regular columns, extensive reviews, poetry, photos, etc. $27.50/six issues, airmail.

Siskiyou Journal
PO Box 741   Ashland, OR 97520 $16/four issues.

Toward Freedom
64 North Street   Burlington, VT 05401
  Report on nonalignment and the developing countries. $10/eight issues.

TRANET
Transnational Network for Appropriate/Alternative Technology
Box 567   Rangely, ME 04970   (207) 864-2252
  A newsletter/directory for people interested in alternative technologies. Coverage is worldwide and subjects include energy, economics, Green politics, bioregionalism, Third World development, environment, and resources. Subscription includes a listing of your name, address, and interests in the annual members' directory. $30/four issues.

Value Line Investment Survey
Value Line, Inc.   711 Third Avenue   New York, NY 10017

Woman of Power
PO Box 827   Cambridge, MA 02238 $22/four issues.

Workplace Democracy
University of Massachusetts
111 Draper Hall   Amherst, MA 01003   Quarterly, $18/year.

World Rainforest Report
PO Box 368   Lismore New South Wales 2480   AUSTRALIA
  $12/four issues.

Also see Organizations for the following listings, since all these groups publish excellent newsletters:
  Co-op America, Institute for Community Economics, Institute for Food and Development Policy, New Alchemy Institute, Regeneration Project, Center for Neighborhood Technology, National Congress for Community Economic Development, School of Living, National Center for Employee Ownership, Citizens Clearinghouse for Hazardous Wastes, Council on Economic Priorities, and Fund for Renewable Energy and the Environment.

About the Author

After nearly a decade of homesteading, Susan Meeker-Lowry became interested in socially responsible investing and the work of GOOD MONEY. Not content with helping to define the least objectionable corporate investments, in 1982 Susan started her own newsletter, *Catalyst*, to report on opportunities for investing in social change. In the quarterly issues of *Catalyst*, Susan discusses all aspects of creating an alternative economy while describing investment opportunities with a wide range of small- or medium-sized businesses and organizations that are in some way helping to create such an economy. Susan is increasingly interested in the possibility of a Gaean, or Earth-based, economy and recently cofounded the Institute for Gaean Economics in Worthington, Massachusetts.

Between issues of *Catalyst*, Susan gives workshops and talks at conferences, cares for her three sons, and spends as much time in the woods as she can. Susan grew up in the White Mountains of New Hampshire and currently lives in Vermont.

For more information about *Catalyst* or the Institute for Gaean Economics, write to 64 Main Street, 2nd Floor, Montpelier, VT 05602.